Rancière and Law

AF694925

This book is the first to approach Jacques Rancière's work from a legal perspective. A former student of Louis Althusser, Rancière is one of the most important contemporary French philosophers of recent decades: offering an original and path-breaking way to think about politics, democracy and aesthetics. Rancière's work has received wide and increasing critical attention, but no study exists so far that reflects on the wider implications of Rancière for law and for socio-legal studies. Although Rancière does not pay much specific attention to law, and there is a strong temptation to identify law with what he terms the 'police order', much of Rancière's historical work highlights the creative potential of law and legal language, with important legal implications and ramifications. So, rather than excavate the Rancièrean corpus for isolated statements about the law, this volume reverses such a method and asks: what would a Rancière-inspired legal theory look like? Bringing together specialists and scholars in different areas of law, critical theory and philosophy, this rethinking of law and socio-legal studies through Rancière provides an original and important engagement with a range of contemporary legal topics, including constituent power and democracy, legal subjectivity, human rights, practices of adjudication, refugees, the nomos of modernity, and the sensory configurations of law. It will, then, be of considerable interest to those working in these areas.

Mónica López Lerma is based at Reed College, USA, and **Julen Etxabe** is based at the University of Helsinki, Finland.

Nomikoi: Critical Legal Thinkers

Series editors:
Peter Goodrich
Cardozo School of Law, New York
David Seymour
School of Law, City University, UK

For a full list of titles in this series, please visit www.routledge.com

Nomikoi: Critical Legal Thinkers presents analyses of key critical theorists whose thinking on law has contributed significantly to the development of the new interdisciplinary legal studies. Addressing those who have most influenced legal thought and thought about law, the aim of the series is to bring legal scholarship, the social sciences and the humanities into closer dialogue.

Other titles in the series:

Deleuze & Guattari: Emergent Law
Jamie Murray

Bruno Latour: The Normativity of Networks
Kyle McGee

Zizek and Law
Edited by Laurent de Sutter

Roberto Esposito: Law, Community and the Political
Peter Langford

Jacques Derrida: Law as Absolute Hospitality
Jacques de Ville

Hannah Arendt: Legal Theory and the Eichmann Trial
Peter Burdon

Adriana Caravero: Resistance and the Voice of Law
Elisabetta Bertolino

Rancière and Law
Mónica López Lerma and Julen Etxabe

Rancière and Law

Edited by Mónica López Lerma and Julen Etxabe

Routledge
Taylor & Francis Group
LONDON AND NEW YORK

First published 2018 by Routledge

2 Park Square, Milton Park, Abingdon, Oxfordshire OX14 4RN
52 Vanderbilt Avenue, New York, NY 10017

Routledge is an imprint of the Taylor & Francis Group, an informa business

First issued in paperback 2019

Copyright © 2018 selection and editorial matter, Mónica López Lerma and Julen Etxabe; individual chapters, the contributors

The right of Mónica López Lerma and Julen Etxabe to be identified as the authors of the editorial material, and of the authors for their individual chapters, has been asserted in accordance with sections 77 and 78 of the Copyright, Designs and Patents Act 1988.

All rights reserved. No part of this book may be reprinted or reproduced or utilised in any form or by any electronic, mechanical, or other means, now known or hereafter invented, including photocopying and recording, or in any information storage or retrieval system, without permission in writing from the publishers.

Notice:
Product or corporate names may be trademarks or registered trademarks, and are used only for identification and explanation without intent to infringe.

British Library Cataloguing-in-Publication Data
A catalogue record for this book is available from the British Library

Library of Congress Cataloging-in-Publication Data
Names: López Lerma, Mónica, editor. | Etxabe, Julen, editor.
Title: Ranciere and law / by Mónica López Lerma and
  Julen Etxabe.
Description: Abingdon, Oxon ; New York, NY : Routledge, 2018. |
  Series: Nomikoi critical legal thinkers
Identifiers: LCCN 2017035344 | ISBN 9781138955134 (hbk) |
  ISBN 9781315666563 (ebk)
Subjects: LCSH: Ranciere, Jacques. | Law—Philosophy.
Classification: LCC K230.R358 R36 2018 | DDC 340/.1—dc23
LC record available at https://lccn.loc.gov/2017035344

ISBN: 978-1-138-95513-4 (hbk)
ISBN: 978-0-367-23245-0 (pbk)

Typeset in Baskerville
by Apex CoVantage, LLC

Contents

Acknowledgements

This edited volume has been many years in the making; too many to remember in detail at this belated hour how the idea might have originated in the first place.

Perhaps it had something to do with a workshop with Jacques Rancière in 2011 organized by the graduate students of the Department of Romance and Literatures at the University of Michigan, where the editors had the chance to meet and interact with Rancière – and engage in conversation over dinner.

The idea was certainly in full bloom in Helsinki, where we organized a first workshop entitled 'Rancière and the Possibility of Law' back in June 2013, thanks to the generous support of the now-defunct Centre of Excellence for the Foundations of European Law. The next year, a follow-up workshop was organized by Susanna Lindroos-Hovinheimo at Queen Mary University of London, where we encountered some old faces and a number of new ones as well. The editors wish to thank the participants in these workshops who have contributed to the volume as well as those who, for one reason or another, were not able to make it in its final form.

We would not wish to forget the unselfish task of those who anonymously reviewed the various chapters; they must remain unnamed, though they certainly know who they are. Dylan Holmes deserves to be mentioned for his invaluable editorial assistance.

Finally we would also like to thank Colin Perrin at Routledge for his enthusiastic reception to our proposal for this volume and, in particular, Peter Goodrich and David Seymour, the series editors of *Nomikoi: Critical Legal Thinkers*, for their encouragement, support, and patience throughout.

Contributors

Petr Agha is Director of the Centre for Law and Public Affairs (CeLAPA), Institute of State and Law, Czech Academy of Sciences and Senior Lecturer at the Faculty of Law, Charles University Prague, Czech Republic. In the past he worked in the Secretariat of the Government Council of the Czech Republic for Human Rights (2003–2006), where he acted as a secretary of the Committee against Racism, and the Committee against Discrimination of Women. Later he worked as an advisory to the vice minister responsible for human rights issues. He has edited a monograph entitled *Human Rights between Law and Politics*, published by Hart Publishing (2017).

Julen Etxabe is Docent in Legal Theory at the University of Helsinki, Finland, and worked as a Fellow at the Helsinki Collegium for Advanced Studies (2014–2017). His book, *The Experience of Tragic Judgment*, was published in 2013 by Routledge. He has also edited several books, including *Living in a Law Transformed: Encounters with the Works of James Boyd White* (with Gary Watt, Michigan Publishing, 2014) and *Cultural History of Law in Antiquity* (forthcoming from Bloomsbury). He was co-editor in chief of *No-Foundations: An Interdisciplinary Journal of Law and Justice* (2012 to 2017).

Tom Frost is Lecturer in Legal Theory at the University of Sussex (UK). He is the editor of *Giorgio Agamben: Legal, Political and Philosophical Perspectives* (Routledge 2015). He was previously a Lecturer in Law at Newcastle University from 2010 to 2013. He is currently working on a monograph entitled *Law, Relationality and the Ethical Life: Agamben and Levinas*, to be published with Routledge.

Eric Heinze is Professor of Law and Humanities, Queen Mary University of London (UK). He has also worked with the International Commission of Jurists and UN Sub-Commission on Human Rights in Geneva and on private litigation before the United Nations Administrative Tribunal in New York. His books include *Hate Speech and Democratic Citizenship* (2016), *The Concept of Injustice* (2013), *The Logic of Constitutional Rights* (2005), *The Logic of Liberal Rights* (2003), *The Logic of Equality* (2003), *Sexual Orientation: A Human Right* (1995) (Russian translation 2004), and the collection *Of Innocence and Autonomy: Children, Sex and Human Rights* (2000). He is currently co-authoring a book with Gavin Phillipson, entitled *Debating Hate Speech.*

Ari Hirvonen is Adjunct Professor in Legal Philosophy and Theory at Helsinki University, Finland, where he acts as the Vice Dean in Research of the Faculty of Law. He was a senior member in the Centre for Excellence in the Foundations of European Law and Polity. He has written extensively on psychoanalysis, political theory, continental philosophy, and phenomenology of law. He is the editor of *Law and Evil: Philosophy, Politics, Psychoanalysis* (with Janne Porttikivi, 2010) and *Polycentricity: Multiple Scenes of Law* (1998).

Susanna Lindroos-Hovinheimo works as Senior Lecturer in Jurisprudence at the University of Helsinki, Finland. Her research focuses on legal theory and EU law. Previously she worked as Lecturer in Law at Queen Mary University of London, where she taught jurisprudence and legal theory. She is the author of *Justice and the Ethics of Legal Interpretation* (Routledge, 2012). Lindroos-Hovinheimo leads the three-year research project The Political Foundations of Privacy Regulation 2017–2019 on the philosophical underpinnings of EU privacy law.

Mónica López Lerma is Visiting Associate Professor at Reed College (Portland, Oregon, USA). She is currently working on a monograph entitled *Sensing Justice: Aesthetics, Politics and Law through Spanish Contemporary Cinema* (to be published with Edinburgh University Press). Her work has appeared in a number of international journals, including *Revue interdisciplinaire d'études juridiques; Southern California Interdisciplinary Law Journal; Politica Comun; Conserveries Memorielles*; and *Journal of Law and Social Research.* Her essay 'Aesthetic Irruptions: Politics of Perception in Alex de la Iglesia *La Comunidad*' appeared in *Rancière and Film*, edited by P. Bowman (Edinburgh University Press, 2013). She was co-editor of *No-Foundations: An Interdisciplinary Journal of Law and Justice* (2012–2017).

Panu Minkkinen is Professor of Jurisprudence at the Faculty of Law of the University of Helsinki, Finland. From 2004 to 2011 he was Professor of Legal Theory at the University of Leicester, UK. He was previously Deputy Director and Fellow at the Helsinki Collegium for Advanced Studies and served a three-year term as Director of the Finnish Institute in London, a charitable trust advancing cultural and academic co-operation between Finland and the UK and Ireland. His books include *Sovereignty, Knowledge, Law* (Routledge, 2009); *Järjen lait* (Tutkijaliitto, 2002); and *Thinking Without Desire* (Hart, 1999).

Wayne Morrison is Professor of Law, Queen Mary University of London, UK, and Barrister and Solicitor of the High Court of New Zealand. He was Director of the University of London's LLB for external/international students from 1999 to 2009 and has travelled and worked globally. His research and publications span criminological and legal theory, including topics traditionally outside the canon, such as genocide and methods of representation and remembrance. He is the author of *Criminology, Civilisation and the New World Order* (Routledge, 2006, Spanish edition 2012) and *The Politics of the Common Law* (with Gearey and Jago, 1st ed. 2009, 2nd ed. 2013).

Introduction

Rancière and the possibility of law

Mónica López Lerma and Julen Etxabe

Jacques Rancière is one of the leading contemporary French philosophers of recent decades. A former student of Louis Althusser, with whom he collaborated and whom he later publicly renounced, Rancière has moved beyond his initial skirmishes in the journal *Révoltes Logiques* and historiographical studies of workers' movements to offer an original and path-breaking way to think of politics, equality, democracy, and aesthetics.[1] In concise and often polemical writings that combine history, politics, literature, pedagogy, contemporary art, and film, Rancière's work challenges traditional disciplinary boundaries, all the while he is helping to reshape contemporary thought, and vocabulary, on all these topics.

Rancière's work has received wide and increasing critical attention.[2] It is not our aim to add to this literature by explaining Rancière's intellectual journey or key terms. While Rancière's work has been illuminated from almost every angle, no study exists so far that reflects on the wider implications of Rancière for law and socio-legal studies. It is true that Rancière does not pay much specific attention to law – and the temptation is strong to associate the law simply with a subgenre of what he terms the 'police order'. Nonetheless, many of Rancière's historical vignettes are legal examples: notably, Rancière has referred to the trial of the revolutionary Auguste Blanqui; to Jeanne Deroin's attempt to participate in an electoral process denied her on account of her gender; as well as to Olympe de Gouges' celebrated riposte that if women are entitled to go to the scaffold, they also ought to be entitled to go to the assembly. These and other similar cases (like the revolt of the plebs on the Aventine Hill) underscore the creative potential of law and legal language, with important legal implications and ramifications. Therefore, rather than delve into the Rancierian corpus for isolated statements on or about the law, this volume reverses the question and asks: what would a Rancière-inspired legal theory look like?

Take for instance the most well-known distinction between police and politics: opposing both Habermasian logic of rational argumentation and consensus as well as Lyotard's differend or absolute heterogeneity, Rancière's work hinges on the construction of polemical stages where heterogeneous logics can encounter each other. These encounters are understood as moments of disjuncture between a given configuration of the perceptible, which he calls the *police*, and a disruptive and unforeseeable force that emerges to interrupt this supposedly natural order, which he calls *politics*. Rancière does not identify the order of the police with the work of governments, state apparatus, or ideology. Rather, the police order is identified with a given regime of the perceptible; an implicit law that regulates the distribution and legitimation of powers, places, and roles. This order determines who is included or excluded, who is counted or uncounted, who has the capacity to speak or not, whose words are significant or not, and what can be said, heard, and seen within it. Politics, on the other hand, occurs when the distribution of the sensible is interrupted by an egalitarian logic that questions its 'naturalness', most notably via the articulation of a 'wrong' not previously perceptible in it. A political act is therefore a specific form of *appearance*: not an 'illusion' opposed to the real, but an emergence in the field of experience of what could not formerly be seen, said, or heard, which, by this very appearance, transforms the entire order of the visible.

One issue often noted by critics is that by privileging the singular and contingent moment of the political act – intermittent acts of *dissensus* – Rancière may not leave room in his thought for the deliberate agency of law or legal institutions. But the question can be reversed: can Rancière help us, differently, to question the very notions of permanence and certainty that are dogmatically reasserted almost every time law is discussed? Can law be thought instead to hinge on similar (dis) junctures? What other terms and motifs might be creatively re-appropriated to shape a different sense of the law? Can law be thought of in terms of regimes of visibility and the distribution of the sensible, of radical equality, democracy and emancipation? Contrariwise, how are we to think of law in terms of arrangement of places, roles, and subjects; of its strategies and practices of consensus; of its determination of legally relevant and irrelevant claims, voices, and ways of being; of its dealings and interminglement with practices of exclusion, representation, and terror?

The aim of this book, therefore, is neither to explain Rancière's ideas about law, nor to apply them to a predetermined field or concept of law, but to rethink law through the help of Rancière. That is, we pursue not solely views of law underlying his thought (law *in* Rancière), but views that his thought may open up (law *through* Rancière). For, while Rancière's ideas can certainly be mobilized to criticize the shortcomings of law and legal institutions and everyday practices, his work may also be fruitfully deployed to explore possibilities of law that are, or remain, invisible as yet. To this end, Rancière is put in conversation with authors who have spoken more openly about juridical questions, pointing out the limits, blind spots, and divergences of opinion resulting naturally from critical engagement with the author. In no particular order, the various chapters examine legal disagreement, the plight and flight of refugees, legal subjectivity, radical equality, practices of adjudication, human rights, constituent power, the power of the constitution, the nomos of modernity, the international law project, street art, and the sensory configurations of law. The goal is not to offer a comprehensive account of Rancière's 'legal theory', but rather to open law up for alternative senses, fictions, images, and practices. In doing so, we seek further to destabilise the grip that the modern nation state and associated notions of sovereignty still hold on the contemporary imagination, and which prevent other views from being heard, seen, said, or done.

The book is structured in four parts:

I. Law without method

One of the most striking aspects of Rancière as a thinker and writer is what he calls his 'method'. At once it can be noticed that his is no method in the ordinary sense. There are indubitable political stakes in his choice of a method that can be called *an-archic*, in the etymological sense of *arkhê* as both commencement and command. It is in the precise sense of invitation without imposition that we call for 'law without method'.

Starting from this basic premise, the introductory chapter by Julen Etxabe addresses what Rancière's 'no-method' might mean for the law. The chapter seeks neither to explain nor apply Rancière's ideas of law to a predetermined concept or field of law. Rather, it seeks to re-enact the legal landscape that Rancière invites us to construct, weaving a theatrical or dramaturgic model of law out of Rancierian threads. A theatrical or dramaturgical conception of law demands attention to the legal scene, not as a return to any primordial or archetypical scene – the killing of the father, the dethronement of the King, glorious moments of revolution, or of mythical founding – but to limit moments of becoming and passing away of law and non-law, where no external position exists for the legal theorist to describe law in its totality, or as a totality. A consistently Rancierian position leads to a radical relativization where law, just as democracy itself, has no proper foundations.

Etxabe's re-creation of the Rancierian topography is based on scenes staged by actors who, acting out of the presupposition of equality, undergo processes of subjectivation that reconfigure the 'sense' of the common. Building on the police/politics distinction, he proposes a doubling similar for law between a given order of *legalism* that distributes roles, places, subjects, and doctrines and an antagonistic *jurisgenerative* impulse that would come to interrupt it. Beyond teasing out the implications of the analogy, which leads to a rejection of both legal positivism and natural law, the chapter critically conceptualizes the stage or space of encounter; the limits to the kind of disagreement susceptible of being thus staged; the obstacles that prevent challenging an order of legalism that does not want to hear; and how a claim perceived to be legally irrelevant can nonetheless be registered as a novel legal inscription, when those in principle without a place in the order of legalism are nevertheless able to reconfigure the sensible texture of law.

Etxabe tests the practical implications of a Rancierian dramaturgy in the context of the post-2008 mortgage crisis in Spain. At this historical juncture, a few judges decided to resist the order of legalism and their putative role as passive enforcers, but instead enacted a jurisgenetic logic that acknowledged a wrong in the distribution of the sensible. The example is able to show how law, despite its strong institutional mechanisms and incentives to close itself down, can be open to jurisgenesis from within.

II. From the rights of subjects to the subjects of rights

In his writings, Rancière valorizes the actions of anonymous men and women who enact their fundamental equality against, or in spite of, a state of affairs that would deny it. In doing so, Rancière invites us to reflect not on how individuals are formed into subjects as does Foucault, but on how they might assert new and transformative subjectivities, which combines elements of *performativity*, *dis-identification*, and *equal intelligence* (Rancière 2012: 213).

The chapters in Part II deal with the subject (as well as the subjects) of rights, one of the few areas where Rancière has explicitly talked about the law. An important thread of his argument is the refusal to accept Agamben's biopolitical diagnosis of bare life and the camp as the *nomos* of modernity, which he takes as a corollary of the Arendtian attempt to preserve the realm of 'pure politics'.

In order to set the Rights of Man on a different footing, Rancière aims to dismantle Hannah Arendt's known paradox that renders those rights either void or tautological – because they represent either the laws of those who have no rights (as apolitical individuals) or else the rights of those who already have rights (as citizens). In contrast, Rancière argues that even those who have no rights can assert the rights that they have not, actually demonstrating that they *do* have those rights (Rancière 2004b). The former depends on processes of subjectivation, where the subject is no longer an ontological human being, but an operator linking the capacity for setting out a dispute about what exactly these rights entail, whom they concern, and in which cases they can be invoked.

But what are the conditions through which rights can function in such a destabilizing and empowering way? How to put to work their emancipatory force and prevent their appropriation by power structures, or their 'neutralization'? Further, to what extent can Rancière's understanding of the subject, and of processes of subjectivation, be incorporated into legal thinking? Does Rancière's analysis of the form of politics help us to assess the merits of different right-claims? These are the questions that Ari Hirvonen, Susanna Lindroos-Hovinheimo and Tom Frost address in their respective chapters.

In 'Fight for Your Rights: Refugees, Resistance, and Disagreement', Ari Hirvonen tackles the so-called European refugee crisis and vindicates the figure of the refugee as a political actor, rather than as passive recipient of state policies. Hirvonen first scrutinizes the policies of the EU and its Member States under the frame of the Rancièrian police order and asks: what functions, places, and ways of being are refugees being allocated in that order? Subsequently, he analyzes Europe-wide refugee protests as instances of politics, which interrupt the consensual distribution where they have no part in society, economy, and politics.

In this context, Hirvonen suggests the need to rethink the potentialities of human rights in a way that differs from humanitarian practices that set refugees as voiceless victims in need of 'protection', and who are supposed to happily embrace the rights to shelter, food, clothing, and health received from their humanitarian hosts. In the analysis, human rights emerge as neither universal, nor as mere ideological constructs, nor as fixed juridical categories. Instead, their existence and effectiveness lies in the back-and-forth movement between the first inscriptions of these rights and their enactments, in dissensual stages in which they are put to the test. These struggles leave a trace in the ever-changing material of the law, the meaning of which they help to expand. Hirvonen analyzes various refugee cases before the European Court of Human Rights, considering the risk that their claims might be simply neutralized in the context of court proceedings, and the possibility that they might not.

The figure of the migrant is the point of departure of the next chapter, 'Rancière and the Legal Subject: Coming to Terms with Non-Existence', fostered by Hanif Kureishi's worrisome image of the migrant without colour, gender, or character that has been lodged everywhere in the collective imagination as a *problem* to be managed. While the faceless and voiceless immigrant can easily be dismissed in the legal field as a non-person, Susanna Lindroos-Hovinheimo halts the near-automatic call to recognize their legal personhood, wondering instead whether something is to be gained from the non-ontological subject that emerges from Rancière. Noting the influences of, and differences with, Althusser, Lindroos-Hovinheimo asks whether a conception of subjectivity not attached to personhood can be transposed to the legal field, and further reorient legal subjectivity towards emancipatory goals. She links this potentiality with the Rancierian axiom of equality, which is a presupposition that must be assumed, as well as continuously reaffirmed and discerned in concrete practices, but that can never be fulfilled, or shaped as a social institution. This axiomatic equality leads to positing the equal capacity of anybody to be(come) a subject. Lindroos-Hovinheimo submits that the reconceptualization of the legal subject as impersonal (i.e., not conceptually tied to personhood) towards emancipatory purposes, sits well with the self-understanding of the critical lawyer trying to open up spaces strategically within the law.

Shifting from the question of the legal subject to the subject of human rights, Tom Frost, in 'Rancière, Human Rights and the Limits of a Politics of Process', begins with a curious *inclusion*: during the drafting of the Universal Declaration of Human Rights, Daniel Defoe's character Robinson Crusoe was evoked by various state representatives as an 'enabling fiction' to conceptualize the relationship between the individual and the community – but which interestingly left out Friday. The anecdote enables Frost to rehearse the Arendtian criticism of the Declaration, on the assumption that politics is only possible within a public sphere in which individuals already recognize each other as equals and distinct. Arendt's critique is then paired with Rancière's counter-critique, where politics cannot be foreclosed in advance.

The debate works as the springboard for the critical question that interests Frost, which is an ethical lacuna he identifies at the heart of Rancière's politics-as-process: if what determines whether an act is political or not is not the outcome, but its form, how can we distinguish between the various acts claiming to be thus defined? Frost points out that the lack of any presupposition other than that of equality – which cannot be rendered into a substantive or 'thick' principle – disables the analytic discernment of their relative merits. Frost takes up the cases of someone prosecuted for inciting racial hatred against Muslims after the September 11 attack (*Norwood v. UK*) and of a French scholar who had denied the existence of gas chambers (*Faurisson v. France*). Given that a society may do well to avail itself of some mechanism to decide these matters, the answer hinges on the responsiveness of the police order, leading to 'better or worse' police. The analysis leads Frost to conclude that Rancière's politics is attractive for opening up the social order to new forms of subjectivation, but limited in its ability to distinguish between them. For Frost, the recognition of a political subject is an ethical act, which Rancière's pejorative description of ethics (as dwelling, way of being, or absolute Other) does not allow us properly to acknowledge.

III. Democracy, constitution, and the state

Rancière rejects the association of democracy with majoritarianism, or with any other rule for registering and institutionalizing popular votes. Likewise, he does not think democracy is a mechanism for managing and administering conflicts, or for producing 'consensus', which inevitably masks the effacement of those who are outside the count. Rather, Rancière associates democracy with the power of a demos – not a given population, collective, or social class – but the generic name of the subjects who stage a wrong in the distribution of the social order, without a specific qualification or entitlement for exercising power. This is why, for Rancière, democracy is not properly a political regime or a form of government, but 'the institution of politics itself' (Rancière 1999: 101).

The chapters by Eric Heinze and Panu Minkkinen critically assess these various claims against the backdrop of the modern liberal state, firstly, by going back to the 'foundational' myths of Plato that Rancière takes as a departure, and, secondly, by running Rancière against the antagonistic concept of the political devised by Carl Schmitt as an attack on the liberal *Rechtsstaat*.

In 'The Constitution of the Constitution: Democratic Legitimacy and Public Discourse', Eric Heinze critically assesses Rancière's views on democracy with the help of a subtle re-reading of Plato, here enlisted in support of the democratic cause. In Heinze's reading, public discourse emerges as the foundation of democratic legitimacy – the 'constitution of the constitution' – with consequences for law that are largely compatible with, yet unacknowledged in, Rancière's theory.

Heinze situates his argument in the twofold demand of legitimacy that government actions reflect people's voices, and the opposite demand for substantive justice, which may require overriding some of these voices. The clash between government and citizenry and manifested as public discourse ensures that the disjunction between citizens and government can never be total. In Heinze's view, public discourse ensures the irreducibly political character of a citizenry distinct from its government, yet remains always constitutive of that government.

Heinze engages with Plato's deflationist foundational myth in the *Republic*, with *The Laws*'s 'exceptional title' of democracy as the power of 'just anyone', and with *Crito*'s subtler inquiry into the legitimating conditions for obedience to law, as a form of immanent critique where democracy is held to account to its own normative standards. While Rancière places the anarchic demos outside, or alongside, government, as 'the ungovernable upon which all government must definitively discover itself to be founded' (2005: 57), Heinze suggests that it is precisely that element before and beyond government, identified as public discourse, which itself constitutes government as legitimate. Still, the crucial feature of a Rancièrian public discourse is not Habermasian or Rawlsian consensus – a fabrication that Rancière views as serving too readily to justify the existence or outcomes of elite managerialism – but rather an anarchic 'dissensus', which forever renews necessary challenges to elite managerialism.

Panu Minkkinen's 'Rancière and Schmitt: Sons of Ares?' attempts to assess Rancière's possible intellectual affinity with Carl Schmitt as belonging to the same agonistic tradition. Rancière hardly writes about Schmitt, and on the one occasion that he openly confronts Schmitt, he explicitly distances himself from the 'formalism' of the friend/enemy distinction. The chapter argues that Schmitt's concept of the political is not quite as formal as it first seems, for Schmitt introduces political substance to his analytical distinction by way of what Minkkinen (here following Badiou rather than Rancière) calls the 'metapolitical necessity' of his theory, which applies both to the concept of the political and to Schmitt's notion of the constitution. The latter results from a constituent-making power through which a constituent subject (a 'people') both establishes the institutions and practices that are essential for its unified political existence, and secures it against potential threats. Schmitt thus introduces an existential dimension into his analytical categories by way of a polemical confrontation with what is being combated, refuted, or negated (and which in Schmitt is not hard to identify with the liberal legalism and certain normative tradition of public law represented by Hans Kelsen).

Minkkinen grants that Rancière's overall project is distanced from Schmitt's state-centric view of the political world; indeed, the disruptive qualities of Rancierian politics would not be welcomed by the conservative thinker. For Schmitt, even exceptional violations of the constitutional order aim in the end to return to the ordered political existence deemed worthy of protection to begin with. Further, Schmitt's substantive political ontology is undermined and thrown into disarray by Rancière's anti-ontological commitments. Notable differences notwithstanding, Minkkinen sees alignment at the metapolitical level of their approach: in the case of Schmitt, a methodological stance where the distinction between friends and enemies ceases to be purely formal, but is interwoven with a prior decision about who or what to oppose; in Rancière, as a 'polemical intervention' against the tradition of political philosophy that attempts to expunge precisely the phenomenon that it claims to be explaining: politics.

IV. Law and aesthetics

A salient aspect of Rancière's thought is the centrality he grants to aesthetics. By this he means not a discipline dealing with artworks, but a 'distribution of the sensible' [*partage du sensible*], that is, a way of configuring sensory experience that identifies what can be seen, heard, felt, and thought. On the assumption that law, too, enacts a certain 'distribution of the sensible', an emphasis on the aesthetics of law might serve to question the sensorial experience of law in modern societies (e.g., boundaries and demarcations of public space, its regimes of visibility, its practices of securitization, and so forth).

That being said, Rancière uses the term 'aesthetic' in at least two senses, one stricter and another broader. On the one hand, aesthetics denotes a specific regime of identification of art, historically determined, which began in the late eighteenth and nineteenth centuries in the works of Hume, Kant, Schiller (and authors such as Victor Hugo, Wordsworth, Flaubert, . . .) and came to full fruition in the twentieth century. What Rancière calls the 'aesthetic regime of art' broke free from and disrupted the hierarchical principles of the earlier '*representative* regime' of Aristotelian origins (where a work of art is arranged under the principles of organic unity and coherence[3]), and from an even earlier '*ethical* regime' described by Plato in the *Republic*, where art was meant to be subservient to truth and to the way of being of a community (Rancière 1998; Rockhill 1998).

On the other hand, aesthetics is used in a broader sense to refer to a general dimension of human experience that comes from the Greek word 'aisthesis', meaning both feeling and understanding (Rancière 2009a: 121; Rancière 2013). Aristotle sought in fact to deduce the political nature of man by linking the capacity of feeling with the capacity of understanding, which ultimately fails to distinguish between the mouthing of pain (*phône*) from the voicing of an argument (*logos*). For Rancière this proves that politics is a matter of aesthetics from the very beginning, to the extent that it deals with the very interpretation of what people do with their mouths (Rancière 2009a: 121).

Rancière makes a threefold, further distinction: first, he speaks of an 'aesthetics of politics' (i.e., the kind of aesthetics that politics is or does) by introducing a dissensual logic in the sensory fabric of the community; in its ways of seeing, feeling, and perceiving; in what is visible or invisible within the community and the boundaries that define what is audible or inaudible. It is important to stress, however, that this has nothing to do with Walter Benjamin's 'aestheticization of politics', where aestheticization is employed to hammer and command a certain ideological point of view (Rancière 2004a: 13). (This is precisely the subject of Wayne Morrison's critique of the use of film during the Nuremberg trials.)

Secondly, Rancière reverses the terms and alludes to a 'politics of aesthetics' (i.e., the kind of politics that aesthetics is or does), by which specific aesthetic acts may 'create new modes of sense perceptions and induce novel forms of political subjectivity' (Rancière 2004a: 9). Rancière suggests that works of art do not perform political action or collective forms of action by themselves, but they can contribute to reframing forms of experience (2009a: 122).[4] They do so not by conveying messages, or by the way they choose to represent society's structures, social groups, and their identities, but by suspending the normal coordinates of space and time (e.g., utopian literature, science fiction) or by displacing conventional links between subjects and roles (Rancière 2009d: 23, 25).[5] While there is no direct causality between the intended effect and its actual result – among other things because the spectator refashions it in their own way (Rancière 2009c: 13) – works of art might 'create new modes of sense perceptions and induce novel forms of political subjectivity' (Rancière 2004a: 9). A Rancièrian-inspired legal theory similarly aims to intervene in the perceptible regime of law and its reconfiguration, which is the topic of Petr Agha's chapter for this volume.

Finally, Rancière uses the term 'aesthetics of knowledge' to describe the kind of discourse necessary to address the intertwinement between the former two dimensions. Rancière argues that many contemporary analyses would dismiss aesthetic suspension as an illusion giving rise to a 'false' sense of equality that blocks the way to 'true' equality. Rancière's riposte is that 'the claim of "true" equality dismisses the reality of the operations of verifications of equality' (2009d: 280). On the one hand, he espouses an 'indisciplinary' practice that suspends the hierarchies between discourses (2009b: 18) and disentangles in every case 'the *as if* that is involved in the "that's the way it is"' (2009d: 280).[6] On the other hand, he vindicates a 'method of equality' 'specifically aimed at detecting and highlighting the operations of equality that may occur everywhere' (2009d: 280–281). In doing so, Rancière's aesthetics of knowledge enables a form of critical intervention in the present (Rockhill 1998: 9–10).

The chapters by Petr Agha, Wayne Morrison, and Mónica López Lerma engage with all these various dimensions of aesthetics and their interactions with law.

Petr Agha's chapter 'Undoing Law: Public Art as Contest over Meanings', revisits some of Rancière's aesthetic ideas to understand how artistic activities as interventions can contribute to ongoing legal, political, and cultural discussions within existing networks, patterns, and spatial arrangements. Agha presents a contrast between public monuments which are 'gaze-repellent', give our feelings a pious direction, and are assigned a concrete place in the dominant narrative, and alternative forms of street-art such as graffiti, which are anonymous, ephemeral, and engage constant public communication, as they are susceptible of being amplified, removed, and painted over.

The chapter examines the work of Rancière against the backdrop of the so-called Lennon Wall located in a central square in Prague. Following John Lennon's assassination, this wall appeared decorated with an image of John Lennon with

Beatles lyrics, which were largely banned during the communist regime. Agha explains how attempts by the authorities to paint over the wall and keep it 'clean' were time and again defeated, as the wall became not only a memorial to John Lennon and his ideals for peace, but also a space for protest against the regime and a symbol of defiance of public authority. After the 1989 Velvet Revolution the Lennon Wall became officialized, slowly morphing into a form of monumental art. However, on the twenty-fifth anniversary of the Velvet Revolution the wall took on unexpected new life when a group of students 'cleaned' the famous landmark to clear space for the next generation of artists. By following the historical, political, and aesthetic changes occurring over three decades, Agha illustrates some of Rancière's key insights into the role of art in the public sphere and the role of art in shaping the contours of societies. Public art may not produce direct political effects, but it can draw an alternative topography and sense of public space, hence disrupting the perceptual and epistemic underpinning of a given police order.

In 'Representing Law "in" the Holocaust or Seeking the Unrepresented: Undoing the Legacy of Nuremberg', Wayne Morrison critically examines the strategies followed during the International Military Tribunal at Nuremberg to represent the Nazi state as completely devoid of law, or lawless. Partly a trial of the accused, partly a pedagogical lesson, and partly an attempt to build the future of international criminal law, the most sought-after effect of the Nuremberg trial, Morrison argues, was to reinforce the belief in the civilizing function of law.

Morrison focuses on two films shown during the trials (the *Nazi Concentration Camps*, compiled by photographers with the Allied Armies as they liberated the camps, and *The Nazi Plan*, a compilation of Nazi propaganda and newsreel images, including extensive footage from Leni Riefenstahl's documentary *Triumph of the Will*). In both cases the films were presented as direct and incontrovertible evidence, so much so that the court immediately adjourned and there was no discussion thereafter. As presented during the trial, however, the films constituted a historically unguided trip into the unspeakable, which did not permit establishing relations of causality and discernment of different actions and purposes. Yet the images were effective and have become the iconic imagery we today associate with the result of the Nazi regime.

Morrison appeals to Rancière to question the politics of this 'visual jurisprudence' that establishes relations between the visible and the invisible, and involves choices and configurations. Morrison's critical stance is addressed to the supposition that Nazi exterminatory violence was driven by lawlessness, or by sadistic or psychotic impulses. This ignores the fact that the existence of the Nazi regime was actually enabled by law: legal principles such as the *Führerprinzip*, laws such as the Law for the Protection of German Blood and Honour, numerous legal decrees, a well-greased administrative and bureaucratic structure, and acts by law-abiding officials.

Nuremberg thus failed to challenge representations of law and sovereignty as commanded by political superiors (Hobbes, Austin), or forms of legal-rational domination (Max Weber). Instead, Nuremberg strove to establish a new paradigm not so much through a confrontation with the Nazi state as a valid and lawful state pursuing radical ('evil') modernity, but by claiming that Nazism was totally devoid of law and civilization. Morrison seeks to take a critical stance on positivistic law as it has been conceived in late modernity.

Mónica López Lerma's 'Justice between Terror and Law' explores the 'aesthetic frames' of national security discourses and imagery in the post 9/11 age of terror, through Enrique Urbizu's (2011) *No habrá paz para los malvados* (*No Peace for the Wicked*). Combining thriller, *film noir*, and post-Western genres, *No Peace for the Wicked* tells the story of Santos Trinidad, a once respected but now drunken cowboy-like cop who, for no apparent reason, shoots three Colombians in a nightclub. Trinidad's hunt for the only witness who manages to escape him leads to uncovering an Islamist cell planning a terrorist attack that Trinidad apparently neutralizes; yet the film ends with an image of a crowded shopping mall where a series of undetected bombs remains active, leaving the viewer with a disquieting feeling of imminent danger.

The events and characters in the film are fictional, but they evoke the places, actions, and strategies behind the 2004 Madrid bombing attacks, underscoring terrorism and anti-terrorism policies, narratives, and images in the wake of the September 11 attacks. The religious overtones and constant cowboy references seem to align the film with President Bush's rhetoric on the 'war on terror'. However, López Lerma situates the film in a post-Western aesthetics that recycles themes, tropes, and styles of classical Western cinema to actively interrupt and modify its assumptions, ideology, and values. Arguing against earlier readings of the film, López Lerma seeks to demonstrate that while at the *narrative* level the film seems to reinforce the moral landscape that Rancière has analyzed under the heading of the 'ethical turn', at the level of its *aesthetics* the film questions and reconfigures the sense(s) of security and justice established by state police forces and the media.

The chapter draws a contrast between management of the public's perceptions of fear and terror as forms of legitimization of a state of permanent insecurity, and the manner in which the film creates opposing 'aesthetic frames' to challenge them. In particular the scrutinizing gaze of Judge Chacón, the embodiment of law in the film, undermines the state's rhetoric of invisible enemies and invites critical examination of the mutually feeding narratives of prevention, protection, and safety. Ultimately, the film raises the question whether a place exists for justice between terror and law.

Notes

1 Rancière's collaboration with Althusser began as a student in one of his seminars on Marx and resulted in the edited collection *Lire Le Capital* (Althusser et al. 1965). After the events of May 1968, Rancière publicly broke with his master and wrote a harsh critique (Rancière 1974). From 1975 to 1981, he was the leading member of a collective

responsible for the journal *Révoltes Logiques*. He also co-edited with Alain Faure *La Parole ouvrière, 1830–1851* (1976). In 1981, he published *Les Nuits des prolétaires* (*Proletarian Nights*, 2012) based on his doctoral dissertation. About the intellectual trajectory of Rancière during these years, see Davis (2010).

2 Rancière has inspired much secondary literature, including a vast number of articles, book chapters, and critical reviews. Recent edited collections include G. Rockwell and P. Watts (2009); P. Bowman and R. Stamp (2011); Deranty and Ross (2012); Bowman (2013); Davis (2013); and Genel and Deranty (2016). Monographs on Rancière include May (2008); Bingham and Biesta (2010); and Chambers (2013). Works of a more introductory nature include Deranty, ed. (2010); Davis (2010); and Tanke (2011). Additionally, a number of special issues are devoted to Rancière: e.g., *Theory and Event*, vol. 6, no. 4 (2003); *SubStance*, vol. 33, no. 1 (2003); *Parallax*, vol. 15, no. 3 (2010); *Symposium*, vol. 15, no. 2 (2011); *Novel*, vol. 47, no. 2 (2014).

3 In the 'representative regime', the choice of subject matter (*inventio*) governs the organization of parts (*dispositio*) and the language used (*elocutio*), and follows generic patterns 'appropriate' to the object in question (the lofty, the noble, the common, the inferior). According to Rancière, the aesthetic regime sought to break with all these principles one by one (Rancière 1998).

4 While aesthetics does not perform exactly the same task as politics, it continuously interferes in politics and 'contributes to weaving the fabric of the political, its words, images, forms of sensibility, etc.' (Rancière 2009a: 122). Rancière calls 'metapolitical' the attempt of art 'to perform that task of politics, the construction of forms of community, by other means' (Ibid).

5 The power of aesthetics consists in the ability to 'neutralize' or 'being indifferent' to social hierarchies: Rancière offers the Kantian example of being able to enjoy the beauty of a palace, which requires suspending what we know about its ownership or the way it was built; he further analyzes the example of the bricklayer who enjoys his craftsmanship, even though he is aware it is being utilized for the benefit of his master (Rancière 2009e: 273ff). For Rancière, aesthetic suspension is not an illusion opposed to the real, but the creation of an alternative 'as if' that both dismantles hierarchical structures of inequality and builds up a new sensible world.

6 In *The Names of History*, Rancière speaks about a 'poetics of knowledge' to underscore that the discipline of history as producer of knowledge crucially depends on elements of fiction to construct and justify its own authority (Rancière 1994).

Bibliography

Althusser, L., Balibar, É., Establet, R., Macherey, P. and Rancière, J. (1965) *Lire Le Capital*, Paris: Editions François Maspero.

Bingham, C. and Biesta, G. (2010) *About Jacques Rancière: Education, Truth, Emancipation*, New York: Continuum.

Bowman, P. (ed.) (2013) *Rancière and Film*, Edinburgh: Edinburgh University Press.

Bowman, P. and Stamp, R. (eds.) (2011) *Reading Rancière*, London and New York: Continuum.

Chambers, S. (2013) *The Lessons of Rancière*, New York: Oxford University Press.

Davis, O. (2010) *Jacques Rancière*, Cambridge, UK: Polity Press.

Deranty, J.-P. (ed.) (2010) *Jacques Rancière: Key Concepts*, Durham: Acumen.

Deranty, J.-P. and Ross, K. (eds.) (2012) *Jacques Rancière and the Contemporary Scene: The Philosopher of Radical Equality*, London and New York: Continuum.

Genel, K. and Deranty, J.-P. (eds.) (2016) *Recognition or Disagreement: A Critical Encounter on the Politics of Freedom, Equality, and Identity: Axel Honneth and Jacques Rancière*. New York: Columbia University Press.
May, T. (2008) *The Political Thought of Jacques Rancière: Creating Equality*, Edinburgh: Edinburgh University Press.
Davis, O. (ed.) (2013) *Rancière Now: Current Perspectives on Jacques Rancière*, Cambridge: Polity Press.
Rancière, J. (1994) *The Names of History: On the Poetics of Knowledge*, translated by H. Melehy, Minneapolis and London: University of Minnesota Press.
Rancière, J. (1998) *Mute Speech: Literature, Critical Theory, and Politics*, translated by J. Swenson with an introduction by G. Rockhill, New York: Columbia University Press.
Rancière, J. (1999) *Disagreement: Politics and Philosophy*, translated by J. Rose, Minneapolis and London: University of Minnesota Press.
Rancière, J. (2004a) *The Politics of Aesthetics: The Distribution of the Sensible*, translated with an introduction by G. Rockhill, London and New York: Continuum.
Rancière, J. (2004b) 'Who Is the Subject of the Rights of Man?', *The South Atlantic Quarterly*, vol. 103, no. 2–3, pp. 297–310.
Rancière, J. (2005) *La haine de la démocratie*, Paris: La Fabrique.
Rancière, J. (2009a) 'A Few Remarks on the Method of Jacques Rancière', *Parallax*, vol. 15, no. 3, pp. 114–123.
Rancière, J. (2009b) 'The Aesthetic Dimension: Aesthetics, Politics, Knowledge', *Critical Inquiry*, vol. 36, pp. 1–19.
Rancière, J. (2009c) *The Emancipated Spectator*, London: Verso.
Rancière, J. (2009d) *Aesthetics and Its Discontents*, translated by S. Corcoran, Cambridge: Polity Press.
Rancière, J. (2009e) 'Afterword: The Method of Equality: An Answer to Some Questions', in Rockhill, G. and Watts, P. (eds.) *Jacques Rancière: History, Politics, Aesthetics*, Durham and London: Duke University Press, pp. 273–288.
Rancière, J. ([1974] 2011) *Althusser's Lesson*, translated by E. Battista, London and New York: Continuum.
Rancière, J. ([1981] 2012) *Proletarian Nights: The Workers' Dream in Nineteenth-Century France*, translated by J. Drury with an introduction by D. Reid, London and New York: Verso.
Rancière, J. (2012) 'Work, Identity, Subject', in Deranty, J.-P. and Ross, K. (eds.) *Jacques Rancière and the Contemporary Scene: The Philosopher of Radical Equality*, London and New York: Continuum, pp. 205–216.
Rancière, J. (2013) *Aisthesis: Scenes from the Aesthetic Regime of Arts*, translated by Z. Paul, London and New York: Verso.
Rancière, J. and Faure, A. (eds.) (1976) *La Parole ouvrière, 1830–1851: textes rassemblés et présentés*, Paris: Union Générale d'éditions.
Rockhill, G. (1998) 'Introduction: Through the Looking Glass: The Subversion of the Modernist Doxa', translated by J. Swenson, in Rancière, J. *Mute Speech: Literature, Critical Theory, and Politics*, New York: Columbia University Press, pp. 1–28.
Rockhill, G. and Watts, P. (eds.) (2009) *Jacques Rancière: History, Politics, Aesthetics*, Durham and London: Duke University Press.
Tanke, J. (2011) *Jacques Rancière: An Introduction*, New York: Continuum.

Part I

Law without method

Chapter 1

Jacques Rancière and the dramaturgy of law

*Julen Etxabe**

> When it comes to the appreciation of a thinker, there are two levels of investigation. One can examine his/her ideas, test their consistency, compare them with other thinkers' ideas and judge the good or bad effects that they can produce when going from 'theory' to 'practice'. But, at another level, one examines the way these 'ideas' are produced, the issues they address, the materials they select, the givens they consider significant, the phrasing of their connection, the landscape they map, their way of inventing solutions (or aporias), in short their method.
>
> (Jacques Rancière 2009a: 114)

1. The method of Jacques Rancière: setting the scene

In the remarkable essay 'A Few Remarks on the Method of Jacques Rancière', the reader and critic Jacques Rancière writes about the well-known philosopher and author Jacques Rancière in the third person, trying to elucidate what might be distinctive about the latter's method. Contrary to grammatical expectations, the third person is used here to create not a separation between author and critic, but rather the opposite, confusion between these two roles. Confusion between speakers is actually an important stylistic trait of much of Rancière's writing, where without markers he introduces the words of speakers – the radical pedagogue Joseph Jacotot in *The Ignorant Schoolmaster*, the romantic historian Jules Michelet in *The Names of History*, the nineteenth century joiner Louis Gabriel Gauny in *The Proletarian Nights* – with whom his own voice merges almost to the point of indistinctiveness (Ross 1991: xxii). The strategy serves not only to disavow a position of authority from which a method is being 'explained' to the reader, but fundamentally also to flesh out an important Rancièrian presupposition: the equality of intelligence between the one who creates sentences and the one who understands them.[1]

What Rancière means by 'method' is not an investigation into an author's propositions – what an author says, the internal consistency of what the author says, and the consequences that follow – but rather the kind of issues it addresses, the materials and givens it considers, the phrasings it articulates, the landscapes it portrays, and the solutions or aporias it generates. This sense of a method does not proceed by Cartesian simplification into clear and distinct ideas, for it entails selecting, discriminating, valuing, intervening, and indeed inventing. Rancière (2009a: 114) writes:

> A method means a path: not the path that a thinker follows but the path that he/she constructs, that you have to construct to know where you are, to figure out the characteristics of the territory you are going through, the places it allows you to go, the way it obliges you to move, the markers that can help you, the obstacles that get in the way. [. . .] This idea of what 'method' means should never be forgotten when it comes to Jacques Rancière.

Note first here the shift from the third to the second person, where 'you' can refer either to the critic trying to make sense of the author's writings, to the author trying to explain his own method to the critic, or to both. Additionally, 'you' also alludes to the reader – say you or me – trying to make sense both of what Rancière the author does generally in his writing and of what Rancière the critic says about it in this particular essay.

As a path that the author constructs rather than follows, a method does not exist in the past in a way that prefigures, and guides, the author's activity. Rather, the path is constituted towards the future, as an invitation to see things one way rather than another; a suggestion to consider certain issues, perspectives, connections, ways of looking – or others. A method thus enables us who wish to trace it to move within the apperceptive sensorium of another human being and inhabit their ways of seeing and judging reality.

Rancière speaks of method in terms of spatial categories of place, territory, and landscape, delimited by markers and prevented by obstacles, which is why a method often has a normative component that 'allows', 'obliges', 'helps', or 'gets in the way'. But a method also features a *temporal* dimension, for it allows you to 'move' and 'go through', while neither the path nor its stepping stones remain unchanged from beginning to end.[2] Rancière defines a method as a form of travel that 'continuously discovers new landscapes, paths or obstacles which oblige to reframe the conceptual net used to think where we are' (Rancière 2009a: 120). Accordingly, '[w]hat he does himself is to construct a moving map of a moving landscape, a map that is ceaselessly modified by the movement itself' (Ibid). To ascertain the characteristics of this landscape requires more than the tools of the prospector trying to extract minerals from the soil. To grasp this 'moving landscape' requires developing a sense of orientation to figure out where you are, where you are going, and where you can go with it, all of which cannot be represented as a still image. To 'map' it is neither to produce a flat cartography, nor to freeze it in time, but to get in on with its movement, in order to recreate a method's 'topography of the thinkable,' which 'is always the topography of a theater of operations' (Rancière 2009b: 19).

My purpose in this chapter is to re-create such a Rancièrian topography in order to elaborate a theatrical or dramaturgic model of law out of it. Indeed,

Rancière has been said to espouse a theatrical model of politics based on scenes staged by actors who, acting out on the presupposition of equality, undergo processes of subjectivation that reconfigure the 'sense' of the common (e.g., Hallward 2009). Disavowing a purified or ontological concept of the political, Rancière instead proposes a *dramaturgy* conceived out of limit-scenes that stage its appearance and disappearance (Rancière 2009a: 119). Consistently,

> Rancière is only interested in ideas at work: not 'democracy' for instance, but 'democracy' voiced in sentences that stage its possibility or impossibility, not 'politics' in general but discourses and practices which set the stage of its birth or of its fading away.
>
> (Rancière 2009a: 116)

In a similar manner, I, too, venture to offer neither an explanation of his ideas nor an application of his thoughts to a predetermined concept of law but a re-enactment of the legal landscape he invites us to traverse.

The analysis focuses on jurisgenerative moments of dissensus, where those in principle without a place in the order of legalism are nevertheless able to stage a disagreement that reconfigures the sensible texture of law. Beyond teasing out the implications of the argument, I inquire how a claim perceived to be legally irrelevant could nonetheless be *heard* and registered as a novel legal inscription. This will lead us to consider a (non-Aristotelian) poetics of expression and of reception, including the role of judges as audiences of improper legal claims, and to test the practical implications of a Rancièrian dramaturgy of law in the case of the post-2008 mortgage crisis in Spain. In the final analysis, a consistently Rancièrian position leads to a radical relativization where law, just as democracy itself, has no proper foundations. My aim is not so much to persuade the reader about this position as about the usefulness of entertaining it, as a possibility for critical intervention.

* * *

Before moving on to the rest of the argument, it is necessary to consider the role that scenes play in Rancière's overall project, for they take centre stage in legal dramaturgy as well. This role is fourfold: first, scenes provide the *texture* of the argument, for 'Rancière always constructs his argumentation as a re-staging of a limited number of such scenes' (Rancière 2009a: 117). Scenes may include the narrative of the Plebs on the Aventine Hill, the aphorism of Aristotle about the political animal, a manifesto of tailors on strike demanding relationships of equality, or the comments of an ordinary joiner about the work of a bricklayer. 'This is an unusual texture for a theoretical discourse' (Rancière 2009a: 117), and departs equally from syllogistic forms of reasoning and from systematic theory building. Rancière purports to construct not a theory of politics, or democracy, or aesthetics, but a *dramaturgy* (Rancière 2009a: 117 and 119). Contrary to conceptual, universalizing discourses where time is suspended, a dramaturgy is necessarily situated. The same is true about Rancière's well-known categories of analysis: police and politics, distribution of the sensible, aesthetics, etc., are neither ontological determinations nor ahistorical essences, but ways of disentangling inherited classifications (Rancière 2009d: 287; Rancière 2010: 205).

Second, a scene is a 'general mode of intelligibility' that helps to frame significant turning points in history, politics, aesthetics, democracy, and so forth, without the need of a universal vantage point (Rancière 2015). A scene is a *site of circulation* that creates a certain configuration of sense, namely, a form of linkage between perceptions, decisions, and meanings (Rancière 2009: 120). 'The main point is not what they explain or express, it is the way in which . . . they create a commonsense: things that the speaker and those who hear it are invited to share – as a spectacle, a feeling, a phrasing, a mode of intelligibility' (Rancière 2009a: 117).[3] Rancière does not enclose scenes in a historicist box, but nor does he hypostasize a unified 'time out of joint' (Rancière 2011a: 13) either. Instead, the analysis 'must implement, at the same time, a principle of historicization and a principle of untimeliness, a principle of contextualization and a principle of de-contextualization' (Rancière 2009d: 282). That is, 'you must make words resound in their concrete place and time of enunciation . . . [b]ut you must also draw the line of escape' where the poor bricklayer meets the aristocratic philosopher of antiquity (Ibid).

Third, scenes are exemplary 'limit-moments' where the appearance and disappearance of subjects, phrases, modes of being, roles, and powers are made visible or invisible (Rancière 2009a: 117–118). They are exemplary not by virtue of models of conduct worthy of imitation but insofar as they are able to disclose their objects to their fullest force and intensity (e.g., equality, politics, democracy, aesthetics, or emancipation). For example, Rancière suggests that the 'power of the people' can be best understood from moments where that power appears in its utmost effectiveness, namely, from moments of disruption of the hierarchical order (Ibid: 118). Likewise 'what politics means can best be understood from the moments when the power of anybody emerges most significantly' (Ibid: 120). In doing so, Rancière draws inspiration from the 'panecastic method' of Joseph Jacotot, which is based on the assumption that 'you can see the whole in a very small fragment' (Rancière 2015).[4] This does not mean that everything is in the scene, but that what appears most forcefully in it (e.g., the demonstration of equality, the power of anybody, the aesthetic reconfiguration of the sensible) can exemplify similar processes everywhere and at any time. As a result, the exemplarity of the scene lies not at the level of mimetic representation (what the scene is shown to portray), but of poetic enactment (what it sets in motion to produce).

Finally, for scenes to deploy their full effects they must be read in a certain way, that is, their effects can be felt only on condition that one pulls different threads together (Rancière 2009a: 119). Scenes thus require the critic 'to follow these fluctuations of perception and speech and to try to *let their power and their stakes be felt*' (Rancière 2011b: 240–241, emphasis added). The critic becomes not a passive onlooker but, rather, a(n) (emancipated) spectator, with the responsibility to perceive, and not overwrite, their potential happening. A poetics of critical reception consists in the double movement of detecting and highlighting the operations (of equality) that shatter supposedly incontrovertible situations (of inequality) and of presenting alternative 'as ifs' that overturn the logic of those situations.[5] This alternative 'as if' is no illusion opposed to the real, but, rather, a redistribution of the 'regime of the sensible' that opens up what can be seen, felt, and thought (Rancière 2009b: 8). The discourse of the critic is effective neither as description (is) nor as prescription (ought), but as potentiality (might be). Accordingly, '"It might be" is a formulation consistent with Rancière's peculiar practice of "theory"' (Rancière 2009a: 119).

To sum up, scenes offer a texture for 'theoretical' argument; a frame of interpretation for intersecting configurations of sense; an occasion for an exemplary appearance of objects in question; and a counterforce to inegalitarian expressions of 'what is'. A theatrical or dramaturgical conception of law finds its correlative in the legal scene, where no external position exists for the legal theorist to describe law in its totality, or as a totality. In order to gain a synoptic vision one has to go through the scene of law as an experience, rather than as an external object, field, or social subsystem. A dramaturgy of law also connects scenes from diverse origins, making them resound in their particular context of enunciation without refusing to draw lines of relevance beyond it. Scenes are chosen for their salience and ability to signify, just as 'hard cases' illuminate not only themselves but the entire legal landscape. To be sure, scenes may have blind spots and some events may not be seen on the stage. And yet absences, omissions, gaps, and silences often leave traces of their absence that are to be interpreted, and can even be sensed, like a chill in the air, an ominous silence, or violence in Greek tragedy, which is not shown on stage, but must be re-enacted. Lastly, a dramaturgy of law critically engages 'not only the "is" and the "ought", but the "is", the "ought", and the "what might be"' (Cover 1983: 10; Etxabe 2010).

2. Politics and jurisgenesis

> Politics is not primarily a matter of laws and constitutions. Rather it is a matter of configuring the sensible texture of the community for which those laws and constitutions make sense.
>
> (Jacques Rancière 2009b: 8)

While on a first reading, law and politics appear not to be 'a matter of' each other, the preceding quotation actually keeps law and politics *connected* through the sensible texture of the community for which they make sense. This calls for a reformulation of both terms. To begin with politics, Rancière develops a particular understanding of politics not as 'the set of procedures whereby the aggregation and consent of collectivities is achieved, the organization of powers, the distribution of places and roles, and the systems for legitimating this distribution' – which he renames *police* (Rancière 1999: 28). Politics, by contrast, is a process whereby a given regime of visibility – an order that regulates what is 'common-sensical' within a society – is interrupted by an egalitarian and dissensual logic that disrupts its naturalness. As an activity, then, politics 'undoes the perceptible divisions' (Rancière 1999: 30) and 'makes visible what had no business being seen, and makes heard a discourse where once there was only place for noise' (Rancière 1999: 30).[6]

Rancière offers multiple examples: Olympe de Gouges' famous declaration during the French Revolution that if women were entitled to go to the scaffold they were also entitled to go to the assembly; Jeanne Deroin when in 1849 she tried to present herself as a candidate to an election where women were not legally allowed to do so; or Rosa Parks when she refused to give up her seat to a white passenger in Montgomery, Alabama. Rancière also draws on little vignettes: during the trial of Auguste Blanqui in 1832, when asked by the magistrate to name his profession, Blanqui defiantly responded 'proletarian'. The magistrate replied that to be a proletarian is not a profession, to which Blanqui retorted: 'But it is the profession of thirty million Frenchmen who live off their labor and who are deprived of political rights!' After this unexpected rejoinder, the judge instructed the clerk to list proletarian as a new profession.

A favourite is the scene of the Plebs of the Aventine Hill in 494 BC, their retreat from the city as a result of the harsh rule of Appius Claudius, their failed negotiation with the patricians who denied them their status as proper interlocutors, and their eventual reintegration into the city with creation of the office of tribune of the plebs. Rather than follow Livy's account, however, Rancière goes for the nineteenth-century retelling by Pierre-Simon Ballanche, who objected to Livy's inability to think of the event as anything other than as an uprising devoid of all political meaning. In contrast, Ballanche restages the conflict as one in which 'the entire issue at stake involves finding out whether there exists a common stage where plebeians and patricians can debate anything' (Rancière 1999: 23). The plebeians claim a symbolic place in the city in which they as yet have no representation, while the patricians are compelled to acknowledge them despite their harsh rejection.

Contrary to what some commentators suppose, Rancière's examples are not always heroic. Sometimes they are small, almost imperceptible events, and range from a modest meeting of nine persons in a London tavern to create a 'Corresponding Society', to a slight modification of the timetable of a worker's evening. Each action seems to require some measure of courage – not least the conviction and determination to follow it through – but not a martyrology of self-sacrifice. Nor does politics consist in moments of hysterical upheaval after which everything becomes calm again. In fact, politics may begin with a 'tiny modification in the posture of the body' (Rancière 2009d: 275), even though major consequences can follow. What these examples have in common is that the political *actor*[7] must do something 'unimaginable' from the perspective of the given order; something to which they are not in principle entitled, but which ends up rearranging the community's configuration of sense.

Politics acts on the police. By police Rancière means not the petty police or the state apparatus, but a more general 'order of the visible and the sayable' that arranges the tangible distribution of society. As reformulated by Rancière, 'police' is a nonpejorative term which defines, often implicitly, 'that a particular activity is visible and another is not, that this speech is understood as discourse and another as noise' (Rancière 1999: 29). Thus, '[p]olicing is not so much the "disciplining" of bodies as a rule governing their appearing' (Ibid). Additionally, however, the police order designates a specific type of saturated community that rules out any supplement or empty spaces, with the motto: 'a place for everything and everything in its place' (Davis 2010: 78). In this restricted sense, police and policing are specific ways of partitioning the sensible [*partage du sensible*] which are antagonistic to politics. Surely, then, the negative overtones of police/ing do not entirely disappear, nor are they erased under the new terminology.

To weave a dramaturgy of law out of Rancièrian threads is not simply to apply the analysis to an already constituted realm of law but to reformulate the latter as well. Some potential avenues are to be resisted: the first is simply to identify law with the police order, for dissensual logic is often expressed in the language of law. On the other hand, the task cannot be a simple reversal either, turning law into politics (e.g., law-as-resistance), for the idea of institutional arrangement cannot be realistically extricated from law altogether. Yet a third red herring would be to posit a differentiated sphere for 'the juridical', separated from the economy, society, and so on.[8] Law cannot be sealed off from the rest of social life, nor does a determinate set of issues exist that are by nature legal.

If law is conceived neither as a form of police, nor as politics, nor as a separate juridical sphere, I want to suggest a fourth possibility in the notion of law as the encounter between two heterogeneous processes. Just as Rancière argues that nothing is political in itself, but anything may become political if it gives rise to a meeting of logics never set up in advance (Rancière 1999: 32), I suggest that nothing is legal in itself, but anything can *become* legal if it gives rise to such an encounter.

I would propose for law a doubling similar to that which Rancière articulates for police/politics: in lieu of the police we would have the order of *legalism*, namely, a set of procedures for the aggregation of consent, the organization of powers, the distribution of places and roles, and the system of legitimizing that distribution. Judith Shklar defines legalism as an ethical attitude of rule-following, coupled with an ideology of agreement that evacuates dissent from 'the right and true view' of the law (Shklar 1964: 1, 10). Legalism is associated with a culture of formalism that establishes a sharp distinction between law and non-law, values consistency, predictability, and procedural correctness, and where the (moral) evaluation of law is irrelevant for its application. Both as a set of practices that constitute (the dominant image of) the rule of law and a particular ideology that pushes out manifestations of law other than the state's, legalism can be identified with the state as 'an institution whose operation tends to transform the political scene into purely a matter of police management' (Rancière 2011b: 249).

In the opposite direction, we could set a process that interrupts legalism which, borrowing a term from Robert Cover (1983), we may call *jurisgenesis*. The jurisgenetic (or jurisgenerative) impulse would come to interrupt the logic of legalism and challenge its distribution of roles, places, subjects, and doctrines. Despite legalism's attempt to saturate the normative space, its completion can never be fully accomplished: 'the juridical inscription that should set things in order . . . constantly lend[s itself] to the construction of unforeseen trajectories of looking and speaking' (Rancière 2011b: 243). This means that jurisgenesis is always a possibility. Jurisgenesis points to the existence of a *wrong* in the legalistic order and challenges the very boundary between law and non-law.

Jurisgenerative capacity is not the privilege of those who hold institutional office or who are otherwise vested with legal authority to act. In the wake of normative pluralism, this power is acknowledged of anyone whomsoever who, undergoing a process of subjectivation, instantiates a wrong in the fabric of legalism and reconfigures the legally sayable, thinkable, and doable.[9] The corollary of this theatrical conception of law is a rejection of legal positivism as an order consisting of a posited, gapless system; but it is equally separated from any idea of natural law as pre-existing, for the law is to be created together with the stage where it is to be understood. The resulting image is not a purified jurisgenetic law, for jurisgenesis is always mixed with legalism.

How norm-generative moments might emerge in specific legal settings calls for elaboration. Taking the cue from Rancière's article 'Who Is the Subject of Human Rights?', a promising avenue may be found in the double existence of rights (and arguably of written law in general), which are first inscriptions in the regime of the visible, but then require to be activated in their potential by those who can make something out of that inscription (Rancière 2004a: 302). The staging calls for a poetics of expression and 'legal imagination' (White 1973), which never develops in a vacuum: it 'draws on forms of juridical inscription or forms of labour [sic] relation, on religious narratives, on models taken from school books, on ways of being alone or of meeting others that are put into circulation by literature, on definitions of bodily health and corruption circulated by life sciences, on ways of seeing and hearing formed by metropolitan cultures' (Rancière 2011b: 242–243), in short, an 'excess of words' that turns humans into 'literary animals' (Ibid: 248; see further Chambers 2013: ch 3). And yet the jurisgenerative impulse is not just world-creating, for it must take into account the material conditions and the limitations upon which it must act. In other words, the creation of litigious worlds is an aesthetic event, not a mere invention of languages, for an argument must always be won on pre-existing and constantly re-enacted distribution of languages (Rancière 1999: 45) and take into account the expected behaviour of those who might likely oppose it.

3. The law of disagreement: putting two worlds in one

> A dissensus puts two worlds – two heterogeneous logics – on the same stage, in the same world. It is a commensurability of incommensurables.
>
> (Rancière 2009b: 11)

A dramaturgic conception of law builds on scenes of disagreement between heterogeneous normative worlds. In Rancière's terminology, a dis-agreement [*mésentente*] is not a simple case of misunderstanding when one of the parties does not understand the meaning of terms, or of misconstruction, when one of the parties does not know what she is saying through dissimulation, ignorance, or delusion. Nor is it a case of someone who says white and another who says black. Rather, 'it is the conflict between one who says white and another who also says white but does not understand the same thing by it or does not understand that the other is saying the same thing in the name of whiteness' (Rancière 1999: x). A parallel term for it is *dissensus*, which is a division in the *sense* – sensory experience and meaning – of the common (Rancière 2010: 38). A dissensus cracks open a situation from within and reconfigures it in a different regime of perception and signification (Rancière 2009c: 48); it does so by inscribing one perceptual world into another – for example, the world in which proletarians and women can participate in the other world in which they are either uncounted as a collective or relegated to domesticity (Rancière 2003b: 226). Disagreement and dissensus are not Schmittian confrontations between friends and enemies, or the opposition of interests or opinions, but fractures over constitutive questions such as 'where are we?', 'who are we?', 'what makes us a we?', 'what do we see and what can we say about it that makes us a we, having a world in common?' (Rancière 2009a: 116).

Rancière situates his argument between Habermas and Lyotard (and thus between two opposing ideas of modernity and the role of reason/unreason in it). Arguing explicitly against the Habermasian model of communicative action, which presupposes equal partners in a horizon of shared understandings, the specifics of dis-agreement are that its partners are no more constituted than the object or the stage itself (Rancière 2010: 38). Indeed, '[p]arties do not exist prior to the conflict they name and in which they are named as parties' (Rancière 1999: 27). According to Rancière, before any confrontation of interests and values, 'the place, the object, and the subjects of the discussion are themselves in dispute and must in the first instance be tested' (Rancière 1999: 27). Therefore, 'it is necessary to simultaneously produce both the argument and the situation in which it is to be understood, the object of the discussion and the world in which it figures as object' (Rancière 1999: 57). This represents a most peculiar platform, for 'the speaker has to behave *as though* such a stage existed, as though there were a common world of argument – which is eminently reasonable *and* eminently unreasonable, eminently wise and resolutely subversive, since such a world does not exist' (Rancière 1999: 52).

On the other hand, the stage(ing) of disagreement cannot be said to be unbridgeable as a *differend*, which is Lyotard's (1988) neologism to describe a kind of conflict that cannot be resolved for lack of a rule of judgment applicable to both parties, and/or where applying a single rule of judgment would wrong one of them.[10] In such cases, the wrong 'consists not only in the fact that a party is harmed but that the injured party is divested of the means to make visible this injury as an injustice' (Schaap 2009: 210). Amidst the inevitable heterogeneity of language games, and the impossibility of subsuming them all under a single, neutral genre of discourse,[11] Lyotard's differend is marked by absences: of a common language between the parties; of a common procedure to channel their conflict; of an equitable rule of judgment; of an appropriate remedy to redress the harm.

Rancière's main objection to Habermas and Lyotard alike, as Fiona Jenkins explains, is that 'they presume a situation of separation and then raise the question whether it can be justly constructed', whereas Rancière 'denies the primacy of separation by placing both contesting claims in a common situation structured by disagreement' (Jenkins 2009: 191). This is what Rancière examines under the heading 'rationality of disagreement', which does not mean that the conflict itself is bound to rules of rational discourse (in the procedural or deliberative sense) or that the participants themselves argue 'rationally' (as opposed to emotionally). What Rancière means is that the disagreement can be placed in a mutual space of encounter or common stage, which is why 'a disagreement may not be settled, *but it can be processed*' (1999: 39, emphasis added).[12]

If a disagreement puts 'two worlds in one and the same world' (Rancière 2004a: 304), how can we conceive this space of encounter – and where does it 'take place'? Samuel Chambers rightly argues that no need arises to posit a logically prior third space of encounter (Chambers 2013: 59; cf. Deranty 2003: para 6).[13] In his view, the disagreement happens within the established order (of the police) itself (Ibid: 62). While partially correct, this does not quite capture the 'newness' that a political or jurisgenerative act introduces in the place in question, which it reconfigures in a different regime of perception and signification. Therefore, even though '[p]olitics 'takes place' in the space of the police' (Rancière 2011a: 8), for Rancière this 'means reshaping those places' (Ibid). There appears to be a double sense of 'place' at work here, at once material and *theatrical* (or virtual but not illusory) (Rancière 2007: 50). While in the first sense 'there is no place outside of the police' (Rancière 2011a: 6), in the latter, the stage of this theater of operations is transformed accordingly. We might say that the encounter 'takes place' not so much within, but *upon* an order (of police/legalism) that the dissensual-jurisgenerative logic simultaneously reconfigures. (We will come back to this later.)

Having suggested that the stage of disagreement also reconfigures the place of encounter, several questions remain: first, do limits exist to the kind of disagreements susceptible to being thus staged? Second, what would it mean to bring a Rancièrian disagreement to the legal arena? Jean-Louis Déotte reflects on the first question by setting up Rancière against Lyotard (Déotte 2004). He argues that the blind spot in Rancière's dis-agreement is that this genre of political discourse (which he equates with 'the deliberative') remains insensitive to cases of intercultural differend, for which no common scene of interlocution would be available. He cites the example of a Malian mother responsible for the genital excision of her daughter, who is condemned by a French tribunal of child abuse or sexual mutilation. Déotte argues that the conflict is not political in the modern sense of the term, for she has no pretension to inscribe her law into the virtual community of deliberation and furthermore she will never be able to justify herself according to such norms. At the very most, Déotte writes, 'an enlightened judge will attempt to render intelligible the words of the mother accused of excision; he will invoke her ethnographic baggage, but only in order to reproach her for her archaic submission to the norms of a traditional group' (Ibid: 88). Thus, the legal system requires her to accept a norm of discourse that is not that of the community that formed her identity, and hence to abandon her own relationship to the law. For Déotte, this example 'demonstrates how insurmountable is the différend between those whose life on earth is predestined by stories and "us", who . . . know that we must deliberate over everything' (Ibid: 87). In other words, disagreement presupposes that the cultural-legal differend has been dealt with, for '[t]here can only be political disagreement between those . . . who share the same sense of history' (Ibid: 88).

This passage contains much to unpack, but the argument rests on an initial mischaracterization. Déotte subsumes Rancière's disagreement into a genre of discourse, the deliberative, which is ill suited to capturing the ruptural logic that the Rancièrian disagreement is meant to introduce.[14] On the one hand, dis-agreement employs forms of demonstration that include bodily gestures, role-playing, mimicking, ironic tossing back, poetic world-openers, and dramatizations, none of which fit easily with abstract models of deliberation. On the other hand, the genre of the deliberative does not exhaust Rancièrian dis-agreement, which is not a conflict of values and interest, but of making visible what had no business being seen.

Mischaracterizations aside, Déotte's analysis has the further consequence of essentializing some kind of conflicts (ethnic, cultural, religious, . . .). Rancière rejects the implicit fatalism of a claim that plunges these conflicts into a sense of archaic destination, excluding them from history. Déotte contrasts the case of the Malian mother with the Roman plebeians, nineteenth-century women, and the proletariat. True, the Malian mother may have no intention of inscribing her custom as law, but living in a society where genital excision is generally seen as aberrant, she will be confronted with the disjunctive of either retracting or defending her position when challenged.[15] She could then decide to withdraw and give up the practice, or else defend it, in which case she would be asking for a reconsideration of the societal norms according to which her action is judged to be aberrant. Herein would lie the potential *jurisgenerative* aspect of her claim, which has nothing to do with her eventual success or failure in doing either.

Conversely, in a context where plebeians were not considered 'creatures of speech', women could not participate in the electoral process, and workers were not thought to constitute a collective subject, can it really be said that they all *already* shared a sense of history with the patricians, the enfranchised men, or the factory owners who denied them? The ability to dramatize a conflict, to place a conflict on a common stage, has nothing to do with the supposedly lesser severity of the conflict, nor does it justify postulating a category of cases (cultural, ethnic, etc.) naturally excluded from being thus staged. At any rate, to stage a dis-agreement does not automatically neutralize or co-opt one's claims, or require accepting the terms of debate, norms, and language of the state as neutral (see

Woodford 2015: 824–825). In fact a dissensus opens up a fracture in the common sense for previously unsayable demands, for which a novel language is required that 'sets the conditions for its own proper reception' (Frank 2009: 89).

This leads to our second general question: What would it take to stage a Rancièrian disagreement in law? The ideology of legalism presents itself as providing a neutral forum and a language in which all claims can be made without loss. However, contemporary life is fraught with examples where the legal system imposes a language that silences some claims and precludes others from even being raised. For example, Andrew Schaap relates how the claim of aboriginal sovereignty in Australia was dismissed out of hand as an 'absurd proposition' (Schaap 2009). The state responded to nascent aboriginal claims in a manner that exemplifies both the silencing and the impossibility of articulating the injustice being committed.[16] Likewise, Emilios Christodoulidis alludes to so-called political trials, where the arguments of dissenters (or 'subversives') are shut down and not even registered (Christodoulidis 2004). Paradoxically, some forms of inclusion are complicit in the silencing. For example, James Tully refers to practices of assimilation where subjects are permitted and often encouraged to participate and yet they are constrained to deliberate in a particular way, in particular places, or over a particular range of issues (but not others), so that their discussion serves to reinforce rather than challenge the status quo (Tully 2002: 223).

The central issue from a Rancièrian perspective is therefore not simply to denounce the law of state-legalism as partial, but to make legalism a party to the disagreement – also transforming the stage where such conflict can happen. That is, to turn a disagreement *in* law into as a disagreement *of* law, where not even the space of the encounter can be taken for granted, or foreclosed in advance as I have already suggested. The practical difficulty is how to challenge an order of legalism that does not want to hear, frames the discussion to the disadvantage of one party, denies a party the status of interlocutor, or more simply, claims that there is anything to discuss.

4. The poetics of expression and the legal hearing

> To happen, events must be perceived and acknowledged as such.
>
> (Ross 2009: 29)

If the gist of dis-agreement is to stage unreasonable and previously unthinkable demands, the established order will presumably not budge, countering that the claims are irrelevant, lack standing, are out of bounds, or unreasonable. Certainly the mere enunciation of a wrong, its appearance in the realm of visibility, does not guarantee that it will produce the desired outcome, as it cannot be assumed that the order of legalism will bend accordingly (Rancière 1999: 44).

How to assess whether the act (demonstration, verification, or claim) succeeds properly as an act? Rancière does not wish to make its success depend upon what the given order does or does not do. As Todd May reminds us, it is important not to confuse the existence of the act with its effects (May 2009: 116). At the same time, Rancière acknowledges that the verification of equality 'becomes social', that is, it is imbued with 'a real social effect, only when it mobilizes an *obligation* to hear' (Rancière 2007: 86, emphasis in original). While Rancière is not explicit about this, there appears to be a gap between the enunciation of a wrong and the hearing it compels, between its expression and the response it elicits: on the one hand, something has effectively to change in the realm of the addressees for the act to come to fruition. On the other hand, its success cannot be made entirely dependent upon those at whose door it lays the question, for then it would suffice to ignore the claim altogether to derail it. So what exactly must happen for an act to succeed as an act? Can it succeed even if the effects are not exactly those intended? And if (some form of) hearing appears necessary, how can it be mobilized as an 'obligation' when the interlocutor 'refuses to hear'? In the context of law: what does it take to for a jurisgenetic act to make a dent and reconfigure the order of legalism?

We might begin to disentangle these questions, first, by focusing on an example of failure. Indeed, that a political demonstration *can* fail gives us important clues as to what stands in the way of its success. Rancière offers the example of a Scythian slave-revolt (Rancière 1999: 12–13). As narrated by Herodotus (iv.3), the Scythians customarily put out the eyes of those they reduced to slavery, the better to restrict them to their task as slaves, which was to milk the livestock. However, this order of things was disturbed after the Scythian army left for a long war-expedition. After nearly three decades battling away against the Medes, the Scythian army returned home to discover a new generation of sons fathered by their own slaves, and raised with their eyes open. Looking around the world, the slaves had reached the conclusion that there was no particular reason why they should be slaves. Accordingly, they built trenches and armed themselves, determined to prove they were equals to the warriors. Initial skirmishes to reconquer them by force failed, but then one of the warriors addressed his brothers thus: 'So long as they see us with arms in our hands, they imagine themselves our equals in birth and bravery; but let them behold us with no other weapon but the whip, and they will feel that they are our slaves, and flee before us' (Herodotus iv.3). And so it was done with immediate success, Herodotus tells us, and the slaves took to their heels without a fight.

The slaves' initial egalitarian demonstration at first unsettles the masters, but when the masters once more show signs of superiority the slaves have no comeback: they are 'unable to transform equality in war into political freedom' (Rancière 1999: 13). This would suggest that, to come to fruition, an act could require a further constellation of accompanying events to fully disclose itself, particularly in the face of likely opposition of the hierarchical order. Some commentators are led to distinguish between the moment of disruption and the moment of reconfiguration, so that the slaves could be said to have interrupted, but not reconfigured, the established order. There is no need for such a distinction: to count, an act must achieve the reconfiguration of the social order it seeks to interrupt, and vice versa. In other words, an act (a demonstration, a claim, a disagreement) 'stops the current' only if, and insofar as, it simultaneously transforms the hierarchical distribution of the sensible. The Scythian slaves failed, first, because they did not articulate another distribution of the sensible, a new distribution that would translate their newly acquired equality of arms (based on force) into a different equality, based on nothing other than the equality of anyone with anyone else and the sheer contingency of the hierarchical order.

But how does the ingenious response of the masters figure in the failure? The warriors asserted their claim to superiority by showing their whips, which made the slaves feel that they were indeed slaves and not the warriors' equals. If the slaves had at any point uttered a claim of equality, surely they were not successful in compelling the obligation to hear. Note, however, that the case was not properly a failure of hearing. The masters heard the claim and heard it exactly as it was initially intended, but acted *as if* they had not heard it, pretending to demonstrate with their demeaning behaviour that the slaves' assertion was null and void. The warriors tested whether the slaves were earnest in asserting a common space of representation with the warriors, and the slaves' return to their former roles without a fight demonstrated they were not. We could say the masters enacted a lie that closely parallels Plato's myth of the three metals (Rancière 2003b: 17–21), and which is equally designed to justify (and perpetuate) a system of social inequality. Here, too, the slaves had their say when believing the master's lie, for 'struck by the spectacle' (Rancière 1999: 12) they failed to stage an alternative 'as if' that would dismantle the master's performative ruse.

That (some sort of) hearing is presupposed in the act can be seen, *a sensu contrario*, in Rancière's favourite story of success. In Ballanche's restaging of the scene of the Aventine, the acknowledgment of the plebs comes almost naturally. The wise men of the senate realize that when a cycle is over it is over, whether you like it or not, and so they are led to conclude that 'since the plebs have become creatures of speech, there is nothing left to do but to talk to them' (Rancière 1999: 25–26). Rancière remarks on Ballanche's sense of historical inevitability, derived from Vico, of cycles that can be progressively recognized by their own signs. We know, however, that for Rancière the recognition of speech as meaningful is never unproblematic, but itself the beginning of politics. Signs, Rancière argues, are not immediately recognizable by all as signifying, but raise a dispute over their status as either signifying (*logos*) or simple noise (*phônê*). Therefore, there is nothing automatic in hearing: it is not that someone utters speech and it is automatically acknowledged. This 'suffices to show that some type of activity, whatever it may be, is involved in the process [of hearing]' (Citton 2009: 122) and opens up the interesting problematic of reception (see Norval 2012).

In sum, what Rancière calls politics (and we are analyzing as jurisgenesis) is a complex social act that requires both uttering and hearing to come fully to fruition. As Marianne Constable has recently elaborated with the help of Adolf Reinach, social acts require being heard or apprehended, but necessitate no particular response in order to be completed (Constable 2014; reviewed in Etxabe 2015). Thus social acts initiate new states of affairs and can instigate responses, but the speaker can never completely determine how a social act, or the state of affairs it initiates, will be taken up – or for how long it will endure (Constable 2014: 91). This creates a potential mismatch between the act and its dissemination, in the echoes, resonances, reverberations, or amplifications by which any act projects itself towards the future.

At the level of enunciation, these acts share features of the performative utterances famously elaborated by John Austin (1986). Still, they are not subject to the 'felicity conditions' Austin imagined.[17] Rancierian claims are spoken by those who are not 'entitled' to speak and hence spoken inappropriately, at the wrong time or in the wrong place, and with no regard for conventions or procedures. Moreover, they encroach upon the listener's sensorium in a way that remained outside of Austin's purview. In this sense they more closely resemble Stanley Cavell's 'passionate utterances' (Cavell 2005), designed to produce effects upon the feelings, thoughts, or actions of the audience without conventional procedures to accomplish the desired effects (Ibid.: 180–182). In these 'the emphasis is explicitly upon the constitution of a *relation* [with you]' (Norval 2009: 171), for I must declare myself to have standing with you and single you out for a response, thereby making myself vulnerable to your rebuke (Cavell 2005: 185). Building on Cavell, Aletta Norval suggests further that passionate utterances open up a space for novel claims to be heard, even in conventional legal settings, due to the transformative force they carry (Norval 2009: 164, 169). As developed by Cavell/Norval, passionate utterances go a long way towards explaining the transformative effects that a jurisgenerative claim can have on the hearers. And yet, in Rancière a political demonstration has force even *in spite of* or *against* you, forcing us to consider the very different constitutive relation[18] established with the interlocutor who rejects you as a proper interlocutor.

For Rancière, this relation is polemic in the sense that the participants need not share the same goals, intentions, or understanding of the situation. This is a central and original point of Rancière that I want to illustrate with the example of Blanqui's magistrate, which conventional accounts of law-as-neutral(izing)-forum inevitably miss. Readers of Rancière naturally focus on the trenchant rejoinder of Blanqui. Much less noted, though no less important, is the reaction of the magistrate, who instructed the court clerk to register proletarian as a new profession. The magistrate is not simply taking stock of Blanqui's rejoinder and recognizing its validity, because the legal order to which he is committed does not include it in the list of proper legal names.

The significance of the gesture can be noticed when we realize that the magistrate was perfectly within his rights to deny the inscription; he could have refused to add proletarian as a new name, for instance leaving a blank space, or he could have ordered the clerk to translate it into one of the known professions. But he did none of these. Instead he ordered the term 'proletarian' to be written down, thereby inscribing a new name in the list of professions. The point is not to make Blanqui's action dependent upon the magistrate, but rather to realize that the latter's simple gesture is already a form of division in the order of legalism he represents.

The response of the presiding magistrate is decidedly different from that of the public prosecutor (*procureur* Mr. M. Delapalme), who protests energetically because for him proletarian does not signify a profession. The prosecutor, who belongs to the same judicial order as the presiding magistrate, and in principle shares his presuppositions, refuses to hear what the magistrate consents to inscribe. The magistrate's different hearing crystallizes the encounter of heterogeneous logics demanded by legal disagreement.

Note that this does not require the magistrate to be aware of what he is doing, or of the implications as Blanqui means them. The magistrate is unlikely to have shared Blanqui's assertion of proletarian as the profession of thirty million French citizens! Perhaps the magistrate wanted to proceed with the trial, or simply to end Blanqui's charade. At any rate his intent is irrelevant: he need not share the ideals and goals of Blanqui for their encounter to 'take place' on a common stage: to be placed under a common scene of intelligibility does not mean there is agreement of wills and intentions, or a shared horizon of understanding – they may in fact have remained dramatically different. Despite being put in one and the same world, their perspectives have not merged into a unified language or single (deliberative) genre of discourse.

5. The emancipated judge

> We are not debt collectors.
>
> (Juan Luis Ibarra, President of the Superior Court of Justice of the Basque Country, in *El Mundo* 2013)

In this chapter I have presented a Rancièrian legal dramaturgy open to jurisgenerative moments of dissensus that disturb the consensual practices of legalism. That law should thus be open is anathema for those who believe in the purity of law and wish to shield it from external influence. My view also differs, though for different reasons, from critical approaches that situate the potential for openness exclusively outside of law, thereby withdrawing from the challenge of thinking of law differently. I have argued that this task demands attention to the legal scene, which is not a return to any primordial or archetypical scene – the killing of the father, the dethronement of a king, grand moments of revolution, or of mythical founding. Rather, a legal dramaturgy is based on contingent scenes of becoming and passing away that enact significant junctures and turning points that constitute the 'sensible community' of [legal] perceptions, affects, names, and ideas (Rancière 2013: xi). Consistent with this 'method' I want to conclude with a scene where judges, the quintessential representatives of legalism, are invited to dissociate themselves from legalism and become emancipated, as third parties to disagreement. Indeed, 'the play of the third person is essential to the logic of political discussion, which is never a simple dialogue' (Rancière 1999: 48). This example will also help us to show how law, despite its strong institutional mechanisms and incentives to close itself down, can be open to jurisgenesis from within.

The scene takes place in the context of the deep mortgage crisis and foreclosures in Spain, one of the countries where the crisis was felt most acutely, after the bursting of the housing bubble in 2008. The liberalization of land in Spain in 1998 had generated a speculative market, supported by aggressive banking practices which marketed mortgages of 100 per cent or more of a property's value (Roca Cladera and Burns 2000; Gentier 2012). Ease of lending, questionable business practices and a culture of home ownership with the highest rates in the EU meant that, by 2008, household debt for home mortgages had reached 65 per cent of the national GDP (European Mortgage Federation 2013). To put it in perspective, Spain built more houses in the decade between 1997 and 2007 than France, Germany, and the United Kingdom combined (Spanish Ombudsman 2012).

When the housing market collapsed, Spain entered a deep economic depression, with harsh austerity measures, and alarming unemployment rates (26 per cent by February 2014, with 50 per cent youth-unemployment from 2012 to 2015). As a result, many new homeowners were unable to make repayments and defaulted *en masse*, leading to hundreds of thousands of foreclosures (440,000 by the end of 2012) (*El Notario del siglo XXI* 2013: 5). What made matters worse was that in Spain, unlike in countries such as the United States, Germany, or France, no mechanism existed for 'clearing' the debt after foreclosure (e.g., personal insolvency laws, debt restructuring). Article 1911 of the Civil Code declares the unlimited liability of debtors, whereby homeowners not only lose their home but are still liable for the outstanding debt plus interest and legal costs.

When the price obtained at auction is insufficient to cover the debt, the enforcement procedure continues according to article 579 of the Law of Civil Procedure (LEC); a procedure of 'limited cognition', where debtors could not raise allegations of substance – in fact, as will be explained later, inability to challenge unfair mortgage clauses would subsequently be declared contrary to European Union law on consumer protection (Case C-415/11). Therefore, it is fair to say that the structure of legalism was heavily tilted in favour of creditors and banks, which not only could auction off a house by paying 50 per cent of the appraisal but also could seize other properties in the ensuing procedure. In addition, if the bank were to sell the repossessed property at a later date at a profit, the amount was not computed towards payment of the principal debt. This led to painful situations of aged parents who had given their homes as collateral for their offspring's mortgages and now risked eviction, even after the mortgaged house had been repossessed by the bank.[19]

Against this dramatic backdrop – including cases of suicide by evicted homeowners – the scene begins in quite an ordinary fashion: a home loan secured by a mortgage; default on repayment; the bank repossesses the house, auctions it off for somewhat more than 50 per cent of the appraisal, and then applies to continue the enforcement procedure for the outstanding debt. In principle, the case appears clear, almost a formality: the judge must ascertain that the conditions are met (enforceable title, non-payment, amount of debt) and the debtor has very limited means of opposition (mainly based on factual errors). The scene is so common in fact that it has been repeated many times over throughout Spain, always with the same result: the judge rules against the debtor with interest and costs. This time, however, the judge refuses to resume the enforcement procedure, with the argument that once the bank has repossessed the house securing the mortgage, continuing the procedure would be an 'abuse of process' [*abuso de derecho*] (Auto 574/2009).

The outcome is unexpected, all the more so because the judge admits that 'the literal reading of the article [579 of LEC] does not seem to leave any interpretive doubts'. Notwithstanding, she assures that 'this does not mean that it should always and in every case be applied' (Ibid.). The judge notes a disparity between the 'nominal' and the 'real' values of the house, by which she means the gap between the price obtained at auction and the valuation agreed upon at creation of the mortgage, enough to cover the full debt. Moreover, the house is not sold to a third party, but the bank enters it in the balance sheet at the appraised value, not the price paid at auction. Therefore, to continue with the enforcement in these circumstances would be a 'manifest abuse of process' (Ibid.).

The decision is as surprising as the reasoning itself, for the judge challenges the conventional wisdom that when the rule leaves no interpretive doubts there is no room for judicial discretion.[20] According to the standard positivist account, when the rule is clear there is nothing for the judge to do but to follow it.

One can begin to appreciate how remarkable this is when contrasted with the very different language by the Provincial Court of Navarra (third section), quashing an identical decision by the same judge just a month later (Auto 4/2011, on appeal). The third section begins by affirming that the role of judges is to perform their task independently, but 'subject to the law' [*sujeción a la ley*]. After recalling the content of articles 1911 CC and 579 LEC (unlimited liability of debtors and possibility to seize for the remainder), the court does not hide its bewilderment: 'the normative content of the said legal precepts is so evident that it is hardly possible to comprehend the reasons why the judge eluded applying them in the case at hand'. Given that the facts fit perfectly with the rules, 'it is not for the judge to assume the legislative function, but to apply the law to the case at hand, [p]articularly when the decision affects the principle of legal certainty' (Ibid.). On the issue of valuation, the court faults the judge for mistaking the value of appraisal with the real value, which is none other than 'the amount of money someone is willing to pay for it' (Ibid.).

Surely these words come closer to what the legal profession would have understood ex ante as representing 'legal common sense'. Therefore, when the second section of the same Provincial Court – the court actually deciding the appeal at hand – sided with the judge of first instance and rejected the enforcement procedure, a scene which had begun as an isolated incident in a small village in Navarre made major headlines (Auto 111/2010).

How did the second section of the Provincial Court justify its decision to uphold? Admittedly, 'from the perspective of a formal and strict application of the law', it cannot be said that the bank has 'abused the process' (Ibid.). However, rules must be interpreted according to the social context in which they are applied (article 3 of the Civil Code) and, in circumstances of crisis, it is 'morally objectionable' that the bank grounds its claim on the loss of value of the property. The bank agreed to secure the property for a value it had itself appraised, and the mortgage would not have been granted had it not been sufficient to cover the mortgage debt in full. In conclusion, the court adds a personal reflection: the loss of value of properties is due to an economic crisis without parallel since the great depression of 1929 and in which 'it cannot be ignored' that financial institutions played a major part. While the bank may not have technically abused its right, it is 'painful' that their claim is 'grounded on circumstances that have stirred such social sensitivity' (Ibid.).

Once again, these are remarkable statements in a court of law, but the question now facing us is: how can two provincial courts – one quashing the first instance decision, the other upholding it – be(come) such different spectators of the same legal scene? One way to read their divergence is through the traditional discrepancy between literal and teleological interpretation, where the former follows a strict application of law and the latter a purposive one (Atienza 2013). Yet the issue is not merely one of different methods of interpretation (cf. Bengoetxea 2014). This is not a mere dispute about the meaning of rules within a common framework (a disagreement in law), but a dispute over the construction of the stage and the status of the claims that the logic of legalism *does not want to hear* (a disagreement of law). The disagreement extends to the very frame of discussion, which legalism wishes to relegate to the realm of non-law.

The judge of first instance opens up a tear that the third section (the one that quashed it) seeks to close off, by appealing to 'self-evident' rules and facts. In contrast, the second section (the one that upheld it) perceives a fracture in the regime of the sensible, where the judgment cannot be divorced from the underlying conditions where the dispute takes place. Whereas the third section follows the (neoliberal) logic of the market as a proxy for the real value, the second section takes up the value agreed upon at appraisal. The latter has been criticized as a fiction (Atienza 2013: 14). Let us not forget, however, that market value is also a fiction that assumes what the economic crisis has completely shattered, namely a perfect correspondence between supply and demand in conditions of free competition. What the second section actually does is to shed light on the inequality at the heart of this fiction and to replace it with a different, alternative 'as if' that ties the valuation to the mortgage it served to secure, and in default of which it would not have been granted. Whether this valuation is less or more 'real' depends on considerations that the third section is unwilling to entertain. By contrast, the second section enquires into the conditions of enforcement. For this it is not irrelevant that the bank itself made the appraisal, later obtained the house at auction by paying only 50 per cent of the appraised amount, and can still sell it when conditions improve – as banks did subsequently in many instances. In bringing these circumstances to bear, the court offers a new configuration of the sensible which rearranges the equality of arms that the procedural laws slanted in favour of creditors and against debtors.

Finally, the third section's conventional submission to legalism (where the role of the judge is simply to follow the law regardless of its merits) displays a further feature of legalism: identifying the third section's opinion with the 'right and true view' of the law (Shklar 1964: 10). The court cannot fathom that a real difference of opinion can exist and seeks to evacuate dissent from the law. By contrast, the second section turns the role of the judge into an open question. Dissenting from the distribution of places and roles assigned by legalism, the judges of the second section turn the term 'judge' into a litigious name.

This process of subjectivation was most clearly articulated by the President of the Superior Court of the Basque Country, Juan Luis Ibarra, after the Court of Justice of the European Union declared the Spanish enforcement procedure contrary to European Law in 2013. According to Ibarra, the European Court corrected an anomaly in Spanish law that turned judges into debt collectors and made judging impossible, for 'judging is not enforcing, but adjudicating contentious issues'. As he put it vividly: 'We are [judges] not debt collectors' (cited in *El Mundo* 2013). Similarly, turning judgment into an issue, the judges in our scene resisted identification with legalism and their putative role as passive enforcers. Instead, they enacted the logic of emancipation, which enabled them to recognize a wrong in the distribution of the sensible; that is, a fundamental inequality between creditors (banks) and debtors (homeowners).

Contrary to the anxieties of legalism, emancipation in this context does not mean that the judge is let loose to impose his or her will on society: the logic of the emancipated judge actually demands the existence of a 'third thing' to be verified in each and every performance.[21] This third thing in our context is the legal scene that both the parties and the judge share; a common frame of intelligibility under which their conflict is staged and plays out. Against the unfounded worry of 'judicial activism' and the correlative claim of judges blindly following the law – a 'noble lie' for the general public, I am afraid, rarely believed by practitioners – the judge in legal dramaturgy is not unmoored from the legal scene before him. To be responsive to the legal scene, and to the demands it poses, also entails responsibility for the 'inscriptions' judges make, the way they talk about issues, the people before them, and the societal impact of their decisions, cognizant of the material constraints they face and aided by the intelligence they possess.

* * *

The decision to uphold of the Provincial Court was short-lived: subsequent legislative changes and a decision of the Spanish Constitutional Court compelled the court to reverse course and submit to the hierarchical principle – while concluding on a note pointing out legal alternatives still open to debtors (Auto 24/2012). Some may be tempted to conclude from this that legalism shuts down the jurisgenerative capacity of judges, as nothing seemed really to change. A critical dramaturgy, however, makes 'the stakes and power of the scene felt', for this was *not nothing*. The scene was not an isolated incident and other judges, too, resisted legalism.[22] More importantly, though the pressures of legalism are obviously strong, they can crack again. When a judge in Barcelona decided to bring to task the Spanish enforcement procedure before the Court of Justice of the European Union, the entire order of legalism had to reckon with the fact that it failed adequately to protect homeowners, and was forced to change.[23] Therefore, while on its own a scene proves nothing, we can make it count as part of a larger sequence of reverberations, echoes, and amplifications that reconfigure the thick armour of legalism.

Notes

* An earlier version of this chapter was presented during the UCB Townsend working Group on Law & Contemporary Theory at the University of Berkeley, California. I want to thank all the participants in the workshop for their inquisitive questions and in particular Marianne Constable and James Martel for organizing it.

1 The equality of intelligence, borrowed from Jacotot, 'does not mean that every manifestation of intelligence is equal to any other. Above all, it means that the same intelligence makes and understands sentences in general' (Rancière 2011b: 114). Jacotot's simple premise is that 'all people are virtually capable of understanding what others have done and understood' (Hallward 2009: 144).

2 'This is why, indeed, his "concepts" are unstable: police and politics, distribution of the sensible, aesthetics, literature, etc. don't mean the same thing from the beginning of the travel to the end' (Rancière 2009a: 120).

3 For Rancière a common sense 'does not mean a consensus but, on the contrary, a polemical place, a confrontation between opposite common senses or opposite ways of framing what is common' (Rancière 2009d: 277).

4 Rancière defines Jacotot's panecastic method as 'a method for finding in every (*ekaston*) peculiar manifestation of intelligence the whole (*pan*) of its power' (Rancière 2009d: 281). Also Rancière (1991: 39).

5 This entails a first, anti-foundational move 'to disentangle in every case the as if which is involved in the "that's the way it is"' (Rancière 2009d: 280) and a second, constructive move 'specifically aimed at detecting and highlighting the operations of equality that may occur everywhere at every time' (Ibid: 280–281).

6 Central to this understanding of politics are concepts such as *wrong*, *dissensus*, *subjectivation*, *equality*, and *demos*, which is the supplementary name of those who find no place (are 'uncounted') in the given 'distribution of the sensible' [*partage du sensible*]. See Davide Panagia (2010) and the rest of the essays in Deranty (ed.) (2010).

7 Rancière understands political action not in terms of impersonal multitudes, but of actors who undergo processes of *subjectivation*, which is 'the production through a series of actions of a body and a capacity for enunciation not previously identifiable within a given field of experience' (Rancière 1999: 35; cf. Rancière 2012). A subject has no concrete faculties or properties, nor is defined in terms of an 'identity'; it is not a group that 'becomes aware' of itself, finds its voice, imposes its weight on society. Instead, it is an '*operator* that connects and disconnects different areas, regions, identities, functions, and capacities' (Ibid: 40, emphasis added). A political subject is a 'surplus name' that sets out a dispute about who is included in their count (Rancière 2004: 303). For example, in the claim 'we, the people' what is staged is a *gap* between the 'we' that is speaking and 'the people' in whose name this 'we' purport to speak (Rancière 2009b: 11). Thus, the subject is a kind of 'theatrical instance' (Rancière 2004b).

8 This would be the Arendtian way: For the contrast between Rancière and Arendt, see Schaap (2012; 2011).

9 In the legal setting, this raises broad issues of capability, privilege, and access (e.g., Galanter 1974). Rancière's starting point is the opposite in that he wishes to demonstrate that the 'incapable' are in fact capable. This lies at the heart of Rancière's controversy with Bourdieu (see especially Rancière 2003b: ch 9).

10 For Lyotard, 'a wrong results from the fact that the rules of the genre of discourse by which one judges are not those of the judged genre or genres of discourse' (Lyotard 1988: xi).

11 Lyotard argues that each time that heterogeneous phrase regimens are 'linked together,' other possible linkages remain neglected, forgotten or repressed (1988: 136 fn 184). In his view, this is inevitable because no single, universal genre exists to subsume all genres (1988: 128 fn 178; 138 fn 189; also fns 179 and 231).

12 As Rancière writes, 'the incommensurability on which politics is based is not identifiable with any "irrationality". It is, rather, the very measure of the relationship between a logos and the *alogia* it defines' (1999: 43). In other words, the stage(ing) of disagreement is the 'commensurability of the incommensurability' (2009b: 11).

13 Deranty deems this third place of encounter 'the political' [le politique]. To be fair, Rancière himself did 'tentatively' conceptualize it like that, in 'Does Democracy Mean Something?,' first published in Douzinas (ed.) (2007) and reprinted in Rancière (2010: 53).

14 The mischaracterization is part of a larger effort to link Rancière with the Western tradition of Aristotle, Descartes and Kant, bypassing the radical critique introduced at the heart of these three authors – the political animal endowed with logos, the autonomous subject, and transcendental Reason. Déotte turns Rancière into a Hegelian proponent of historical progress, a characterization he has explicitly denied (e.g., Rancière 2003a).

15 In a similar situation to the Malian mother is Antigone, who arguably wanted solely to bury her brother in peace following time-honoured burial rites, but in the process was able to reconfigure the law for the entire community. I have argued at length elsewhere that it is a mistake to suppose she betrays her commitment by the mere fact of arguing her case in a language the citizens too can understand (see generally Etxabe 2013; more specifically, and shortly, Etxabe 2009).

16 As Schaap (2009) explains, the state did so by denying that courts and municipal law were competent to deal with such claims (negation of addressee); that dispossession ever took place (negation of referent); that Aboriginal sovereignty was a legally cognizable or meaningful concept (negation of sense); and that such a thing as an aboriginal nation existed to begin with (negation of addressor).

17 Austin linked the particular success to certain conventional conditions and procedures (e.g. that the procedures are followed, that they are performed by the appropriate persons, that they are done in earnest, with particular intentions).

18 The issue of relation is central to what James Boyd White has coined with the term *constitutive rhetoric* (White 1984), which is none of the senses in which rhetoric has been understood in the Western tradition – as the ignoble art of persuading others of the sophists; as the Aristotelian science of finding the right topoi rescued by modern theorists of argumentations; or as the Ciceronian and medieval art of speaking well. In White's sense constitutive rhetoric is not a mere linguistic endeavour, but the holistic art of creating improbable communities between different worlds, which always entails the need for translation, and hence the possibility of mistranslation. In every rhetorical

engagement, I must set the tone, the context, and my own authority to speak, thus creating a character for myself, my listener, and our relationship, which calls into being a community that can be accepted, declined, misinterpreted, or actively resisted. At any rate, the emphasis lies on the *betweenness*, the relation between the interlocutors and the audience, both immediate and future, constituted by who we are to one another and how we understand our being together.

19 On the effects of the mortgage crisis on vulnerable populations, see Human Rights Watch (2014).

20 Article 3 of the Civil Code provides different interpretive criteria (including the so-called 'spirit of the law'). However, these criteria are meant to clarify the sense of the norms in question; once the meaning is clear, it does not allow discretion not to apply the interpreted rules.

21 In the logic of emancipation 'there is always a third thing – a book or some piece of writing – alien to both and to which they can refer to verify in common what the pupil has seen, what she says about it and what she thinks of it (Rancière 2009c: 15).

22 In Elche (Alicante), a judge conditioned repossession on the use that the bank would give to it (relying on equity) (Providencia of July 28, 2011). In Girona, the court applied the doctrine of unjust enrichment after the bank obtained a benefit from selling the house and still proceeded against the debtor (Auto 113/2009, of April 7, 2011).

23 The request for a preliminary ruling in the Aziz case was raised by Juzgado de lo Mercantil (Commercial Court) Number 3 of Barcelona. For the implications of the CJEU ruling for the Spanish system, see Bengoetxea (2014) (arguing for the benefits of inter-legality to shift our national prism and pierce through hermetic interpretations).

Bibliography

Atienza, M. (2013) 'Los desahucios, los jueces y la idea del Derecho', *El Cronista*, vol. 37, pp. 14–19.

Austin, J. (1986) *How to Do Things with Words*, 2nd edition, Oxford: Oxford University Press.

Bengoetxea, J. (2014) 'Sobre-endeudamiento, desahucio, abuso del derecho y cultura judicial formalista', *El Cronista*, vol. 48, pp. 50–55.

Cavell, S. (2005) *Philosophy the Day after Tomorrow*, Cambridge and London: The Belknap Press of Harvard University Press.

Chambers, S. (2013) *The Lessons of Rancière*, New York: Oxford University Press.

Christodoulidis, E. (2004) 'The Objection That Cannot Be Heard: Communication and Legitimacy in the Courtroom', in Duff, A., Farmer, L., Marshall, S. and Tadros, V. (eds.) *The Trial on Trial*, vol. 1, Oxford and Portland: Hart Publishing, pp. 179–202.

Citton, Y. (2009) 'Political Agency and the Ambivalence of the Sensible', in Rockhill, G. and Watts, P. (eds.) *Jacques Rancière: History, Politics, Aesthetics*, Durham and London: Duke University Press, pp. 120–139.

Constable, M. (2014) *Our Word Is Our Bond: How Legal Speech Acts*, Stanford: Stanford University Press.

Cover, R. (1983) 'The Supreme Court, 1982 Term – Foreword: Nomos and Narrative', *Harvard Law Review*, vol. 97, pp. 4–68.

Davis, O. (2010) *Jacques Rancière*, Cambridge, UK: Polity Press.

Déotte, J.-L. (2004) 'The Differences between Rancière's Mesentente (Political Disagreement) and Lyotard's Differend', *SubStance*, vol. 33, no. 1, pp. 77–90.

Deranty, J.-P. (2003) 'Rancière and Contemporary Political Ontology', *Theory and Event*, vol. 6, no. 4, n. p.

Deranty, J.-P. (ed.) (2010) *Jacques Rancière: Key Concepts*, Durham: Acumen.
Douzinas, C. (ed.) (2007) *Adieu Derrida*, New York: Palgrave Macmillan.
El Mundo (2013) 'Hoy podemos decir que los jueces no somos cobradores del frac', 14 March, Available: http://www.elmundo.es/elmundo/2013/03/14/paisvasco/1363274390.html
El Notario del Siglo XXI (2013) vol. 48, March–April, Editorial: 'La sentencia del Tribunal de Justicia de la Unión Europea y el futuro de la hipoteca en España'. Available: www.elnotario.es/index.php/hemeroteca/revista-48/145-la-sentencia-del-tribunal-de-justicia-de-la-union-europea-y-el-futuro-de-la-hipoteca-en-espana-0–6296839738541133
Etxabe, J. (2009) 'Antigone's Nomos', *Animus: The Canadian Journal of Philosophy and Humanities*, vol. 13, pp. 60–73.
Etxabe, J. (2010) 'The Legal Universe after Robert Cover', *Law & Humanities*, vol. 4, no. 1, pp. 115–147.
Etxabe, J. (2013) *The Experience of Tragic Judgement*, Abingdon: Routledge.
Etxabe, J. (2015) 'Book Review: Marianne Constable's *Our Word Is Our Bond: How Legal Speech Acts*', *No Foundations: An Interdisciplinary Journal of Law and Justice*, vol. 12, pp. 136–145.
European Mortgage Federation (2013) *Hypostat 2013: A review of Europe's mortgage and housing market*. Available: www.hypo.org/portaldev/objects/6/files/hypostat_2013.pdf
Frank, J. (2009) 'Staging Dissensus: Frederick Douglass and "We, the People"', in Schaap, A. (ed.) *Law and Agonistic Politics*, Farnham: Ashgate, pp. 87–103.
Galanter, M. (1974) 'Why the "Haves" Come Out Ahead: Speculations on the Limits of Legal Change', *Law & Society Review*, vol. 9, no. 1, pp. 95–160.
Gentier, A. (2012) 'Spanish Banks and the Housing Crisis: Worse Than the Subprime Crisis?', *International Journal of Business*, vol. 17, no. 4, pp. 342–351.
Hallward, P. (2009) 'Staging Equality: Rancière's Theatrocracy and the Limits of Anarchic Equality', in Rockhill, G. and Watts, P. (eds.) *Jacques Rancière: History, Politics, Aesthetics*, Durham and London: Duke University Press, pp. 140–157.
Human Rights Watch (2014) 'Shattered Dreams: Impact of Spain's Hosing Crisis on Vulnerable Groups', [Online]. Available: www.housingrightswatch.org/sites/default/files/2014-06-01%20Human%20Rights%20Watch%20-%20Spain.pdf
Jenkins, F. (2009) 'On the Rationality of Disagreement and Feeling', in Schaap, A. (ed.) *Law and Agonistic Politics*, Farnham: Ashgate, pp. 179–192.
Lyotard, J.-F. (1988) *The Differend: Phrases in Dispute*, translated by G. Van Den Abbeele, Minneapolis: University of Minnesota Press.
May, T. (2009) 'Rancière in South Carolina', in Rockhill, G. and Watts, P. (eds.) *Jacques Rancière: History, Politics, Aesthetics*, Durham and London: Duke University Press, pp. 105–119.
Norval, A. (2009) 'Passionate Subjectivity, Contestation and Acknowledgement: Rereading Austin and Cavell', in Schaap, A. (ed.) *Law and Agonistic Politics*, Farnham: Ashgate, pp. 163–177.
Norval, A. (2012) '"Writing a Name in the Sky": Rancière, Cavell, and the Possibility of Egalitarian Inscription', *American Political Science Review*, vol. 106, no. 4, pp. 810–826.
Panagia, D. (2010) 'Partage du Sensible: The Distribution of the Sensible', in Deranty, J.-P. (ed.) *Jacques Rancière: Key Concepts*, Durham: Acumen, pp. 95–103.
Rancière, J. (1991) *The Ignorant Schoolmaster: Five Lessons in Intellectual Emancipation*, translated with an introduction by K. Ross, Stanford: Stanford University Press.
Rancière, J. (1999) *Disagreement: Politics and Philosophy*, translated by J. Rose, Minneapolis and London: University of Minnesota Press.
Rancière, J. (2003a) 'Comments and Responses', *Theory and Event*, vol. 6, no. 4, n. p.

Rancière, J. (2003b) *The Philosopher and His Poor*, edited and with an introduction by A. Parker, Durham and London: Duke University.

Rancière, J. (2004a) 'Who Is the Subject of the Rights of Man?', *The South Atlantic Quarterly*, vol. 103, no. 2–3, pp. 297–310.

Rancière, J. (2004b) 'Entretien avec Jacques Rancière', *Dissonance*, vol. 1, [Online]. Available: www.multitudes.net/Entretien-avec-Jacques-Ranciere/

Rancière, J. (2007) *On the Shores of Politics*, translated by L. Heron, London and New York: Verso.

Rancière, J. (2009a) 'A Few Remarks on the Method of Jacques Rancière', *Parallax*, vol. 15, no. 3, pp. 114–123.

Rancière, J. (2009b) 'The Aesthetic Dimension: Aesthetics, Politics, Knowledge', *Critical Inquiry*, vol. 36, pp. 1–19.

Rancière, J. (2009c) *The Emancipated Spectator*, London: Verso.

Rancière, J. (2009d) 'Afterword: The Method of Equality: An Answer to Some Questions', in Rockhill, G. and Watts, P. (eds.) *Jacques Rancière: History, Politics, Aesthetics*, Durham and London: Duke University Press, pp. 273–288.

Rancière, J. (2010) *Dissensus: On Politics and Aesthetics*, edited and translated by S. Corcoran, London and New York: Continuum.

Rancière, J. (2011a) 'The Thinking of Dissensus', in Bowman, P. and Stamp, R. (eds.) *Reading Rancière*, London and New York: Continuum, pp. 1–17.

Rancière, J. (2011b) 'Against an Ebbing Tide: An Interview with Jacques Rancière', in Bowman, P. and Stamp, S. (eds.) *Reading Rancière*, London and New York: Continuum, pp. 238–251.

Rancière, J. (2012) 'Work, Identity, Subject', in Deranty, J.-P. and Ross, K. (eds.) *Jacques Rancière and the Contemporary Scene: The Philosopher of Radical Equality*, London and New York: Continuum, pp. 205–216.

Rancière, J. (2013) *Aisthesis: Scenes from the Aesthetic Regime of Art*, translated by P. Zakir, London and New York: Verso.

Rancière, J. (2015) 'The Politics of Art: An Interview with Jacques Rancière', [Online]. Available: www.versobooks.com/blogs/2320-the-politics-of-art-an-interview-with-jacques-ranciere

Roca Cladera, J. and Burns, M. (2000) 'The Liberalization of the Land Market in Spain in 1998', *European Planning Studies*, vol. 8, no. 5, pp. 547–564.

Ross, K. (1991) 'Translator's Introduction', in Rancière, J. *The Ignorant Schoolmaster: Five Lessons in Intellectual Emancipation*, Stanford: Stanford University Press, pp. vii-xxiii.

Ross, K. (2009) 'Historicizing Untimeliness', in Rockhill, G. and Watts, P. (eds.) *Jacques Rancière: History, Politics, Aesthetics*, Durham and London: Duke University Press, pp. 15–29.

Schaap, A. (2009) 'The Absurd Proposition of Aboriginal Sovereignty', in Schaap, A. (ed.) *Law and Agonistic Politics*, Farnham: Ashgate, pp. 209–223.

Schaap, A. (2011) 'Enacting the Right to Have Rights: Jacques Rancière's Critique of Hannah Arendt', *European Journal of Political Theory*, vol. 10, no. 1, pp. 22–45.

Schaap, A. (2012) 'Hannah Arendt and the Philosophical Repression of Politics', in Deranty, J.-P. and Ross, A. (eds.) *Jacques Rancière and the Contemporary Scene: The Philosopher of Radical Equality*, London and New York: Continuum, pp. 145–165.

Shklar, J. (1964) *Legalism*, Cambridge: Harvard University Press.

Spanish Ombudsman (*Defensor del Pueblo*) (January 22, 2012), 'Crisis económica y deudores hipotecarios: actuaciones y propuestas del Defensor del Pueblo', [Online].

Available: www.defensordelpueblo.es/wp-content/uploads/2015/05/2012-01-Crisis-econ%C3%B3mica-y-deudores-hipotecarios-actuaciones-y-propuestas-del-Defensor-del-Pueblo.pdf

Tully, J. (2002) 'The Unfreedom of the Moderns in Comparison to Their Ideals of Constitutional Democracy', *Modern Law Review*, vol. 65, pp. 204–228.

White, J. B. (1973) *The Legal Imagination: Studies in the Nature of Legal Thought and Expression*, Boston: Little Brown.

White, J. B. (1984) *When Words Lose Their Meaning: Constitutions and Reconstitutions of Language, Character, and Community*, Chicago and London: The University of Chicago Press.

Woodford, C. (2015) '"Reinventing Modes of Dreaming" and Doing: Jacques Rancière and Strategies for the New Left', *Philosophy and Social Criticism*, vol. 41, no. 8, pp. 811–836.

Court decisions

Auto 574/2009 November 13, 2009, of Judge of First Instance and Instruction of Estella/Lizarra Nº 2.

Auto 831/2008 of December 9, 2009, of Judge of First Instance and Instruction of Estella/Lizarra Nº 2.

Auto 111/2010 of December 17, 2010, Provincial Court of Navarre, Second Section.

Auto 4/2011 of January 28, 2011, Provincial Court of Navarre, Third Section.

Auto 113/2009 of April 7, 2011, Provincial Court of Girona, First Section.

Providencia of July 28, 2011, Judge of First Instance Number Five, of Elche (Alicante).

Auto 24/2012 of May 4, 2012, Provincial Court of Navarra, Second Section.

Case C-415/11, *Mohamed Aziz v. Caixa d'Estalvis de Catalunya, Tarragona i Manresa*, March 14, 2013, Court of Justice of the European Union, First Chamber.

Part II

From the rights of subjects to the subjects of rights

Chapter 2

Fight for your rights

Refugees, resistance, and disagreement

Ari Hirvonen

1. Demands of our time

The image of the three-year-old Aylan Kurdi lying lifeless on a Turkish beach after he had drowned on 2 September 2015 provoked Europe into action over the so-called refugee crisis. Suddenly and inexplicably, as Patricia Tuitt puts it, 'the question of human "right" was momentarily divorced from the question of citizenship' (Tuitt 2016; see also El-Enany 2016). Even though there were thousands of refugees fleeing war, terror, persecution, and poverty from Western and South Asia and Africa to Europe to seek asylum who had died before Aylan, only now the European political elite admitted that '[u]rgent action [is] required – a Europe-wide mobilization is urgent' (tweet by PM Manuel Valls, in Tharoor 2015). European liberal democrats promised to 'fulfil [their] moral responsibilities' (David Cameron, in Watt and Wintour 2015).

The humanitarian compassion did not last long. At the beginning of 2016, another image of refugees started to circulate based on the events of New Year's Eve, when men of Arab and North African appearance were alleged to have harassed women in Cologne and some other European cities. The young refugee men were widely targeted by politicians, media, and the voice of public opinion as a conspicuous group that does not respect European universal values, gender equality, secular tradition, or legislation.

Jacques Rancière says that 'any political theory is a discourse on the circumstances of the political – a manner of describing the places and moments of its intervention, the objects brought forth by its action, and the subjects that participate in it' (Rancière 2014: xii). Instead of writing about Rancière's political theory – 'there is no political theory per se' – I will construct a text of circumstance, which aims, as Rancière says, 'to increase the visibility of the ruptures that egalitarian interventions work into the fabric of domination' (Ibid).

My text 'responds to the demands of its time' (Ibid: vii). The context of this response is the contemporary fabric of domination that has produced images, discourses, policies, and instruments related to what is called the refugee crisis. More properly, the circumstance of this text is the polemical space where demonstrations of power – the aforementioned images, the refugee policy, the part the refugees play in contemporary Europe, the ongoing migrant deportations – are all subject to disagreement, *mésentente*. Disagreement is 'a determined kind of speech situation: one in which one of the interlocutors at once understands and does not understand what the other is saying' (Rancière 1999: x). Disagreement supposes that there is some kind of common ground between the conflicting speakers. An English translation does not catch the double sense of the French term, which means first, the fact of not hearing or understanding language, and second, disagreement as 'quarrel', 'dispute'. Together the sense of these two meanings is that the mere fact of hearing and understanding *langue*, a common sharing of language, does not produce any egalitarian effects. No politics emerges from this fact. 'Egalitarian effects occur only through a forcing, that is, the instituting of quarrel that challenges the incorporated, perceptible evidence of an inegalitarian logic. This quarrel is politics' (Rancière 2004a: 4).

The quarrel I will take up is one not only over European refugee policy but also over the situation of refugees in Europe. I will ask what is the relation between the consensual distribution of the sensible (*le partage du sensible*) and the emergence of dissensus that interrupts this consensual distribution, this *sensus communis*. Two specific questions are addressed here. Firstly, can we consider these emergences of dissensus as sequences of politics (*la politique*), instances of emancipation and inventions of political subjects? Secondly, do human rights have any function as part of refugees' political struggles or does the proliferation of abstract rights merely lead to a legalistic culture, juridical formalism, and the legalization of political dissensus?

My claim is that Rancière gives a hint of how to resist the European refugee policy. At the same time, his thinking contributes to rethinking the political potentialities of human rights and the radical emancipation that takes place through refugees' political protests and resistance.

2. Police and refugees

Before answering the aforementioned questions, I will sketch out a map of the present situation to see who is in a position to define the European refugee policy and what kind of position the forcibly displaced people – refugees and migrants[1] – occupy in the European police order (*la police*).

The police is 'a symbolic constitution of the social' that structures the spaces of society (Rancière 2010: 36). On the one hand, it distributes places, tasks, roles, and functions, and makes distinctions between private and public, labour and leisure, political and social, humans and animals. On the other hand, it determines boundaries between the visible and invisible, audible and non-audible, comprehensible and incomprehensible – that is, it draws a line between what is and is not perceptible. The police is, as Rancière says, 'an order of bodies that defines the allocation of ways of doing, ways of being, and ways of saying . . . an order of the visible and the sayable' (1999: 26). The police order is not so much the discipline of bodies and individuals as a rule that governs their appearance. The police refers to various implicit and explicit rules and conventions, to various institutions and practices that regulate the regimes of both symbolic and material sensibility. These rules and practices stem equally from the state functions and the spontaneity of social relations. The essence of the police lies in a certain distribution or partition of the sensible. Distribution (*partage*) should be understood here in the double sense of the word *partage*: on the one hand, that which separates and excludes, and on the other hand, that which allows participation (Rancière 2010: 36).

The police, then, is a fixed distribution of beings and things into public and private, common and particular, familiar and strange. To understand the European refugee and migrant policy, we have to consider how the police, symbolizing the community as an ensemble of defined parts, excludes and includes, defines and identifies, manages and objectifies refugees. What kind of 'functions, places and ways of being' are refugees and migrants allocated in the European police order and what is perceptible in this order (Ibid)?

1) *Function*. Refugees are considered as a group that is 'tied to a specific mode of doing' (Ibid). As Rancière points out, at one point immigrants were called workers, but now their name and identity are reduced to mere otherness, and they are 'nothing but immigrants, people with different skin and moralities' (Rancière 2009b: 42). Refugees are not counted as labour or the proletariat. They are not even considered as unemployed or the precariat.

'You have got a swarm of people coming across the Mediterranean, seeking a better life', David Cameron says (Elgot 2016). Those who are considered to be merely seeking welfare benefits or jobs – alongside swindlers, villains, criminals, and potential terrorists – are to be taken into custody and deported swiftly. Those who are counted as victims are forced to wait in limbo to be granted asylum, given a residence permit, or be deported. Their temporal rhythm is totally determined by the exploitation of their time. The function they do have in society is to kill time. In their 'doing-killing time', their actions, voices, thoughts, and achievements as individuals are made invisible and unheard. However, according to the European Commission, they have clear obligations 'to cooperate with the authorities throughout the procedure' for international protection and there are 'strict consequences to non-compliance with obligations' (COM [2016] 467 final: 4).

They are excluded from public discussions, political activities, and everyday matters. Since they are invisible, they are also nameless. 'Whoever is nameless *cannot* speak' (Rancière 1999: 23). Within the existing distribution of the sensible, they naturally apprehend speech but do not possess it. In Aristotelian terms, they are disposed of human speech (*logos*) by which to make distinctions between justice and injustice, good and evil. Refugees are left with mere prelinguistic animal noise (*phone*) that merely indicates their pain and pleasure (Aristotle 1995: 1253a9–18; Rancière 1995: 13). The police order does not count them as speaking beings. As they lack speech, they are not able to express a shared sense of justice, legality, ethics, and usefulness. In this sense, refugees can be compared with the Roman plebeians who 'do not speak because they are beings without a name, deprived of logos' (Rancière 1999: 23). At the most, refugees are like the plebeians, that is, 'people who fall through the cracks, who are in society without being *of* society' (Rancière 2013: 24). However, since they do not figure even as passive citizen, they do not even have the status of the plebeians in Europe.

In their passivity, some refugees are counted as innocent and vulnerable victims, who are in need of protection. Based on her ethnographic studies, Leena Malkki confirms Rancière's point by showing how humanitarian practices tend to silence refugees and see them simply as mute victims (1996: 378). According to Malkki, refugees remain invisible even if we do see them, since they are regarded merely as an anonymous group, as a mass of bodies without qualities. They 'stop being specific persons and become pure victims in general' (Ibid). Moreover, they are supposed to happily embrace those rights, protection, shelter, food, clothes, and health treatment they receive from their humanitarian hosts.

2) *Place*. What are 'places in which these occupations are exercised' (Rancière 2010: 36)? The police assigns the invisible and voiceless refugees, who have no part in social, economic, political, labour, or cultural activities, to their proper place in society. This non-place is exclusion and isolation.

Since 'killing time' has to take place somewhere, the police, as a rule that governs 'the properties of the spaces where these occupations are distributed' (Rancière 1999: 29), assigns refugees to designated shelters: reception centres, detention shelters, and refugee camps. These places are not public spaces 'regulated by the ways of seeing and saying proper to what is called the public domain' (Ibid).

Perhaps refugees belong 'to a "domestic" space that was separated from public life, one from which only groans or cries expressing suffering, hunger, or anger could emerge, but no actual speech demonstrating a shared *aesthesis*' (Rancière 2010: 38). However, domestic space is part of the distribution of the sensible as a space designated for apolitical activities. The shelters for refugees are not spaces defined by work, consumption, leisure, love, religion, or household matters. In what Rancière calls 'the parcelling out of spaces' (2004b: 38), these shelters become temporary places of exclusion for those who are invisible and unheard, who are not counted in society, who have no share as citizens or residents.

Article 14(1) of the Universal Declaration of Human Rights guarantees everyone's right to seek and to enjoy asylum from persecution, but accessibility of this right has become more and more restricted. The borders have become places of hindrance, barriers, walls, criminalization, exclusion and death for refugees. According to the European Commission, the main issue for the EU is not the protection of refugees' right to life and human dignity but the fact that 'certain Members States do not issue return decisions following a negative decision on an asylum claim or residence permit' (C [2017]1600 final: 11). The solution for the so-called refugee crisis is, as the Commission recommends, building 'a robust and effective system', 'a streamlined and shorter procedure', and 'an accelerated examination process' (COM [2016] 467 final: 4). What is needed is, therefore, a more effective return procedure by removing legal and practical obstacles to deporting refugees from Europe.

The European Commission proves thus that refugees are, as Rancière puts it, counted as those who expose 'the contradiction between affirming free circulation in a world without borders and the practices of keeping borders under surveillance and defining groups of people who cannot cross them' (Rancière 2003: 201). For the EU, it is crucial to remove 'incentives for asylum shopping and secondary movements between Member States' (COM [2016] 467 final: 4). In other words, refugees have no proper place in Europe, or their temporary place is in detention centres and shelters.

3) *Modes of being*. Refugees are tied 'to modes of being corresponding to these occupations and these places' (Rancière 2010: 36). Since refugees are considered passive objects merely waiting for the decision by authorities at the designated spaces, they do not have a world in common with Europeans. They are entities that are just there in European society. As such beings, they are truly those who have no part in anything (Rancière 1999: 9).

Rancière convincingly shows how socialist, revolutionary, progressive, and republican ideals have turned against themselves in Europe. They are no longer weapons in the battle for equality as they used to be. Instead, they have become a means of discrimination, distrust, and contempt directed towards the undesirable refugees, who are counted as backward, communalist, and overly zealous. Republican universalism is thus subverted into a reactionary battery that stigmatizes refugees. Since we in Europe are unable to fight the growth of inequality, Rancière says, we legitimize inequalities by *de*legitimizing those who suffer their effects (2015).

Refugees are not able to take a critical stand on their own behalf since they have fallen into their particular roles, traditions, and beliefs. As a consequence, the mode of being of refugees is characterized by practices, values, and ways of life that are in fundamental conflict with European ones. Thus, they form not merely an individual but a collective threat to Europe.

As this kind of being, a refugee is defined through policing activities. Through this miscount of the role of a refugee, 'the object of [the] problem is transformed into an object of hatred' (Rancière 2009b: 45). The mode of being assigned to refugees by the European police order is then not being what they are. That is, they have a passive and object-like mode of being, one in which they do not contribute to the community through their work, acts, or words. Moreover, they are counted as an undesirable collective being that as an absolute other has no place in European society. The mode of being of refugees is to be undesirable.

This view is explicit in the right-wing identity politics based on the pre-political fantasy of the ethnic and racial nation. Even if European liberal democrats see refugees more as victims than villains, they also consider refugees as objects of law, human rights, and humanitarian protection and not as subjects. However, the division between European liberal democrats and anti-immigrant populists may well be not quite so clear. The xenophobic distribution of the sensible that sees refugees as undesirables comes close to nationalist populism. According to Rancière, the right-wing populism – together with its nationalist and anti-immigration prejudices – is more and more integrated into the prevailing political system. At the same time, the liberal democrats use the denunciation of this very same right-wing populism as a tactic to mask this rapid right-wing drift of European refugee policy (see Rancière 2015). Both populists and liberal democrats deliver migrants as fodder for a disoriented and fearful electorate (see Badiou 2012). The so-called refugee crisis has only accelerated this and it is being used as an excuse for the anti-immigration tendencies that have been explicitly and immanently present in European liberal politics and legislation for decades. It is European liberal democrats that have transformed political choices concerning migration into an objective social and legal problem. At the same time, the blame for the migratory and refugee crises is put on the undesirable refugees (see Rancière 2012). Instead of blaming 'ignorant voters' or anti-immigrant populist parties, the European liberal democrat governments share responsibility for the prevailing repressive refugee and migration policy.[2]

3. Refugee protests

As we have shown, in the distribution (*partage*) of the sensible, refugees are the part (*le part*) of those who have no part (*les sans-parts*) (Rancière 1999: 30). Refugees have no vote in elections. They do not have their representatives in parliaments or city councils. Their political rights are very limited, if existent. Some NGOs and progressive politicians, intellectuals, and human rights lawyers defend refugees and protect *sans-papiers*, undocumented immigrants, making at the same time visible and audible their opposition to the European refugee policy and the surge of neo-nationalism. Even then, refugees remain that part who has no part in politics.

Rancière signs off his *Disagreement* on a rather pessimistic note: 'How some new politics could break the circle of cheerful consensuality and denial of humanity is scarcely foreseeable or decidable right now' (Ibid: 139–140). But is this his last word on the matter? Hardly. '"Where is the left?" the socialists ask', Rancière said in an interview in relation to the surge of xenophobia, 'The answer is simple: it is where they have led it, that is, into the abyss' (2015). To contemplate the possibility of a new politics, we have to look beyond both parliamentary democracy, leftist or green political parties, and NGOs, in general, beyond politics as it is usually understood. Politics that makes a difference is always possible: 'there is no reason for it to be impossible' (Rancière 2003: 197). This kind of possible politics 'is always an alternative to any police order, regardless of both the forms of power the former must develop and the latter's organisation, form or value' (Ibid: 199). There is no reason why refugees may not act politically.

Refugees have been holding protests around Europe against living conditions and isolation at the refugee camps and shelters. They have held demonstrations, gone on hunger strikes, occupied buildings, set up camps, and blocked entrances to centres. All these protests are seen by the authorities merely as moaning sparked by boredom, disappointment with the new environment, or a matter of diet. When refugees refused to eat the food served at the Finnish reception centres, they were reminded that the Finnish children eat the very same institutional food in schools. After the suicide of an Iranian, Mohammad R., in February 2012 at the Würzburg asylum centre, his fellow inmates organized a demonstration in front of the City Hall where one of them declared: 'We are treated like animals' (McGuaran and Hudig 2014: 30). The police transformed their protests into a mere matter of taste, diet, and digestion. This was not an exception but a model for the normal way of policing the refugee protests. The dispute becomes an objectified problem, which 'can be reduced to a simple lack . . . of the means to solve it' (Rancière 1999: 107). The protesters' demands are considered merely as private complaints and not recognized as political demands.

Migrant squatter camps have been bulldozed to allegedly protect migrant's health, safety, and rights, but those assigned the role of a victim or illegal migrant have disputed these positions forced upon them through resistance. The refugee protest at Camp Vienna that started as a protest against inhumane living conditions within a reception centre turned into a wider protest movement against restrictive refugee policy, with various forms of collective action organized by refugees and activists who had joined them at Sigmund Freud Park. Their protest camp made refugees, who had been placed within spatially and socially isolated places, highly visible. The formation of resistance and mobilization that constructed new spaces coincided with the emergence of political subjectivities (Ataç 2016: 629–630). 'We want to be self-sustainable, we don't want to depend on the State. We reclaim our dignity as human beings' (RPCV 2012a). The effect of the resistance was this reclaiming, that is, emancipation.

A refugee bus tour through Germany stopped at various cities politically radicalizing public spaces in city centres. It ended in Berlin, where Refugee Strike Berlin transformed a public square in Kreuzberg into a long-term protest camp, which they used to become visible, voice their struggle, articulate their demands, and emerge as political activists forming alliances with neighbours and squatting movements. The square became both a home and a political space. After the expulsion of the camp, refugees occupied several spaces in Berlin, turning them into sites of resistance. A banner on the roof of an occupied school made by the People of the School read, 'You can't evict a movement' (Bhimji 2016).

In Calais, the cooperation between refugees and anti-deportation No Border Network blurred the distinction between those considered as political activists and refugees as they turned the closely regulated border into the political stage of a spatial struggle. According to Naomi Millner's ethnographical study, the true activists were actually undocumented migrants: 'In the act of crossing the border they assert a claim to a *polis* which includes all migrants' over the police order, where only certain parts are counted (Millner 2011: 326). In a press statement, the migrant hunger strikers in Greece pointed out that even if they made an appeal of support on behalf of everyone suffering exploitation, they 'do not receive "guidance" by anybody' (cited in Topak 2017: 8). In practising a politics of equality, they constructed and verified the universality of equality (Ibid: 6).

Refugee camps – these spaces of physical, social, political, and symbolic exclusion – have been turned into political spaces through various protests, which have also extended beyond the guarded gates and electrified fences. These struggles within camps have created new forms of politics and political subjectivities as the inmates have made visible what had no business being seen (Malkki 1995: 236–238; Malkki 2002: 351–360). I will take up six points on how politics takes place in refugee protests.

1) *Names*. 'Kein Mensch ist illegal' was the name given to a political movement which originated during the early 1990s asylum debates (Bhimji 2016: 449). Now, the slogan 'No One Is Illegal', used in various refugee protests, asserts the equality of all and everyone who moves within and across borders. The *sans-papiers*, undocumented, oppose their legal status by refusing to refer to themselves as clandestine or illegal immigrants. In this way, they politicize their non-status identity (see Nyers 2003). In Vienna, the protesters called themselves refugees and not asylum seekers, and in Berlin they named themselves refugee activists. In Athens, hunger-striking refugees referred to themselves as migrant workers, not merely migrants. These names are surplus names that litigate who is included in the count made by the police order (Rancière 2010: 68). The previously invisible individuals who have to hide and work illegally under constant fear of deportation make themselves visible on purpose. As *sans-papiers* they take the lead in anti-deportation campaigns as they form political stages where they emerge as political subjects (see Hayter 2000: 143; Nyers 2003). 'We are here!' said a slogan on a large banner with a picture of the members of the Amsterdam group of *sans-papiers* who demanded freedom and protested against their inhuman treatment in detention jails. *Sans-papiers* establish a collective basis for their social, political, and economic relations that used to be solely the product of an infinite number of legal relationships between a particular illegal immigrant, and judicial and administrative authority.[3] In this way, *sans-papiers* disrupt the police order and break away from the function, the place, and the being assigned to them to take part in politics.

2) *Spaces*. These protests, which are increasingly linked transnationally, turn roads, streets, squares, piazzas, urban communication paths, buildings, shopping malls, refugee centres and camps into political stages. Refugees resist the symbolic and material orderings and policing of spaces by opening up these spaces to the processes of the verification of equality (see Dikec 2012: 674). On these stages, they break out from the 'regime of enforced invisibility' (Beltrán 2009: 599). The

function of the place is changed, the body is shifted from the place assigned to it and refugees become visible not as victims or villains, as legal or illegal immigrants, but as political subjects. All these various refugee protests and struggles are politics, that is, 'the art of the local and singular construction of cases of universality' (Rancière 1999: 139).

3) *Wrong*. What refugee protests seek to bring forth is political, social, and economic injustices. Refugees demand better living conditions, more doctors and healthier food, an end to deportations, legal rights, and more humane legislation. At the same time, protests go beyond particular demands and manifest what Rancière calls *le tort*, the wrong.[4] There is a wrong in the distribution of the sensible that denies refugees speech, isolates them in designated places, considers their speech and arguments merely as noise and moaning, and excludes them from political discourse. In and through refugee protests, those who are counted by the police order merely as victims or villains, articulate the wrong in the field of logos. As a consequence, the articulation of the wrong creates a political stage. That is, refugees show that, contrary to the position held by the European societies, every voice is articulable as logos.

4) *Equality*. Politics occurs in refugee protests as an effect of 'the presupposition of the equality of anyone and everyone' (Rancière 1999: 17). That is, refugees implement an assumption of their equality with all those counted as citizens (see Ibid: 30). There is no reciprocal recognition between those who have a part in politics and those who have no part in it,[5] but refugees act as if they were equal in an unequal European society. What equality means here is not equality before the law that the state should guarantee. Instead, equality is a presupposition that is verified in and through their political action. Through the events of protest, refugees show that 'they are locals just as authentically as those born with lighter skin' (Rancière 2014: ix). The Refugee Struggle for Freedom that occupied the lounge of the German Trade Union Federation in Berlin demanded both their right to residence and their right to equal membership in society (Bhimji 2016: 445). In a singular spatial struggle refugees made a universal claim about equality of all and verified their equality with those the police counts as citizens.

5) *Subject*. These are subject formation processes in which refugees 'inscribe the count of the uncounted as a supplement' (Rancière 2003: 197). This is what Rancière calls 'subjectivation', which takes place only in political events and moments as they interrupt the consensual distribution of the sensible. Refugees, the surplus subjects, who are counted as the part of those who have no part and added as a supplement to the sum the police has counted, is the demos that intervenes and disrupts the police, forms political stages, and creates a democratic community of sharing. According to Rancière, 'the political exists only through the action of collective subjects who concretely change situations by asserting their creativity and reconstructing the world' (Rancière 2014: ix). Refugees appear as political subjects in and through political action. Becoming a political subject is

the crucial point in politics, since without the emergence of the political collective subject, there is only either the order of domination or disorder. Refugees do not exist as political subjects before political events. Politics does not happen because refugees oppose citizens. It is other way round: politics causes refugees to exist as an entity, as a collective political subject. That is, refugees as political subjects are products of political struggles, like the proletariat. Various protests of refugees lead to the formation of political mobilization and subjectivities.[6]

6) *Bodies*. An Iranian Kurdish refugee, Abbas Amini, went on a hunger strike and sewed his eyes, ears and mouth with a coarse green cotton thread, not merely in protest of the threat of his deportation, but to make a statement on behalf of refugees everywhere. 'I sewed my eyes so others could see, I sewed my ears so others could hear, I sewed my mouth to give others a voice' ('Stitches removed from asylum protestor', 2003). Rancière shares Amini's own affirmation, 'Yes, it was political' (Branigan 2003). Amini was not merely a suffering being – his body was transformed into a stage of political struggle. The police order condemned him to silence. He was not considered capable of speaking about political matters or claiming his rights through public discourse. In such situations, refugees have invented 'paradoxical ways to claim their rights' (Rancière 2016a). In claiming his rights and demanding to be recognized as a refugee he created what Rancière calls 'an artistic political action' by stitching his lips: 'a way of speaking without speaking, speaking without speaking to prove precisely that we are speaking beings' (Ibid). Moreover, he became visible by rendering himself blind. Thus, his act created a heterogeneous stage wherein the lip-sewing protest encompassed the police order and legal rights by interrupting the existing realm of perception that had forced the *sans-papiers* into exclusion and insignificance.

If the political subject is necessarily a collective subject, should we consider Amini, who acted alone, as merely a conscientious objector or an individual in revolt? First, we have to understand the political subject not as a collection of individual subjects but as an operation (*dispositif*) which does not exist prior to the political act and which is always on the verge of disappearing. What is crucial for the collective subject is not the number of individuals but that individual(s) are dislocated from their particular identities, interests and qualities, and created as political subjects in the process of the subjectivation. Second, Amini does not speak for himself or his particular interests but 'for anybody' (Rancière 2006b). His silent speech does invite others – both refugees and European citizens – to join in opposition to the police order. But it is not only an invitation to create a political movement. It is already part of the political process in so far as it is intimately linked to other similar acts of protest around the world in which refugees silently speak for all, in the name of equality. Amini's speech is at the very moment of the act dislocated from his particular person and emerges as a polyphony, as the speech of a collective subject.

4. Who needs mere human rights?

For Rancière, human rights are not the humanitarian rights of victims, who are 'unable to exercise their rights or even to claim any in their own name', and who therefore need the Western democracies to exercise rights in the place of them (Rancière 2010: 62). These kinds of humanitarian rights, Rancière says, creates 'the "right to humanitarian interference"' (Ibid: 74).

Are human rights claims merely a façade for the hegemony of global liberal democratic capitalism? If so, we would come back to Marx. In *On the Jewish Question*, Marx considers the rights of man (equality, liberty, property, and security), which differ from the rights of citizens exercised in community with other men, as the rights of an egoistic and private individual separated from other individuals and the community. According to him, the political emancipation related either to human or civil rights is inadequate. It reduces human beings, on the one hand, to the egoistic individual, and, on the other hand, to the citizen, a legal person. For Marx, rights as a means of political emancipation do lead to freedom from the modern state based on these rights (see Marx 1978).[7]

Rancière does not subscribe to the 'Marxist symptomal reading' (Žižek 2005: 129) of human rights. Having made this clear in 'Who Is the Subject of Human Rights?', he turns his attention to one of his main polemical targets, Hannah Arendt, who considers that real rights cannot be the rights of the human as a mere human being. According to her, the growing number of refugees fleeing all over Europe, who had 'lost all other qualities and specific relationships – except that they were still human', should have been bearers of human rights (Arendt 1973: 299). Arendt goes on: 'If a human being loses his political status, he should, according to the implications of the inborn and inalienable rights of man, come under exactly the situation for which the declaration of such general rights provided' (Ibid: 300).

Immediately after saying this, she adds her crucial point, 'Actually the opposite is the case' (Ibid). For Arendt, the abstract conception of human rights, which would spring immediately from the nature or essence of being human, has no political or legal relevance. People displaced from their political community were deprived of rights since they were merely human beings without a political community where they would exercise their rights as citizens. Thus, there is no political community and legal order that would protect stateless beings – those thrown back 'on their natural givenness' (Ibid: 302) – and ensure their intrinsic rights. The paradox is, Arendt says, that 'the loss of human rights . . . coincides with the instant when a person becomes a human being in general . . . deprived of expression within and action upon a common world' (Ibid). A mere human being without citizenship, profession, opinion, and 'deed by which to identify and specify himself' has nothing to fall on but their inborn rights (Ibid). And these rights are the rights of those who are nothing but human beings, which are the rights of those who have no rights. For Arendt, the concept of human rights is meaningful only if it is understood as 'a right to have rights', that is, the right to be a member of a political community (Ibid: 296).[8] This is what refugees lacked. Therefore, human rights ought to be redefined as the right to human condition, which depends upon belonging to a human community.

As Rancière explains, Arendt's paradox – the rights of man are the rights of those who have no rights – is based on the Aristotelian separation she makes between two spheres and forms of life. On the one side, there is the political sphere and life, public action, speech and appearance. On the other side, we have the sphere of necessity, private and abstract life. For Arendt, according to Rancière, the rights of man are not idealist fantasies of the French revolutionaries, as Edmund Burke would claim, but 'the paradoxical rights of the private, poor, de-politicized individual' (Rancière 2010: 63). Rancière goes so far as to claim Arendt's critique of abstract rights are a critique of democracy, since her critique is based on the assumption that 'modern democracy was spoilt from the beginning' because the revolutionaries felt pity for the poor and confused 'political freedom, opposed to domination, and social freedom, opposed to necessity' (Ibid). For Rancière the fundamental problem with Arendt's thinking is her rigid dichotomy between public and private realms. All in all, Arendt founds politics, Rancière says, 'on the essence of a mode of life, on the idea of a *bios politicos*' (2010: 92). As a consequence, she ends by making an ontological distinction between political and non-political, the conditions of plurality and the conditions of life in need of sustenance and reproducibility (Schaap 2011: 31). Thus, her regime of political *praxis* is reserved merely for 'equals who are in possession of the power to . . . begin anew' (Rancière 2010: 29).

According to Rancière, Giorgio Agamben's critique of human rights basically 'relies on Arendt's contrast between two kinds of lives . . . between *zoe* and *bios*, between natural and human life' (Rancière 2010: 64–65). But Agamben goes beyond Arendt as he transforms Arendt's aforementioned paradox by 'means of a series of substitutions that equate it, first, with Michel Foucault's theory of biopower and, second, with Carl Schmitt's theory of the state of exception' (Ibid: 64). As a consequence, Agamben situates *zoe* at the centre of politics and brings sovereign power and biopower, which regulates and governs biological life, together. For him, bare life that is situated originally at the margins of politics coincides with the political realm (Agamben 1998: 9). Politics vanishes 'in the pure relationship between state power and individual life' in the de-politicized sphere of exceptionality (Rancière 2010: 67). 'Political conflict, properly speaking, thus comes to be replaced by a correlation between sovereign power and bare life' and political practices are 'always already caught in the biopolitical trap' (Ibid: 66). As a consequence, all claims to human rights or struggles enacting them are immediately trapped in the polarity of bare life and the state of exception. Instead of emancipation, the various declarations of human rights represent the figure of the inscription of bare life onto the juridico-political order of the nation-state (Agamben 1998: 127). The bearer of rights is the new subject of politics, that is, bare life, the exception which has become the rule defining everyone's life in contemporary society. Once bare life has been positivized by human rights declarations and it has penetrated political life, it becomes a line, a threshold that must be constantly drawn to identify and isolate 'a new living dead man, a new sacred life' (Ibid: 131; see also Agamben 2000: 21). The true subject of human rights is the refugee, the abandoned *homo sacer*. The refugee is 'not simply set outside the law and made indifferent to it but is rather *abandoned* by it, that is, exposed and threatened on the threshold in which life and law, outside and inside become indistinguishable' (Agamben 1998: 29). Refugees are both excluded from the political community and totally subjugated within the state. Since human rights define us in the terms of bare lives, the more we invoke rights in political struggles, the more we subject ourselves to the state power and are included within the state in the form of our exclusion (Schaap 2008: 2; Lechte and Newman 2012: 523). This Agambenian view ends up as an ontological destiny: we are all refugees in the camp, which is, as Catherine Mills says, 'a general logic of contemporary politics' and is not 'limited to the geographical space of confinement' (2008: 84–85).

5. Dissensus over human rights

What Rancière attempts to do is rethink human rights without reducing them to depoliticized rights. Rancière takes us back to the revolutionary figure of Olympe de Gouges, who argued that even if women were born equal, they did not have political rights and were not equal as citizens. This situation was justified by the difference between domestic life, the realm of women's bare life, and public life – the realm of the citizen's political life where the freedom and equality of the *Declaration of Rights of Man and the Citizen* is implemented. She disagreed with this *a priori* clear division between the political and the bare life. Since women were entitled to go to the guillotine to lose their bare life, they were also entitled to go to the National Assembly: 'If they were as equal "as men" under the guillotine, then they had the right to the whole of equality' (Rancière 2010: 69).

Rancière does not accept Arendt's axiom that is either a void – the rights of man are the rights of non-politicized individuals, those who have no rights – or a tautology – the rights of citizen are the rights attached to the fact of being a citizen of a constitutional state, that is, the rights of those who have rights. Rancière states a third assumption: 'the Rights of Man are the rights of those who do not have the rights that they have and have the rights that they do not have' (Ibid: 67, translation modified). The first part of the sentence combines a negation of human rights and an affirmation of them: human rights are the rights of those who do not have the rights they have. In the context of the contemporary refugee 'crisis', this means that human rights are the rights of refugees who in the contemporary European police order are deprived of these rights they do have under human rights conventions. The second part is the other way around: human rights are the rights of those who have rights they do not have. In this way Rancière turns the paradox that human rights are deprived exactly when one is reduced to a mere human being, that is, the true bearer of universal human rights regardless of one's citizenship or lack of it, into the possibility of political subjectivation. Human rights are the rights of refugees who through their political action show that they have been deprived of these rights by policy-making, legislation, other norms, and judicial and administrative practices. Therefore, as refugees act as subjects that do not have the rights that they have and that have rights that they do not have their case conflates two worlds, and this is political dissensus. As Mohamed, a refugee occupying a school in Berlin, said: 'We are human beings and we need our rights. That is why we are here and are fighting' (in Bhimji 2016: 441). Hunger strikers staying at the Faculty of Law in Athens, who demanded to be legalized, stated that '[their] existence is not recognized' but they had come 'to fight, for as long as our bodies . . . allow us, for our rights' (MHS 2011b). In another statement, they declared, 'we ask for the same political and social rights and obligations as Greek workers' (MHS 2011a). The statement by protesting refugees in Vienna reads: 'We the refugees from Traiskirchen now raise our voices and demand our rights' (RPCV 2012b). It is not merely a demand for litigation so that an Austrian court could guarantee their specific rights. They name themselves as political subjects making their dissenting voice heard and demand rights that are already their rights, since they belong equally to everyone. Instead of being merely a particular claim, it is to be understood as a declaration of the universality of basic rights. 'Right to Live', a 2017 demonstration camp at Helsinki Railway Square, which continued for 141 days without interruption, called for a halt to deportations which violate the non-refoulement principle and demanded the respect of their human rights. The protesters also alleged that the asylum decision process violated the right to fair trial. While this camp made refugees visible and heard, it demonstrated that all refugees regardless of their legal status have rights that are denied from them by the Finnish authorities and law.

For Rancière, human rights are not some universal natural rights based on reason, nature, human dignity, or being. He would share Foucault's view, who at the same time rejected any notion of human nature or essence as a basis for human rights and affirmed rights as contingent, contestable, and revisable (Foucault 2014: 265). A recipe for protecting them as depoliticized humanitarian rights or guardians of global capitalism and liberal neo-colonialism is to elevate them to the realm of political correctness or universal moral language (see Mutua 2002: 157). For William Twining, a source of strength in human rights discourse theories is that they consider debates as 'part of the discipline of human rights, which allows for considerable internal diversity, indeterminacy, and disagreement' (Twining 2009: 223). Does Rancière go along with these theories that prefer an open public deliberation over a substantive universality? Whilst there is disagreement about indeterminate human rights, Rancière goes far beyond discourse and deliberation. I will take up four points.

Firstly, the true subject of rights for Rancière is neither the essential human being nor the citizen. Instead of coinciding with a definite subject or particular identity, the subject of human rights is 'defined by interval[s] between identities, whether these identities are determined by social relations or juridical categories' (Rancière 2006a: 301). It emerges in the interspace between the human being and the citizen, and this emergence takes place as a process of subjectivation. Thus, the subject of human rights is a subject in 'specific scenes of dissensus' (Rancière 2010: 70). Or, as Andrew Schaap says, it 'emerges through political action and speech that seeks to verify the existence of those rights' (Schaap 2011: 34). The subject of human rights is '*demos*, which is the generic name of political subjects' (Rancière 2010: 70). Consequently, we have to redefine the human being and the citizen: they do not designate collections of individuals. Instead, they are 'merely' litigious names that 'set out a dispute about who is included in their count' (Ibid: 68).

Secondly, this subject of human rights as the process of subjectivation bridges the interval between human rights as legal norms and rights-in-practice. Human rights are part of the ever-changing legal material. As a normative 'writing of the community as free and equal' human rights are part of 'the configuration of the given' (Ibid), which does not consist only of the inequality of the contemporary European police order but also 'contains an inscription that gives equality a form of visibility' (Ibid). Even though law prescribes human rights, there is no one true interpretation and meaning. Instead, they are open political predicates, which open up disputes about what they entail, whom they concern, how they are interpreted and applied. In this way, human rights order is arguably contingent.

Rancière comes close to Claude Lefort, for whom human rights cannot be reduced to abstract and formal rights of atomized individuals but are part of the political and, hence, struggles for human rights have a political character (Lefort 1981; see also Lacroix 2012). Both Lefort and Rancière understand the Marxist gap between the formal democracy and rights, and the social and economic reality of exploitation in a subversive way. Human rights are not merely an ideological construction. Instead, they possess actual efficiency as they are taken over by political subjects as a means to articulate wrongs, disagreement, and equality (Žižek 2005: 130).

Thirdly, human rights argumentation is inscribed in the field of the language and the law. This takes place as a result of political struggles, which 'expand the text of the law' (Déotte 2004: 81). Human rights struggles are not vanquished after revolutions, ruptures, and the events of resistance, but rather they leave traces in the law as the police order integrates the improbable at the point at which the political subject formed in and through a human rights struggle articulates new conceptions of human rights (Ibid).

Fourthly, human rights 'can never be simply identified with some kind of juridical category that would be part of [the] police order' (Rancière 2016a). Their existence and effectiveness as human rights lies in the back-and-forth movement between the first inscriptions of these rights, generated by political struggles, and their enactments in the dissensual stages whereby these rights are put to the test. On the one hand, there is the inscription of abstract human rights norms; on the other hand, we have a political polemic over the validity, inclusiveness, and substance of human rights, that is, over their verification. Human rights exist 'in so far as there is an effective movement which can grasp' these rights and bring them into existence retroactively (Rancière 2003: 197). The subject of human rights should not only use these rights but also build cases to verify the power of their inscription. This is inevitable if the subject of human rights is defined as a political subject, that is, a subject in a specific scene of dissensus.

All in all, in refugee protests where rights claims are made, the refugee acts neither as legal subject nor as bare human being but as political subject, who appears due the staging of a dissensus over the 'who' and 'what' of human rights. This kind of politics of human rights brings 'the inscription of rights to bear against situations in which those rights are denied' (Rancière 2010: 69). As a consequence, political subjects 'construct the world in which those rights are valid, together with the world in which they are not' (Ibid). Human rights are the rights of those who make something out of these inscriptions. Through political protest, refugees, as political subjects *rather than* as a particular group, show that since they can 'enact those rights, they actually possessed them' (Rancière 2010: 57). For Rancière, the *sans-papiers* movement is exemplary political action since it makes something out of the right to have rights, since they act as if they have the rights they lack. This is world-disclosing since 'it puts two worlds into one: the world where "no one is illegal" into the world where there are *sans-papiers*' (Schaap 2011: 39).

Political dissensus over human rights does not merely use the existing rights but also, and more importantly, both reconfigure and invent rights. As Rancière says, 'politics is always a way of extending the field of rights. Police order is trying, on the contrary, to narrow, to shrink, or to suppress this field of possible extension of rights' (Rancière 2016a). The question is not merely who is counted as the subject of rights but also what is included in the notion of equal rights.

We still have to answer the costly question of whether political struggles that involve human rights claims may be fought in courtrooms. What if refugees build cases to verify the power of the inscription in law courts and through trials? Does this turn a political disagreement into a legal case? Rancière makes a difference between political wrong that cannot be assimilated and a 'juridical wrong that a court of law can address on the basis of laws' (Rancière 1995: 97). 'Juridical wrong' refers here to specific legal disputes in which the judgment corrects the juridical wrong. In a legal process, particular individuals or groups, who have presented their problems and claims, are ultimately granted their legal status and specific rights. Part of this legal process is the endless production of laws and legal norms 'designated to foresee and regulate all grievances' (Ibid: 98). This is not, for Rancière, emancipation through the process of subjectivation. Should refugees' resistance keep clear of the courtrooms?

I will answer this question by analyzing two European Court of Human Rights (ECtHR) cases. First, *Cisse v. France*. On 28 June 1996, a group of around two hundred *sans-papiers* occupied St. Bernhard Church in Paris, ten of whom decided to go on a hunger strike to draw attention to the difficulties they had in obtaining a review of their status and the laws that put them in a legal limbo. Madjiguène Cissé, a spokeswoman of the movement *Sans-Papiers de St Bernhard*, says that their fate as an underground movement, whose members had to conceal and hide themselves, had been either to take part in the process of integration or 'be deported like cattle' (Cissé 2003: 40). Through their struggle they 'made [them] selves visible to say that [they] are here, to say that [they] are not in hiding but [they]'re just human beings' (Ibid). Humanitarian organizations that wanted to help them repeated the logic of the police order. According to Cissé, these organizations did not want them to gain autonomy but insisted on speaking on their behalf. Thus, 'we had to say, "But we can explain it very well ourselves"' (Ibid). They refused to be labelled as illegals, highlighted the inhuman situation they experienced and demanded the repeal of laws that restricted the rights of foreigners even further. The popular support in France grew when people understood that their struggle was raising questions which went beyond the regulation of the *sans-papiers*. As Cissé says, 'New questions have gradually emerged: "Do you agree to live in France where fundamental human rights are trampled on?"' (Ibid).

On 23 August, they were forcibly evacuated on the grounds that the occupation constituted a risk both to the health and safety of those involved in the church protest and public order more generally. After the case had been in the French courts, Cissé lodged an application to the ECtHR complaining that the breach of her right to the freedom of peaceful assembly with others to protest their treatment violated Article 11 of the European Convention on Human Rights. The Court held that the interference with Cissé's right to the freedom of assembly was not disproportionate since the hunger strikers' health had deteriorated and sanitary conditions had become wholly inadequate. There was no violation of Article 11. However, the Court criticized the methods used by the police and, more significantly, declared that neither the fact that Cissé was an illegal immigrant nor the peaceful protest against the legislation itself constituted a legitimate aim for a restriction of the right to the freedom of assembly. Moreover, the Court recognized 'the symbolic and testimonial value of the applicant's and other immigrants' presence' in the church protest as demonstrators.

In another case, *Hirsi Jamaa and Others v. Italy*, the ECtHR considered a case where the Italian authorities had, on 6 May 2009, intercepted vessels carrying more than two hundred people on the high seas. The occupants of the vessels were transferred onto Italian military ships and returned to Libya, the point of their departure. This violated Article 3 of the Convention that categorically prohibits torture and inhuman or degrading treatment or punishment, since both in Libya and in their countries of origin, Eritrea and Somalia, they faced a risk of being tortured or detained under inhuman conditions in refugee camps. In addition, the removal of the occupants was in breach of Article 4 of Protocol No. 4 to the Convention, which prohibits the collective expulsion of aliens, and of Article 13 of the Convention, which demands an effective remedy before national authority for those whose rights are violated. The Court's assessment gave 'more weight to the applicant's version' than the Italian government's. Moreover, the Court considered it important that the potential asylum seekers had access to information to facilitate asylum procedures and substantiate their complaints. Once again, the Court recognized the human rights of refugees and the equality of competence that 'lies in the acts [testimonies, complaints] which make manifest [their] effectiveness' (Rancière 2003: 198).

The European Convention on Human Rights and the ECtHR could be considered to be part of the police order, and as such these judgments contributed to the existing distribution of the sensible. These two judgments solved particular legal problems and enforced the rights of specific individuals or groups.

At the same time, the ECtHR may use human rights to guarantee rights to those who seemingly did not have rights they did in fact have. Since not all potentialities of human rights have been actualized in preceding cases, the ECtHR may realize potentialities that are immanent in the law. Moreover, the ECtHR may offer a place for those who have no part in the political society. A courtroom may become a stage where it is possible 'to make the invisible visible, to give a name to the anonymous and to make words audible where only noise was perceptible before' (Rancière 1995: 85). In the *Cissé* case, the Court depoliticized the occupation by considering the immigrants as bare life in need of protection and incapable of making decisions concerning their life (health and living conditions). However, the Court recognized the occupation as a political demonstration, and Cissé and her fellow protesters as actors.

However, in arriving at its judgment, the ECtHR did not transform the political struggle into a mere legal case. Insofar as it recognized the human rights claims of the applicants, it recognized the applicants as 'an additional group to be recognized as part of society' (Rancière 2008). The legal processes or judgments in themselves do not create political subjects, who are the subjects of human rights. However, politics and political subjectivation may take place during (and in spite of) the legal process.

In the *Cissé* case, the legal process in the French courts and the ECtHR was not merely a legal case but also, more importantly, a political one. The political struggle continued in the courts. The courts were turned into political stages where the *sans-papiers* manifested the wrong, verified their equality and transformed human rights claims into presentations of lines of resistance towards the actual distribution of human rights in the consensual distribution of the sensible. The *sans-papiers* showed that they have human rights as they set out a disagreement over the 'who' and 'what' of human rights. Even if the Court did not judge the complainants to have suffered a violation of Article 11, it was forced to recognize the political status and rights of those who had previously been invisible, underground. The political disagreement changed the distribution of the sensible, and the judgment has produced effects well beyond the particular case and legal field. Even if the Court had concluded its decision with a more emancipatory interpretation of law and human rights and, thus, reconfigured the distribution of the sensible, it would have not spelt any kind of final victory for refugees' human rights. Political dissensus would once again disrupt this new distribution of the sensible.

In the *Hirsi Jamaa* case, the ECtHR judgment marks a new inscription of human rights that can be used in forthcoming political struggles. However, this case seems to be a legal one about the rights of specific individuals and groups. That is, the judgment reconfigured the distribution of the sensible, but – and *perhaps* – there was not that kind of political subjectivation as in the *Cissé* case, which was part of the ongoing political struggle of *sans-papiers*, who employed 'the competence of the so-called incompetents' (Ibid). In other words, in the *Hirsi Jamaa* case there was, *perhaps* 'no real political proposition', which would require that subjects act and think 'for anybody' (Rancière 2006b).

6. Conclusion

Millions of refugees are fleeing war and terror, thousands have died attempting to reach Europe, the EU reinforces the security of its external borders, and deportations violate the non-refoulement principle, among other human rights. Arendt's conception of human rights seems to be, once again, a relevant springboard to think about the contemporary global situation. Refugees in Europe seem to find themselves 'out of legality altogether' (Arendt 1973: 294). For Arendt, rights depend on the declaration that everyone has the right to be recognized as a member of the political community. Nowadays, the right to have rights is an urgent claim. One could conclude, like Justine Lacroix does, that Arendt paves the way for a political concept of human rights as she outlines the conditions of their effectiveness (see Lacroix 2013). In this case, Rancière's conception of human rights could be seen as an extension of Arendt's framework (see Ingram 2008).

I have to admit that Rancière's dissensual way of reading Arendt – or Agamben, does not always do justice to them. However, I have considered Rancière as a more relevant springboard than Arendt – or Agamben – to think about the contemporary situation: on the one hand, the police order marginalizes refugees as victims and illegals – and on the other hand, refugees act as political subjects, extending their protest and presenting the equality of all. In accordance with Rancière, I consider human rights as the rights of those who do not have the rights that they have and have the rights that they do not have. As a consequence, refugees – even undocumented migrants – are not out of legality altogether. Under international law, human rights are universal and applicable to all subjects under the jurisdiction of a state – that is, to all refugees and migrants regardless of their legal status. The same applies to most of the constitutional rights. Despite this, as Gregor Noll says, undocumented migrants are unable to participate in the universality of human rights since 'human rights are practically inaccessible to them' (Noll 2010: 241). Even though refugees have formal human rights, they cannot claim them from state institutions because of the risk of deportation. The fear of deportation is only one reason why human rights are inaccessible to refugees. The police order systematically denies the rights refugees do have, and politics is the fight for the rights that the EU and its Members States are denying.

Politics requires that there are, as Rancière puts it, 'two distinct and perceptibly opposed ways to describe the common situation and to count the players involved' (Rancière 2014: viii). On the one hand, the police assigns and distributes functions, places, and modes of being for refugees. On the other hand, the processes of equality – created by those who have no entitlement to exercise power or participate in public discussions as they declare an intelligence that belongs to anyone and everyone – is at the heart of politics. Anyone is able to argue politically about a wrong. Thus, the 'confirmation of equality is inscribed in the setting up of a dispute' constructed by refugees (Rancière 1999: 30).

In and through various protests and struggles, refugees partake in that which they previously had no part. By occupying places and constructing demonstration camps, refugees create stages of disagreement, tears in the common fabric of the police order, and processes of wrong and litigation. Designated ways of speaking, acting, and being – given the division between public and private, political and social, speech and noise – all are disrupted by their visible presence in various cities. The existing distribution of the sensible is interrupted by sewing lips or refusing to eat. Heterogeneous assumptions are implemented that demonstrate 'the sheer contingency of the [police] order, the equality of any speaking being with any other speaking being' (Ibid: 32). As the axiomatic status of a given refugee policy – be it liberal democratic, neo-nationalistic or a combination of these two – is challenged, new possibilities are opened up as a result of the political stages refugees create. Through their action in public spaces as collective subjects, refugees 'concretely change situations by asserting their creativity and reconstructing the world' (Rancière 2014: ix). Due to demonstrations, refugees manage to redesign 'the map of [the] possible' and to contribute to 'the political community through their words and struggles' (Ibid: ix, xiii). These new political ideas and possibilities are – and must be – made sensible. Through their political action, refugees invent a new sensitivity, a new aesthesis, a new distribution of the sensible.

It is through these processes of political dissensus verifying the axiom of equality that radical emancipation takes place. It is crucial to realize that 'the people who suffer oppression have to fight against their own submission – you can't liberate people on their behalf. [. . .] It can only happen by way of mass, democratic movements' (Rancière 2015).[9] Emancipation is always possible since refugees themselves have the capacity for staging scenes of dissensus.

We have shown how human rights may become an integral part of these scenes of political struggles but if, and only if, there is first a dissensual approach to human rights that is not based on any determination of human essence or pre-existing legal subject, and second, their emancipatory potential is activated in the processes of political events that interrupt the distribution of the sensible, the dominant normative way to understand law and human rights. Through political struggles political subjects are formed, and human rights emerge as politically effective instruments or weapons. These two coincide. The precondition for this is that human rights claims are not merely claims about legal injustices; they are the manifestations of wrong in the name of axiomatic universal equality by the political subject that appears through the process where the dissensus over human rights takes place. Moreover, this political subject is not defined as the subject of abstract and formal universal rights, a proposition which would bring us back to the Marxist reading of rights.

Even though the police and politics are opposing spheres and have a different logic, there is not an absolute difference between them. Politics is 'when you create a stage where you include your enemy' (Rancière 2006b). The dissensual interruption of the dominant human rights doctrine and the consensual distribution of the sensible confront each other in the political dissensus concerning human rights.

In his earlier political works, Rancière set up a rather strict opposition between the police and politics and came close to the logic of identity and difference which he elsewhere attacked. Therefore, one may easily misread this opposition as meaning that there is total difference between political and human rights, or legal discourse in general. In *Aesthetics and Its Discontents*, this division is not so evident. As Gabriel Rockhill says, he now emphasizes that, on the one hand, politics is both the distribution of the sensible and a potential redistribution of the sensible, and, on the other hand, the consensual distribution of the sensible includes dissensual elements (see Rockhill 2009: 201–202). For Rancière, there is no absolute difference between politics and police, between various genres of discourse, between human and inhuman other, bare life and citizen, social and political, private and public, voice and speech, the sensible and reason. There is no pure politics, but a tension between politics and the police. Therefore, the double condition of politics is that there is 1) a consensual distribution of the sensible, a *sensus communis* and 2) the suspension of the consensual agreement between the sensible and the thought, the disruption of this distribution. Taken together, these two mean that politics is the dissensual renegotiation and reproduction of the distribution of the sensible. Politics invents a new *sensus communis*.

Human rights are inscribed in the law as a result of legislation and case law. As such they are part of the consensual distribution of the sensible, the *sensus communis*. However, these inscriptions are often due to political struggles. As part of the law, human rights are always already open to alternative legal interpretations that challenge their consensual understanding. But human rights cannot be reduced to mere legal questions, even critical ones. What is most important in Rancière's reading of human rights is that they are the rights of political subjects who act in scenes of political dissensus as they put human rights to test. The politics of human rights is disagreement over the 'who' and 'what' of these rights. Political dissensus ends up in new rights or a wider application of human rights, that is, in a new distribution of the sensible but also its future disruption by emerging political subjects. The strength of human rights lies in this kind of ongoing movement between their inscription and political dissensus.

Finally, let us return to our two images, which are part of the consensual distribution of the sensible. A refugee – whether a victim or a villain – is reduced to a silenced object in the European societies. A dissensual image that presents a disagreement is offered by Sylvain George's documentary *Qu'ils reposent en révolte* ['May they rest in revolt'], which presents the dreadful situation of refugees and migrants in the so-called jungle in Calais. It makes visible the living conditions of those who suffer injustices due to the local authorities, police force and right-wing militants. However, refugees and migrants do not present the figure of the silenced victim but prove themselves to be subjects capable of telling their histories and taking care of their situation. The documentary is, George says, 'about standing up, about contesting these grey zones'. The most importantpolitics of George's films is

> not only in showing the capacity of the 'wretched of the earth' to live and think in accordance with the violence they are subjected to, but also in making them antecedently inhabit this world that is refused to them, the worlds where everyone has access to everything.
>
> (George 2016)

However, as Rancière says, migrants and refugees are not there as political subjects, since they are in Calais primarily to get to somewhere else. A migrant in this situation is solely a migrant who has to deal with an order of policing that impedes his journey, *but* 'he is also a potential political subject the moment he claims the right to live exactly where he is, the way everyone else does' (Rancière 2016b). Refugees share political community as equals and the law exist for them. Fight for rights continues.

Notes

1 *Refugee* and *migrant* have different meanings. Refugees are considered as persons fleeing armed conflicts or persecution. They have specific protection guaranteed under both national and international law. Migrants fleeing poverty, social injustices, unemployment, and for other reasons are dealt with by national immigration laws. Blurring these two terms may serve to distract from the specific legal protection refugees require (UNHCR 2016).

2 Both Rancière and Badiou share this view (see Rancière 2015; Rancière 2009b: 39–45; Badiou 2012).

3 This is how Rancière describes the activity of nineteenth-century workers in his *Disagreement* (Rancière 1999: 30).

4 Rancière's *tort* differs from Jean-François Lyotard's *tort*, since for Lyotard the victim of wrong is unable to put the wrong done in phrases within the discourse.

5 Arendt sees the reciprocal recognition of equality as the precondition of politics. Thus, the only possibility for refugees is a struggle for liberation, where action is subordinated to freeing themselves from domination (Arendt 1990: 29; Schaap 2011: 35).

6 See Critical Citizenship Studies, (Ataç 2016; Isin and Nielsen 2008; Nyers 2003).

7 David Leopold argues that Marx was not merely hostile towards human rights. Marx's genuine human emancipation does not merely negate political emancipation but sublates (*aufhebt*) it and thus there are some kind of rights in the fully emancipated society (2007; see also Boyd 2009).

8 According to Richard Bernstein, Arendt's experiences as a stateless person taught her 'why it is so essential to be a citizen in a polity to live a fully human life' (Bernstein 1996: 54).

9 Rancière admits that the situation of women in the Muslim world is problematic, but that it is for the women concerned to decide what they consider oppressive.

Bibliography

Agamben, G. (1998) *Homo Sacer: Sovereign Power and Bare Life*, translated by D. Heller-Roazen, Stanford: Stanford University Press.

Agamben, G. (2000) *Means without End: Notes on Politics*, translated by V. Binetti and C. Casarino, Minneapolis and London: University of Minnesota Press.

Arendt, H. (1973) *The Origins of Totalitarianism*, New York: Harcourt Brace Janovich.

Arendt, H. (1990) *On Revolution*, Harmondsworth: Penguin.

Aristotle (1995) *Politics*, translated by E. Barker, Oxford: Oxford University Press.

Ataç, I. (2016) '"Refugee Protest Camp Vienna": Making Citizens through Locations of the Protest Movement', *Citizenship Studies*, vol. 20, no. 5, pp. 629–646.

Badiou, A. (2012) 'Le racisme des intellectuels', *Le Monde*, 5 May 2012. Available: http://www.lemonde.fr/election-presidentielle-2012/article/2012/05/05/le-racisme-des-intellectuels-par-alain-badiou_1696292_1471069.html.

Beltrán, C. (2009) 'Going Public: Hannah Arendt, Immigrant Action, and the Space of Appearance', *Political Theory*, vol. 37, pp. 595–622.

Bernstein, R. (1996) *Hannah Arendt and the Jewish Question*, London: Polity Press.

Bhimji, F. (2016) 'Visibilities and the Politics of Space: Refugee Activism in Berlin', *Journal of Immigrant & Refugee Studies*, vol. 14, no. 4, pp. 432–450.

Boyd, C. M. J. (2009) 'Can a Marxist Believe in Human Rights?', *Critique*, vol. 37, no. 4, pp. 579–600.

Branigan, T. (2003) 'Kurdish Poet Finds His Voice', *The Guardian*, 31 May. Available: www.theguardian.com/uk/2003/may/31/immigrationandpublicservices.immigration

C/2017/1600. *Commission Recommendation (EU) 2017/432 of 7 March 2017 on making more effective when implementing the.* Directive 2008/115/EC of the European Parliament and of the Council.

Cissé, M. (2003) 'The *Sans-Papiers*: A Woman Draws the First Lesson', in Notes from Nowhere (ed.) *We Are Everywhere: The Irresistible Rise of Global Anticapitalism*, London and New York: Verso, pp. 38–45.

COM (2016) 467 final. Proposal for a *Regulation of the European Parliament and the Council establishing a common procedure for international protection in the Union and repealing* Directive 2013/32/EU.

Déotte, J.-L. (2004) 'The Differences between Rancière's Mésentente (Political Disagreement) and Lyotard's Différend', translated by R. Lapidus, *SubStance*, vol. 33, no. 1, pp. 77–90.

Dikec, M. (2012) 'Space as a Mode of Political Thinking', *Geoforum*, vol. 43, pp. 669–676.

El-Enany, N. (2016) 'Aylan Kurdi: The Human Refugee', *Law and Critique*, vol. 27, no. 1, pp. 13–15.

Elgot, J. (2016) 'How David Cameron's Language on Refugees Provoked Anger', *The Guardian*, 27 January. Available: www.theguardian.com/uk-news/2016/jan/27/david-camerons-bunch-of-migrants-quip-is-latest-of-several-such-comments

Foucault, M. (2014) *Wrong-Doing, Truth-Telling: The Function of Avowal in Justice*, translated by S. W. Sawyer, Chicago: Chicago University Press.

George, S. (2016) 'Dissent!', *Auguste Orts* [Electronic]. Available: www.augusteorts.be/discourse/33/DISSENT-Sylvain-George

Hayter, T. (2000) *Open Borders: The Case Against Immigration Controls*, London: Pluto Press.
Ingram, J. (2008) 'What Is a "Right to Have Rights"? Three Images of the Politics of Human Rights', *American Political Science Review*, vol. 102, no. 4, pp. 401–416.
Isin, E. F. and Nielsen, G. M. (eds.) (2008) *Acts of Citizenship*, London: Zed Books.
Lacroix, J. (2012) 'Droits de l'homme et politique, 1980–2012', *La Vie des Idées* [Electronics]. Available: www.laviedesidees.fr/Droits-de-l-homme-et-politique.html
Lacroix, J. (2013) 'Arendt, Human Rights and French Philosophy', *Social Science Research Network*, American Political Science Association 2013 Annual Meeting, Chicago. Available: http://ssrn.com/abstract=2300419
Lechte, J. and Newman, S. (2012) 'Agamben, Arendt and Human Rights: Bearing Witness to the Human', *European Journal of Social Theory*, vol. 15, no. 4, pp. 522–534.
Lefort, C. (1981) *L'Invention démocratique*, Paris: Fayard.
Leopold, D. (2007) *The Young Karl Marx: German Philosophy, Modern Politics, and Human Flourishing*, Cambridge and New York: Cambridge University Press.
Malkki, L. (1995) *Purity and Exile: Violence, Memory and National Cosmology among Hutu Refugees in Tanzania*, Chicago: The University of Chicago Press.
Malkki, L. (1996) 'Speechless Emissaries: Refugees, Humanitarianism, and Dehistoricisation', *Cultural Anthropology*, vol. 11, no. 3, pp. 377–404.
Malkki, L. (2002) 'News from Nowhere: Mass Displacement and Globalized "Problems of Organization"', *Ethnography*, vol. 3, no. 3, pp. 351–360.
Marx, K. (1978) 'On the Jewish Question', in Tucker, R. (ed.) *The Marx-Engels Reader*, New York: Norton & Company, pp. 26–46.
McGuaran, K. and Hudig, K. (2014) 'Refugee Protests in Europe: Fighting for the Right to Say', *Statewatch Journal*, vol. 23, no. 3–4, pp. 28–33.
Migrants on Hunger Strike (MHS) (2011a) *Statement of the 3000 migrant workers on hunger strike, January 25, 2011*, Wordpress [Electronic]. Available: https://allilmap.wordpress.com/2011/01/20/statement-of-the-300-migrant-workers-on-hunger-strike-from-25-january-2011/
Migrants on Hunger Strike (MHS) (2011b) *Press release: Decision of the assembly of migrants on hunger strike, January 27, 2011*, Wordpress [Electronic]. Available: http://hungerstrike300.espivblogs.net/2011/01/27/press-release-decision-of-the-assembly-of-migrants-on-hunger-strike/
Millner, N. (2011) 'From "Refugee" to "Migrant" in Calais Solidarity Activism: Re-Staging Undocumented Migration for a Future Politics of Asylum', *Political Geography*, vol. 30, pp. 320–328.
Mills, C. (2008) *The Philosophy of Agamben*, London: Continuum.
Mutua, M. (2002) *Human Rights: A Political and Cultural Critique*, Philadelphia: University of Pennsylvania Press.
Noll, G. (2010) 'Why Human Rights Fail to Protect Undocumented Migrants', *European Journal of Migration and Law*, vol. 12, pp. 241–272.
Nyers, P. (2003) 'Abject Cosmopolitanism: The Politics of Protection in the Anti-Deportation Movement', *Third World Quarterly*, vol. 24, no. 6, pp. 1069–1093.
Rancière, J. (1995) *On the Shores of Politics*, translated by L. Heron, London and New York: Verso.
Rancière, J. (1999) *Disagreement: Politics and Philosophy*, translated by J. Rose, Minneapolis and London: University of Minnesota Press.
Rancière, J. (2003) 'Politics and Aesthetics: An Interview', translated by F. Morloch, *Angelaki: Journal of Theoretical Humanities*, vol. 8, no. 2, pp. 191–211.

Rancière, J. (2004a) 'Introducing Disagreement', *Angelaki: Journal of Theoretical Humanities*, vol. 9, no. 3, pp. 3–9.

Rancière, J. (2004b) *Malaise dans l'esthétique*, Paris: Galilée.

Rancière, J. (2006a) 'Democracy, Republic, Representation', *Constellations*, vol. 13, no. 3, pp. 297–307.

Rancière, J. (2006b) 'Our Police Order: What Can Be Said, Seen, and Done: Interview with Truis Lie', *Eurozine* [Electronic], 11 August. Available: www.eurozine.com/our-police-order-what-can-be-said-seen-and-done/

Rancière, J. (2008) 'Jacques Rancière and Indisciplinarity', interview by M.-A. Baronian and M. Rosello', translated by G. Elliot, *Art & Research: A Journal of Ideas, Contexts and Methods*, vol. 2, no. 1. Available: www.artandresearch.org.uk/v2n1/jrinterview.html

Rancière, J. (2009b) *Moments: Interventions 1977–2009*, Paris: La Fabrique.

Rancière, J. (2010) *Dissensus: On Politics and Aesthetics*, translated by S. Corcoran, London and New York: Continuum.

Rancière, J. (2012) 'Hablar de crisis de la sociedad es culpar a sus victimas: Entrevista de Jacques Rancière', *Público*, 15 January. Available: http://www.publico.es/culturas/hablar-crisis-sociedad-culpar-victimas.html

Rancière, J. (2013) 'A Precarious Dialogue', translated by O. L. Fraser, *Radical Philosophy*, no. 181, pp. 18–25.

Rancière, J. (2014) *Moments Politiques, Interventions 1977–2009*, translated by M. Foster, New York: Seven Stories Press.

Rancière, J. (2015) 'Les idéaux républicains sont devenus des armes de discrimination et de mépris', interview with E. Aeschimann', *L'Obs*, 4 April. Available: http://bibliobs.nouvelobs.com/essais/20150403.OBS6427/jacques-ranciere-les-ideaux-republicains-sont-devenus-des-armes-de-discrimination-et-de-mepris.html

Rancière, J. (2016a) 'Polyphonic Discussion with Jacques Rancière', HIAP Gallery Augusta, Helsinki.

Rancière, J. (2016b) *The Method of Equality: Interviews with Laurent Jeanpierre and Dork Zabunyan*, translated by J. Rose, Cambridge and Malden: Polity Press.

Refugee Protest Camp Vienna (RPCV) (2012a) *Urgent demands, November 25, 2012*, Noblogs.org [Electronic]. Available: https://refugeecampvienna.noblogs.org/

Refugee Protest Camp Vienna (RPCV) (2012b) *Demands by the protesting refugees, November 26, 2012*, Noblogs.org [Electronic]. Available: https://refugeecampvienna.noblogs.org/

Rockhill, G. (2009) 'The Politics of Aesthetics: Political History and the Hermeneutics of Art', in Rockhill, G. and Watts, P. (eds.) *Jacques Rancière, History, Politics, Aesthetics*, Durham and London: Duke University Press, pp. 195–215.

Schaap, A. (2008) 'Political Abandonment and the Abandonment of Politics in Agamben's Critique of Human Rights', Open Research Exeter [Electronic]. Available: https://ore.exeter.ac.uk/repository/handle/10036/42438

Schaap, A. (2011) 'Enacting the Right to Have Rights: Jacques Rancière's Critique of Hannah Arendt', *European Journal of Political Theory*, vol. 10, no. 1, pp. 22–45.

'Stitches Removed from Asylum Protestor', *BBC News* (30 May 2003). Available: http://news.bbc.co.uk/2/hi/uk_news/england/nottinghamshire/2949896.stm

Tharoor, I. (2015) 'Death of Drowned Syrian Toddler Aylan Kurdi Jolts World Leaders', *The Washington Post*, 3 September. Available: www.washingtonpost.com/news/worldviews/wp/2015/09/03/image-of-drowned-syrian-toddler-aylan-kurdi-jolts-world-leaders/?utm_term=.443c41af8e6b

Topak, Ö. E. (2017) 'Migrant Protest in Times of Crisis: Politics, Ethics and the Sacred from Below', *Citizenship Studies*, vol. 21, no. 1, pp. 1–21.

Tuitt, P. (2016) 'A-Legality and the Death of the Refugee', *Law and Critique*, vol. 27, no. 1, pp. 5–8.

Twining, W. (2009) *General Jurisprudence: Understanding Law from a Global Perspective*, Cambridge: Cambridge University Press.

United Nations High Commissioner for Refugees (UNHCR) (2016) 'Refugee or Migrant', *The UN Refugee Agency* [Electronic]. Available: www.unhcr.org/uk/news/latest/2016/7/55df0e556/unhcr-viewpoint-refugee-migrant-right.html

Watt, N. and Wintour, P. (2015) 'David Cameron says UK Will Fulfil Moral Responsibility Over Migration Crisis', *The Guardian*, 3 September. Available: www.theguardian.com/uk-news/2015/sep/03/david-cameron-says-uk-will-fulfil-moral-responsibility-over-migration-crisis

Žižek, S. (2005) 'Against Human Rights', *New Left Review*, vol. 34, pp. 115–131.

Chapter 3

Rancière and the legal subject

Coming to terms with non-existence

Susanna Lindroos-Hovinheimo

1. Introduction

This chapter discusses legal subjectivity.[1] The main question asked is whether a Rancièrian understanding of the political subject can be transported to the legal field and, if so, what ramifications this would have for contemporary legal thinking. Overall, it is clear from the outset that Rancière's project does not merge with mainstream jurisprudence to form any simple constellation, if indeed the two can interact at all.[2] Why should his ideas, then, be of interest to legal scholars or others working with the law? What can we gain from reading him or what can we learn from him?

Two Rancièrian themes can be especially fruitful for legal theory: equality and subjectivity – and the two are interdependent. His strong emphasis on equality is notable, not only because it is indeed a worthy ideal, but also in the way he structures his argument. His view on equality is markedly different from how the concept usually operates in political theory. Rancière introduces a form of *a priori* equality, equality as a presupposed principle instead of an aim. As it has traditionally been conceived, the idea of equality has not been successful in producing actual equality in society. Of course, much more is needed in order to achieve equality than the mere reconfiguration of concepts, but concepts, categories, and principles also require rethinking. There is a need for a novel understanding of equality and of institutions that define, promote, and protect it, and Rancière's work offers a way of thinking where equality is not only seen as a goal to be achieved, but also as a principle that is always already in operation.

The aim of this chapter is to show that the fascinating – albeit complex – understanding of the political subject that emerges from Rancière's writings could help us reconsider legal subjectivity. When legal definitions of subjectivity and personhood are put into question in a Rancièrian setting, it may be possible to shed new light on current problems pertaining to legal practice, especially the legal definition of citizenship, which dictates participation and exclusion. This chapter endeavours to question what the legal subject is and what it can be. The purpose is to consider whether legal theory could benefit from Rancière's understanding of subjectivity and, if so, what avenues of thought are opened up by this analysis. The discussion presented here thus comes with a critical aim: to reconfigure the concept of the legal subject from the point of view of equality in an attempt to assess the strengths and shortcomings of the legal subject.

The main argument developed is that the subject can be understood without a necessary connection to individual personhood. If the equality of everyone is understood in its most radical sense, then anybody, whoever they may be, can be a (political) subject. There is, strictly speaking, no subject, and subjectivity is not founded on anything. The political subject, as well as the legal subject, are in an important sense impersonal[3] categories. The legal subject is an empty place, like a hollow tree. The tree has been there forever, an ancient oak as old as the law. But it nevertheless contains no life. By accepting the emptiness of the category of the legal subject, we can put it to use in various ways. This view of subjectivity might introduce the equipment necessary for a legal recognition of the non-recognized – that is, those who do not count.

2. Migrant personhood

In a beautiful newspaper piece, the author Hanif Kureishi once expressed his worry that the migrant, who in contemporary public debates has no colour, gender, or character, has not only migrated from a country to others, but *from reality to the collective imagination*, where he has been transformed into fiction. The migrant has no face and no story. An interesting passage in Kureishi's text echoes Rancièrian themes:

> It is impossible to speak up for the immigrant or, more importantly, hear him speak for himself, since everyone, including the most reasonable and sensitive, has made up their mind that the immigrant is everywhere now, and he is too much of a problem. There is, of course, always good reason to be suspicious of agreement: there is nothing more coercive and stupid than consensus, and it is through consensus that inequality is concealed.
>
> (Kureishi 2014)

Consensus is coercive and it conceals inequality. These ideas are compatible with a Rancièrian point of view. Consensus that is hostile towards difference and disagreement may be coercive. And consensus is a powerful way of upholding unequal social conditions.

According to Kureishi, 'the immigrant is easily dismissed and denigrated since he is now *no longer a person*. [. . .] The migrant has no face, no status, no protection and no story' (Kureishi 2014, emphasis added). The idea here seems to be that an immigrant is easily dismissed because his personhood is not recognized. The notion is familiar: only persons are taken seriously in politics or law. They are the ones who count. Everyone and everything else has secondary status. The unusual thought to be learned from Rancière is, however, that the political does not have to be understood in such a person-centred way.

Having no recognized personhood or, alternatively, no easily categorized identity does not necessarily mean impotence in the political sphere. When reading Rancière, one might be surprised that he sees an opening for political subjectivity for these non-persons precisely in the fact that they do not count. The interpretation of his theory put forward in this chapter argues that 'nobodies' can act politically, thereby becoming political subjects. The migrant may be seen as an exemplary figure, whose lacking status as a person can guide us towards an understanding of the subject as founded on non-existence.

3. A dramaturgy of politics

Before going into the complexities of subjectivity, we need to pay attention to Rancière's overall project and methodology. He is adamant that his aim is not to engage in political philosophy. He is not drafting a theory of politics, or even a philosophy of the political.[4] His method consists of reading others, that is, analyzing historical progresses and situations, debates and narratives. Even though he occasionally does draw general conclusions from some of his examples, and we can undoubtedly classify several of his texts as theoretical, he emphasizes that he is not engaged in general theory, or in making deductions from a theoretical framework to the understanding of politics, art, or literature (Rancière 2009a: 114–117).

This position, where he places himself outside the philosophers, the theorists, the wise who tell us how things are, is perhaps the only one available to him. Otherwise, his whole work could be caught up in an infinite regress of position taking against position taking, while his aim is really to question the prevailing positions from which people present their views. For him, there can be no 'theory' that explains things separate from 'practice' founded on the lessons of theory. His task, as he sees it, is to move from particular examples to tentative models for how things might be.

> 'It might be' is a formulation consistent with Rancière's peculiar practice of 'theory'. As I mentioned earlier, even when he writes 'theses on politics', he does not say what politics is but what it might be. He does not build a theory starting from the ontological principle of politics to deduce its consequences.
> (Rancière 2009a: 119)

How things might be is the end of the process, not the beginning. By analyzing occurrences that seem paradoxical, Rancière constructs a picture of what the term 'democracy' might mean, how equality can be understood and what the intricate collaborations between disruption and order could be. He posits formulas, but they are to be understood as tentative answers derived from enquiries into temporally and spatially situated themes. He uses words such as 'the dramaturgy of politics' (Ibid: 119, 120), 'a moving map of a moving landscape' (Ibid: 120), or 'topography' (Rancière 2006: 49) to refer to what he is trying to achieve. A certain hesitancy, as well as an aversion of dogmatism, is evident here.

While drawing up the landscape of the political, the main focus for Rancière is not so much what people – authors, politicians, workers – express, but the things they do, create, or make visible by their expressions and actions. He is intrigued by the stage they set as well as the way they create a 'common sense' that the speakers and listeners may share (Rancière 2009a: 117).

The subject is an important motif, but Rancière regards it a difficult topic to approach theoretically. In a short text entitled *Work, Identity, Subject*, he calls the question of the subject 'monstrous':

> Who plays the part of the subject who incarnates, represents or symbolizes work: that is the way in which, in the end, the 'question of work' has presented itself for me. It is also the way in which I have been able to address that monstrous question that has always terrorized me in the same measure as my contemporaries made it paramount: the 'theory of the subject'. This explains why I have only ever addressed it but from the side, through a specific aspect; namely, the relationship between subject and identity.
>
> (Rancière 2012: 206)

So, Rancière is not seeking a new theory of the subject. The 'question of the subject' is too difficult, too all-encompassing. It can only be approached in a roundabout way. He addresses only a specific aspect, namely the questionable relationship between subject and identity. In this way, he engages in critiques of identity. In order to understand how, it may be helpful to consider his background and the intellectual context in which he writes.

Some of Rancière's influences derive from Althusser, which may be rather evident,[5] and some from Sartre, which is perhaps less evident but highly interesting, and may equally help us understand Rancière's approach to subjectivity. Althusser's description of subject formation as interpellation has become a classic and still has relevance for contemporary political theory. His central thesis on the structure and functioning of ideology is that ideology creates individuals as subjects. Ideology is a complex concept, but for Althusser it primarily refers to the ways in which reality is represented. Ideology is here used in a similar sense to 'world view'. Althusser notes that it refers to an imaginary relationship of individuals to their real conditions of existence (Althusser 1971: 162). Ideologies do not necessarily correspond to any reality. People need ideologies and will always have them, because they need to make sense of their lives and the world they inhabit. Ideologies are indispensable, even though they are imaginary (see, e.g., Ricoeur 1994: 56–57).

How do individuals, then, live in a determinate ideology – for example, a religious, legal, ethical, or aesthetic one? An individual may believe in God, Duty or Justice. The belief is the individual's own and derives from his consciousness. Because of his ideology, the individual acts in certain ways and participates in practices that are those of his freely chosen ideological apparatus, for instance the church. If he believes in Duty, he will basically act accordingly. If he believes in

Justice, he will submit to the rules of law and may want to defend them if they are threatened (Althusser 1971: 166–167). What is noteworthy here is that the subject is (more or less) conscious of his acts and the reasons for them, and he makes his own choices. However, when the subject takes part in practices organized by the church or the legal system, the ideas guiding his choice of belief tend to disappear. The ideology underlies the practice, but is not predominantly reflected on in the acts carried out in rituals and habitual behaviour. This means that rather than the subject acting from an ideological conviction of how things are and what the world is, he is in fact acted upon by the ideological apparatus.

Althusser ends up in a position where the category of the subject is the constitutive element of ideology. There is no ideology except for concrete subjects, and it is made possible by them. A double bind appears. Ideology is for the subject, but the category of the subject is constitutive of all ideology – and every subject is necessarily an ideological subject (Althusser 1971: 171).

> [Y]ou and I are *always already* subjects, and as such constantly practice the rituals of ideological recognition, which guarantee for us that we are indeed concrete, individual, distinguishable and (naturally) irreplaceable subjects.
> (Althusser 1971: 172)

All ideology interpolates or hails individuals as subjects through the way the category of the subject functions. Ideology 'recruits' subjects among individuals and 'transforms' them into subjects. The process can be imagined in his famous example, where a police officer hails, 'Hey, you there!' Happening in the street, it will make the individual turn around, and in that instance become a subject.

> By this mere one-hundred-and-eighty-degree physical conversion, he becomes a *subject*. Why? Because he has recognized that the hail was 'really' addressed to him, and that 'it was *really him* who was hailed'.
> (Althusser 1971: 174)

It may seem as though the hailing takes place outside of ideology, in the street, that is, on neutral ground. This is not the case; it takes place in ideology. Those who are in ideology tend to think of themselves as outside it. This is one of the most curious but rather common-sensical ways in which ideology functions: one of its effects is the denial of the ideological nature of ideology. Ideology never says 'I am ideological'; nor does it have an outside (Althusser 1971: 175).

State apparatuses have two aspects. They may be repressive or coercive, like the prison system, or they may be simply ideological, like education or culture. In some cases they are both, like the law. However, the state itself is both repressive and ideological. It interferes in both the public and the private. A seemingly private issue, like family or ethical belief, is not outside the state's influence (Ricoeur 1994: 52). This is obvious in law, which functions as a repressive system but also as a symbolic system transmitting values, duties and beliefs – that is, ideology.

There are several differences between Althusser's and Rancière's conceptions of the subject. Only one will be highlighted here. For Althusser, individuals are in a fundamental sense always already subjects,[6] whereas for Rancière, subjects are in a remarkable way non-existent, which is the central and rather astonishing idea explored in this chapter.

In addition to Althusser, Rancière takes inspiration from Sartre. Rancière is concerned with identitarian fixations, that is, fixing identities, an idea that brings to mind a Sartrean notion of freedom.[7] Sartre rejects fixed identities and makes a distinction between doing things and making oneself. This, according to Rancière, was the framework for his own first readings of Marx (Rancière 2012: 207).

Rancière wants to understand and explain how alienation is related to an understanding of the subject as expelled from itself and attached to an alien identity (Rancière 2012: 207). Having conducted a great deal of research on workers, Rancière notes that not even a worker's identity is fixed. He has a capacity, or perhaps it may even be called freedom, to contest the alien identities that are given to him. The 'process of subjectivization is a process of disidentification or declassification' (Rancière 1992: 61). In this way, the political subject can come into existence through the denial of identity. Thus, the idea of subjectivity points to an intricate structure of non-presence.

> [A] subject is an outsider or, more, an in-between. Proletarians was the name given to people who are together inasmuch as they are between: between several names, statuses, and identities; between humanity and inhumanity, citizenship and its denial; between the status of a man of tools and the status of a speaking and thinking being.
>
> (Rancière 1992: 61)

A subject is an outsider or an in-between. But how can people who are between names, statuses, and identities be political subjects? Does not the whole idea of political subjectivity, as well as the concept of political action, presuppose somebody whose presence is acknowledged, somebody who counts, somebody who takes part in conversations? Even though it might sound nonsensical, especially for lawyers, Rancière invites us to rethink the subject as *not there*, as in important ways *non-existent*. It can come into being in political action, but it *is* nothing prior to politics.

It is worth noting that the subject is not here discussed in an ontological, existential or psychological sense, but as a political actor. For this reason, non-existence is not to be understood as an ontological category or attribute. The existence or inexistence of a political subject is not a discussion that can take place on the same plane as the existence of, say, objects such as cars or mountains. In a Rancièrian framework, ontology can be seen as order when it uses fixed categories of being and non-being. Politics, on the other hand, implies opposition to ontology, because it requires at least some kind of disruption. Politics opens up the space for disagreements about existence and non-existence, being and non-being, subjects and objects, among other things. It entails the activity of causing splits and ruptures in ontological divisions and definitions (see Ieven 2009: 50–51). And the political subject does not pre-exist this activity. Rancière does not see the political subject as a definable and existing *being* who would have consistency and a self-related identity. Politics concerns relations between subjects who are not yet there as recognized units (see Rancière 2016: 85–95).

Because ontology is not Rancière's primary concern, it is natural that he is interested in human beings[8] first and foremost in the political sense. Subjectivity is best understood as a *process* and not, for instance, as a state or an attribute.

> Political subjectivity [. . .] refers to an enunciative and demonstrative capacity to reconfigure the relation between the visible and the sayable, the relation between words and bodies: namely, what I refer to as 'the partition of the sensible'.
>
> (Rancière 2000: 115)

Political subjectivity entails an enunciative and demonstrable capacity. On the one hand, this does not sound like much: only a capacity? On the other, it is clear that subjectivity demands a great deal. The idea underlying this definition of subjectivity is Rancière's conception of equality.

4. Axiomatic equality

The subject does not pre-exist politics, but comes into being in reconfigurations of the visible and the sayable. Equality enjoys a central (or even *the* central) place in Rancière's thought. He describes it as a principle. It has no world of its own, he states (Rancière 2010: 213). It is nothing in the world in the sense of being fixed, defined, or laid down. It is a presupposition, not a goal to be attained. Equality is something that Rancière takes as a given: we are all equal, whether that ever shows, or whether it is realized or not.

In the text 'The Community of Equals', we find an example of how Rancière understands *inequality*. An unequal relationship can be illustrated by one in which a person explains something to another. I explain something to you assuming that without this explanation you would not understand. Here, I assume the role of the one with more knowledge. Explanation establishes a specific bond between people, a bond that upholds inequality: one knows more or understands better than the others. Any hierarchical constructions, where people assume roles according to their status, disguise the fact that ultimately everyone is equally valuable (Rancière 1995: 84).

Actual equality can be advanced on two conditions. It has to be *assumed*, taken for granted, and endlessly reaffirmed. But a community of equals can never achieve the form of a social institution. It is relevant for legal philosophy to notice that juridical instruments such as legal regulation can only get us so far in achieving equality in practice. The idea is that as soon as we feel comfortable in our institutions, providing for equal measures and protecting equal interests, we risk losing equality. Equality is a principle that needs to be assumed and continuously reaffirmed, but can never be fulfilled. There will not come a time when we can announce that we finally live in an equal society (Rancière 1995: 82–84). Again, as with the subject, we see an interesting logic where emphasis is put on the non-present, the not-there.

What is unique in Rancière's thought is that he does not see equality as something that happens *to* people. Traditional political theories often understand equality as received from the state or some other instance with power. Rancière's view is different. We do not *receive* equality, nor is it given to us from a source outside ourselves. It is not granted to us as a right. It cannot be handed to us: we have to grab it. Equality is *done*. It is created by us, not for us. This feature of his thinking is sometimes referred to as his radical anti-liberalism. For instance, Todd May argues that Rancière's understanding of politics is the inverse of traditional liberal political theory. Equality comes from the people. It is a presupposition out of which they can act in the political sphere (May 2010: 72). 'What is at issue in politics is the equality of those who seek to participate' (May 2010: 75). Political action makes the equality of everyone visible and audible.

Equality is a concept whose precise reference cannot be defined. All it says is that everybody is equal. It is a principle anterior to the practical field of politics. Its application, however, is undetermined, so it can operate in various ways, mainly disrupting pre-existing divisions of power or definitions of status and identity. '[T]he egalitarian axiom defines the practices, the modes of expression and manifestation that are themselves always determined by a particular state of inequality and by the potential for equality' (Rancière et al. 2000: 6). Equality is always possible in principle, a potential waiting to be fulfilled. Thus, the *presupposition* of equality has positive world-altering potential. There are moments when equals declare themselves as such, no matter what the actual conditions in society might suggest.

5. Political speech

How is it that certain people in certain times manage to declare themselves equal in societal conditions that suggest otherwise? Let us bring back the migrant. He has no voice and no place. How does he suddenly recognize his equality when his life is one of political (and legal) inequality? The issue is connected to the capacity of staging a scene, making oneself heard, demonstrating one's denial of identity. Where does that capacity come from? Probing into these issues is in an interesting way irrelevant within the framework of Rancière's thought, because circularity is introduced the moment we ask 'who?' as in 'who has the ability to dissent?'[9] This is so because when inquiring into the 'who' of politics, we are already either acting politically or affirming the *status quo*. A political act can be a mere question. Politics is not a field or a place *out there*. It can always happen here. It takes place when we put into motion the definitions and categories that are in force. There is, properly speaking, no political subject, because politics is precisely the act of putting into question our definitions of political subjects.

Rancière is not primarily interested in revolutions if we understand them as singular upheavals or ruptures. He says that he is not a thinker of the event but 'rather of emancipation as something with its own tradition, with a history that isn't just made up of great striking deeds, but also of the ongoing effort to create forms of the common different from the ones on offer from the state' (Rancière 2011: 80–81). A world-altering act can be tiny. It does not have to happen on a barricade.

Philosophy is one example of revolutionary action. According to Rancière, the

> critical practice of philosophy is an inseparably egalitarian, or anarchistic practice, since it considers arguments, narratives, testimonies, investigations and metaphors all as the equal inventions of a common capacity in a common language. Engaging in critique of the instituted divisions, then, paves the way for renewing our interrogations into what we are able to think and to do.
> (Rancière 2010: 218)

Philosophy, when it criticizes divisions, opens up possibilities for new or different ways of thinking and acting. In this way, philosophy can take part in changing the world. But do you have to be a philosopher to change the world? Certainly not. Anybody can question the given order of things. And the political subject is born *in this questioning*.

Understood in this way, politics may be rare, but this does not mean that it only happens in exceptional moments with times of apathy in between. Politics is rare because it does not happen naturally or automatically merely because of the fact that there are relations of power. In order to understand how politics as an affirmation of equality can happen, we need to study moments when the power of *anybody* emerges. According to Rancière, politics is 'almost everywhere and in every time interlocked, if not confused, with police' (Rancière 2009a: 118). It can be difficult to notice and analyze political acts for this very reason. Dissensus tends to be entangled with consensus, and it is by studying specific situations – usually after they have taken place – that we can distinguish between them.

Rancière pays quite a lot of attention to language, communication, speech, and writing. For instance, he thinks that speech can be political. But it is not language itself that is political; it is the action of speaking or writing, especially in the sense that it questions the distinction between legitimate and illegitimate speakers (Rancière and Panagia 2000: 114; Rancière 2010: 152–153; Rancière et al. 2000: 7–8, 12). Categories such as 'worker' or 'immigrant' can be rearranged by taking a talking subject's position. What is required is to put into circulation words that do things or sometimes just to use words in ways that are contested by those who claim to speak correctly. The capacity to speak gives us the possibility to disagree and disrupt the hierarchical order.

According to Rancière, in order to become a political subject, one has to stage a scene. For politics to happen, we must invent a scene upon which words may be audible, objects may be visible and individuals may be recognized (Rancière and Panagia 2000: 116). Presupposed equality makes this staging and restaging possible. It enables constitutive rethinking (Rancière and Panagia 2000: 120). Without a stage or a scene, there cannot be disagreement. Rancière speaks of May 1968 like this when he states, 'what is required is a staging of this mythico-philosophical event that marks the advent of thinking for those who were not initially destined to think' (Rancière and Panagia 2000: 121).

Therefore, politics has an aesthetic dimension because it entails a struggle for how things are seen or heard.[10] Political acts disrupt what is visible and audible. They interfere with the partition of the sensible. The aesthetic dimension of politics means the 'staging of a dissensus – of a conflict of sensory worlds – by subjects who act as if they were the people, which is made of the uncountable count of the anyone' (Rancière 2009b: 11).

6. Political subjectivization as a logic of otherness

Before moving on to law, let us summarize how the subject is understood by Rancière. As subjectivization means the enactment of equality, it is an emancipative process or act. Thus, equality is actualized in subjectivization. This can happen in different ways.

Firstly, political subjectivization is a heterology, *a logic of the other* (Rancière 1992: 62). It does not entail only the simple assertion of identity. It is always at the same time the denial of an identity given by an other, by the prevailing order. Where policy and order are about 'right' names, names that put people in their places and dictate their social roles, politics is about 'wrong' names. These are misnomers that 'articulate a gap and connect with a wrong' (Rancière 1992: 62). So, politics is about naming, but not about right names, rather, *other* names. Demos, or 'the people', is a helpful concept to be applied here. It refers to being that is non-being. The demos consists of people who are not identified with anybody, they are nobody, that is, the masses.

Secondly, political subjectivization is a demonstration, which always supposes an other (Rancière 1992: 62). There has to be a common place that is shared with the other, even though the place only serves as a stage for dissensus. It may not be a place for dialogue, but subjectivization still happens in relation to an other. One of the examples provided by Rancière takes place on the Aventine, where plebeians and patricians occupy the same place for disagreement. The disagreement regards not only the objects of debate, but also the status of the speakers. The patricians do not understand the noises that come out of the plebeians' mouths. In order to be heard and understood, the plebeians have to stage a scene of argumentation, where the patricians understand them as sharing a world (Rancière and Panagia 2000: 116). To become a political subject, one has to demonstrate one's existence, that is, political non-existence, *to somebody* by inventing a scene where that demonstration can be experienced.

Here, we become attentive to the flexibility of the term 'other'. Otherness has a varying meaning in Rancière's thought, depending on point of view. The other can refer to the political others, the ones who do not fit the order and do not count. For instance, today the immigrant is such an other, often having no political existence at all. But the term 'other' can be applied in different directions. It can refer to the countless masses, or to the rulers and policymakers. This way of using the term is understandable insofar as we regard it in connection with the presupposition of equality. That everybody is equal means that anybody can be exchanged for an other. Equality includes the idea of substitutability. We are all equally valuable and our roles in society could, in principle, be reversed at any time. To sum up, political subjectivization entails a demonstration of otherness. It is an act that displays visible or audible otherness. This demonstration is always done keeping in mind an other – the patricians or the capitalists or the majority – whoever that other may be.

Thirdly, political subjectivization entails an impossible identification (Rancière 1992: 62). This is perhaps the most complex issue of political subjectivization: it happens in the interval between identities. One does not become a political actor by changing one's identity from this to that, say from immigrant to citizen. Fixing things is not politics. What seems to matter for Rancière is the in-between. Here, in the non-determined space where we do not really know who anybody is or what their role is, emancipatory politics can have a chance.

> The process of equality is a process of difference. But difference does not mean the assumption of a different identity or the plain confrontation of two identities. The place for the working out of difference is not the 'self' or the culture of a group. It is the *topos* of an argument. And the place for such an argument is an interval. The place of a political subject is an interval or a gap: being *together* to the extent that we are *in between* – between names, identities, cultures and so on.
>
> (Rancière 1992: 62)

When referring to this peculiar logic of difference, it is worthwhile to distinguish Rancière's position from that of Derrida. Where Rancière sees his own understanding of democracy as political, he accuses Derrida of a view that amounts to a lack of politics. Even though Rancière sees merit in Derrida's theory, his concern is with Derrida's concept of 'democracy to come'. In Rancière's reading, it is not a political concept but ultimately an ethical one. Derrida's democracy is actually a democracy without demos. What is absent is the idea of the political subject. This is, according to Rancière, caused by the fact that Derrida cannot endorse the idea of substitutability. The equivalence of the same and the other is a central idea of Rancière's – perhaps even the most central idea for his concept of equality – and it does not find a place in Derridean thinking.

Derrida's understanding of politics is, according to Rancière, not the exercise of the capacity of everybody, because his notion of the political subject cannot be an undefined and neutral whoever. Democracy to come does not mean a community of substitutable persons, as Rancière would have it. Democracy to come can oppose the practice of nation states through commitment to an absolute other. This other is not the same as us and can never become the same as us. Derrida's other is wholly other, not someone substitutable for me (Rancière 2009b: 11–13). What Rancière wants is a democracy where anyone can act as political subject, staging their otherness, taking different roles and making visible the fluid boundaries between the other and the same.

There are indeed differences between the two thinkers. Derrida's other is conceptualized as wholly other, and the separation between the same and the other is somehow absolute. Rancière's understanding of political subjectivity is built around the idea of differences between the same and the other, but the two can constantly change places. Roles, names, and identities are continuously being renegotiated and reconfigured. A political subject can show that there is no difference between the same and the other by taking the role of anyone or the people. This display of substitutability is a display of equality and a way to change the relationship between the included and the excluded.

For Rancière, democracy has a built-in logic of heterogeneity (Rancière 2010: 50–53). But 'democracy' is here understood neither as a form of government nor a form of social life. Democracy *is* politics. It is the principle that says that the power to rule is founded on nothing. The basis for power is that there is no basis, because we are all equal. Why then do some have the position of ruler, while others are ruled? Many patterns may dictate this, for instance birth, wealth, or force. But democracy, politics proper, means the rule of the demos. A radically democratic government would be one where the governors are chosen by drawing lots (Rancière 2009c: 40–49).

Political acts display the power of those who are no more qualified to rule than those who are being ruled. 'Democracy' refers to an anarchic structure where the rulers and the ruled are the same and can at any time change places. Politics as dissensus or disruption means that all qualifications are supplemented by the power of the unqualified (Rancière 2010: 53; Rancière 2009a: 118). The essence of the power of the people, and thus of democracy, is the power of those who have no qualification. It does not matter what individual features they have, what kind of persons they are, whether they are skilled, wise, good, or bad. The power of the people is impersonal. Hence, the political subject, the demos, can be described as a singular universal: a singular that appears as a stand-in for the universal (see Žižek 2008: 221, 282).

7. Rancièrian legal subjects

The political subject, as we have seen, is closely tied to the principle of equality. The process of subjectivization means the enactment of equality, which tends to require disruption of the prevailing order of things, knowledge, roles, and power relations. Law, however, is the guardian of order. Is law, then, necessarily an antipode to politics? Such a conclusion sounds strange to critical legal scholars, who generally understand law as intertwined with politics. Indeed, after the lessons learned from legal realism and critical legal studies, it is difficult to see how there could be law devoid of politics.

Rancière himself sees very little emancipatory potential in law. For him, the legal system represents above all order and hierarchy. He is also highly sceptical of human rights (see Rancière 2010: 62–75). Both views may be transported to legal theory of the critical variety. It is likely that the ideas of the non-existent subject and democracy as the power of anyone are most difficult for lawyers. It is difficult to reconcile an understanding of politics as dissensus, including constant openness of roles and positions with law, which at least on the surface seems to operate with definable categories and rules, as well as clear roles such as 'party to the contract', 'citizen', 'defendant', or 'judge' (see Rancière 1999: 108–112). Still, while digging deeper into the foundations of law, possibilities for Rancièrian understandings may perhaps be found.

The legal subject is a category used to demarcate between who counts in law and who does not. It draws boundaries between those whose agency the law recognizes and those who are excluded or reduced to the status of objects, such as animals. It also defines who has the capacity to speak in law. The concept is a gatekeeper. In itself it explains no specifics about the subjects it refers to, but simply defines whether someone or something has legal agency or not.[11] One might say that the legal subject is nothing but an empty place designating a possibility of subjectivization (cf. Esposito 2013: 29).

The legal person is a 'dry, sterile and artificial character, all law and no life' (Naffine 2009: 42). Some critical legal theorists want to reconfigure the legal subject, often by uniting it with life by giving it a more nuanced existence. They want to emancipate the concept of legal personhood from its generality. These strategies are familiar, for instance, in feminist legal studies or critical race theory. However, it may not always be a disadvantage in the face of emancipation if legal personhood remains sterile, dry and artificial. Being what it is, there is room for manoeuvring the way the concept is used. The more general it is, the more flexible it can be. Impersonal legal personhood allows for substitutability and heteronomy. If anyone and whoever can occupy the position of the subject, then there is a chance for egalitarian shifts, changes and ruptures within the hierarchies of legal systems.

The law does many things. It produces, upholds and polices order. But this is not all that it does. Deconstructing the category of legal subject, we see that it can be reconciled with presupposed equality. The theoretical construction that we find in jurisprudence – and then used in a variety of ways in legal practice – is one where, in principle, almost anybody can fit. It can be seen to denote a very fundamental equality presupposing basically equal powers, equal intelligence[12] and equal humanity – for anyone, similarly for babies and for the handicapped, and for firms and companies. This abstract definition of subjectivity is fictitious, but perhaps Rancièrian ideas can be combined with jurisprudence in order to embrace the fiction. Because of the way the legal conception of subjectivity operates, there may be space for political disruption inside the fabric of law. When disagreements arise about who counts as a legal subject, politics necessarily steps in.

To become a subject whose equality is recognized, one needs to demonstrate dissensus *to somebody* by inventing a scene. Is there a way that the law could function as that scene? A migrant may make himself heard and demonstrate his existence by speaking up in the media. Openly disagreeing with the role that he has been given can be a political act in the Rancièrian sense. How about the migrant speaking in a court of law? Can this be a political act? In order to use the legal system as a forum, a speaker must adhere to the pre-given hierarchical order of society and accept the norms that govern it, at least to some extent. In this sense, legal acts cannot be political acts. Nevertheless, if legal acts interfere in the drafting of the political landscape by defining concepts and categories, influencing attitudes and reconfiguring power relations, then they can be political. The claim here is not that law enables political action, but rather that it can in some instances, most specifically in some *cases*, contribute with a platform, from which the fabric of the social can be questioned. Law can work as a medium through which this questioning can be made audible (see Lindroos-Hovinheimo 2012: 153–155).[13] Attention to situations, cases, and instances is required in order to determine whether equality has been affirmed or not: 'Politics is the art of warped deductions and mixed identities. It is the art of the local and singular construction of cases of universality' (Rancière 1999: 139).

Still, in a Rancièrian setting, the legal system is clearly identified as order and the police. Similarly in *The Ticklish Subject*, Slavoj Žižek makes a difference between what he calls the 'culture of complaint' and the 'true radical/revolutionary act'. The subject tends to blame the big Other, for instance the state, for its failures. By doing so, the subject asserts his dependence on it. The basic feature of a culture of complaint is a call addressed to the big Other to intervene and put things right, that is to compensate for a wrong in society. What is crucial in such complaining is that it does not undermine the position of the big Other in any way; on the contrary, it affirms that position. Interestingly, it tends to have a legalistic nature. Complaints are expressed in legal terms so that the need for retribution is translated into a legal obligation to make amends. The Other is made responsible. According to Žižek, 'by translating their demand into the terms of legalistic complain, they *confirm the Other in its position in the very gesture of attacking it*' (Žižek 2008: 441). There is a decisive difference between complaints and true radical acts. Instead of reaffirming the Other when demanding actions of it, the radical or revolutionary act suspends the legal frame and accomplishes the act itself (Žižek 2008: 441). The worry is thus that by using our available legal instruments in contestations and disagreements, we only end up upholding the *status quo*.

This is indeed a concern, but it may be over-emphasized when law is considered, as both Rancière and Žižek tend to do, as something definite, that is, a system, an order, a definable *something* that carries clear meanings and definite concepts. However, when the other side of law, the uncertain side of gaps, difficult cases and the judges' role as ideological actors are considered, then the view becomes blurred (Lindroos-Hovinheimo 2012: 157–162). It is difficult to see the legal system purely as a servant of the *status quo* if the system itself is a multifaceted, complex mess always including elements that may be interpreted as pointing in several different and even mutually exclusionary decisions. There is definitely room for struggle inside the law.

Rancière himself maintains that dissensus is often entangled with consensus and politics with order. The two cannot be conceptually separated. This idea sits well with the self-understanding of a critical lawyer, who sees his or her task as including active usurpation of legal principles and concepts. Law is a tool used, not an order given. No legal rule or principle applies itself, which leaves room for interpretation and disagreement. That is exactly what many lawyers are trained to do: to disagree. Their craft consists of using legal concepts as instruments for strategic purposes, thus taking advantage of the leeway of language while simultaneously causing meanings to fluctuate.

8. A legal demos?

Rancière's view of democracy as the power of anyone may be the most problematic part of his theory for a legal theorist. Radical equality entails the rule of the demos, that is, the power of those who are no more qualified to rule than those who are being ruled. This anarchic structure simply does not fit Western jurisprudence.[14] It is difficult to merge with a lawyer's understanding of government and the rule of law depending on a prearranged system of norms. The justifiable exercise of power is based on specific rules and pre-given roles for legislative bodies, decision-makers and administrators.

Legal rule tends to rely on experts. Understandably, Rancière is weary of their power. Even questions of equality are submitted to legal experts to decide.

> The trouble is that experts in law exist whereas experts in equality do not – or, more exactly, that the power of equality begins only when the power of the experts ceases to hold sway. Wherever the vaunted triumph of law and of the legal state takes the form of recourse to experts, democracy has been reduced to a caricature of itself – to nothing more than government by wise men.
>
> (Rancière 1995: 89)

The power of the law indeed entails government by men (and women), wise or not, but occupying expert positions nonetheless.

Still, through reconfiguring the concept of the legal subject, there are possibilities for emancipation. Continuously asking who the legal subject is, or demonstrating non-identification with the way legal concepts are used in legal practice, can be a form of disagreement.[15] The excluded or the surplus may not become automatically or even easily included through these acts, but at least they have a chance to be noticed as the ones who do not count. Who notices? Well, in a legal case, primarily the experts, but in order for there to be a political act one has to demonstrate one's existence – that is, political non-existence – *to someone*, and that demonstration has to be experienced *by someone*. Experts will do as a primary audience if the political act penetrates their understanding of order.

The legal subject is a fiction reflecting the migrant as described by Kureishi. The migrant has no colour, gender or character. He has migrated from reality to the collective imagination, where he has been transformed into a fiction. The same goes for the legal subject, whose stereotype is a healthy, adult, rational, conscious human being, but in a magnitude of cases something quite different, ranging from an unborn child to an artificial person. The legal subject is not definite enough to ever refer to anyone specific, and it can refer to a most diverse group of beings. The legal person is, in a sense, non-existent.

9. Conclusions

> Politics exists when the figure of a specific subject is constituted, a supernumerary subject in relation to the calculated number of groups, places, and functions in society. This is summed up in the concept of the *demos*.
>
> (Rancière 2006: 51)

This chapter has considered whether Rancière's understanding of the political subject can be useful for legal theory. We have seen that subjectivization is understood as enactment of equality. Politics is a constant struggle for names and identities. The exemplary figure has been that of the migrant, who today tends to have no face, no body, and no existence as a person. Demos is the collective name for those who are nobody and do not count as political subjects. It denotes being that is non-being, because the people are those who are not identified with anybody. They are the rest, the surplus. Likewise with the migrant; it has become the name of an outcast, a non-person. There are significant echoes of the radical definition of demos in the migrant.

Rancière's understanding of political subjectivity assumes differences between the same and the other, but they are not absolute. The same and the other can constantly change places. Hierarchies and roles are continuously being renegotiated and reconfigured. A subject can show that there is no difference between the same and the other by taking the role of anyone. This display of substitutability is a display of equality and a way to disrupt the relationship between the included and the excluded.

This chapter has argued that non-presence, which can be found at the heart of Rancière's understanding of the political subject, can be discerned in the category of the legal subject as well. This view of legal subjectivity requires, however, that the equality of everyone is taken for granted. Equality as a presupposed principle is the foundation for anybody's subject status. Because equality is something that underlies all human contact and communication, it generalizes but also reduces all humans to the same level. It leads to an understanding of subjectivity that is not founded on individuality, singularity, or personhood. The subjectivity of anyone and whoever is possible because we are all already equal.

Notes

1 Some of the arguments presented in this chapter have been developed in a case study on the famous 'right to be forgotten' ruling by the European Court of Justice. See Lindroos-Hovinheimo (2016).

2 The relationship between Rancière and the mainstream is contentious at best, as well as his relation to political theory or philosophy. Perhaps one of the best attempts to situate him is to see him in 'a position of mainstream marginality in contemporary thought' (Watkin 2014: 418).

3 The impersonalism of Roberto Esposito is similar to the ideas presented here (see, for instance, Esposito 2012). He sees the centrality of the category of the person as a hindrance to equality. An increasing focus on persons is a move away from democracy. The ideological underpinnings, the concepts and the very logic of democratic rule do not fit the biopolitical person-centred thinking of today. Democracy concerns a totality of equal subjects, not individual bodies. Esposito uses the concept of Third Person to refer to a non-personal person or a non-person. He or she is somebody, but that somebody is anybody and does not occupy the position of a speaker or actor. He or she is never the unique subject who utters something to somebody in a particular dialogue, but an anonymous 'whoever'. It is simply a name we give to someone who does not occupy the role of subject.

4 In 'From Politics to Aesthetics?' published in 2005, he refers to the research he has previously conducted, for instance in his doctoral dissertation La Nuit des Prolétaires (The Nights of Labour), as 'historical' and 'political'. He also states that he is no more a political philosopher than he is a philosopher of art (Rancière 2005: 13, 18).

5 Rancière was Althusser's student at École Normale Supérieure in the 1960s, but his thought later developed in directions that differ quite considerably from his teacher's. See his remarks on Althusser in (Rancière and Panagia 2000: 113–116; Rancière 2010: 37–40). For discussions of the two philosophers' similarities and differences, (see, e.g., Corcoran 2010: 1–24; Parker 2003: ix–xxviii). For a discussion of the Althusserian legal subject, (see, e.g., Buonamano 2014).

6 See, for example, Buonamano (2014: 234–235) for an illuminating discussion of this theme.

7 Sartrean freedom can be understood as indeterminate being-for-itself, a way of being that is not necessarily defined by the roles we are made to play or the identities that are given to us. Everybody defines themselves, instead of being defined by the ways in which they are subjected (Hallward 2006: 110).

8 Rancière rarely uses this term, so it may seem out of place. However, for want of a better term, I use it here with caution. He seems to prefer words like 'man', 'humanity', 'people', 'bodies', or even 'the human animal'.

9 And is the 'who' necessarily human? If Rancière does not accept any pre-given definition of the subject, then is it possible to conceive non-human actors such as dolphins

and computer programmes as such? The question is difficult, but because Rancière puts so much emphasis on (human) language, it perhaps becomes understandable that the answer has to be 'no'. However, Jane Bennett argues that even if Rancière himself denies that the political subject could be anything but human, there is an opening for non-human actors to gain the subject position in Rancièrean political theory (Bennett 2010: 105–106).

10 And art *can be* one medium through which politics happens. In an interview from 2014, he says that art 'is a work on the distribution of the sensible. Sometimes, but not very often, it rearranges the set of perception between what is visible, thinkable, and understandable, and what is not. This is the politics of art. I always try to question mainstream ideas on this subject, especially the assumption that artists' work can have precise, intended effects. When practices of art affect the sensible, it is not simply as a result of artists' intentions' (Replace ref. with: (Rancière 2015: n.p.)

11 Legal subjects can indeed be 'things', such as firms or companies.

12 Equal intelligence is arguably the foundation stone of equality. See, for example, Méchoulan (2004: 3), '"Equally intelligent" – both terms are important: they lead the reflection towards the status of political equality, and the legitimacy of ordinary people appearing as intelligent'.

13 Interestingly, some of Rancière's own examples of when a reconfiguration of the partition of the sensible has taken place are juridical, or at least have close affinity with some form of law.

14 It is indeed easy to agree with Rancière's criticism of current Western democracies. They are not democratic in the sense that power would belong to everybody and anybody equally, including those who have no qualification to rule (Rancière 2009c).

15 See also Gunneflo and Selberg (2010: 173–191). They put forward a similar argument when discussing European migration law, drawing on Rancière.

Bibliography

Althusser, L. (1971) *Lenin and Philosophy, and Other Essays*, New York: Monthly Review Press.

Bennett, J. (2010) *Vibrant Matter: A Political Ecology of Things*, Durham and London: Duke University Press.

Buonamano, R. (2014) 'The Legal Subject in Althusser's Political Theory', *Law & Critique*, vol. 25, pp. 231–248.

Corcoran, S. (2010) 'Editor's Introduction', in Rancière, J. *Dissensus: On Politics and Aesthetics*, London and New York: Continuum, pp. 1–24.

Esposito, R. (2012) *Third Person: Politics of Life and Philosophy of the Impersonal*, Cambridge and Malden: Polity Press.

Esposito, R. (2013) *Terms of the Political: Community, Immunity, Biopolitics*, New York: Fordham University Press.

Gunneflo, M. and Selberg, N. (2010) 'Discourse or Merely Noise? Regarding the Disagreement on Undocumented Migrants', *European Journal of Migration and Law*, vol. 12, pp. 173–191.

Hallward, P. (2006) 'Staging Equality: On Rancière's Theatrocracy', *New Left Review*, vol. 37, pp. 109–129.

Ieven, B. (2009) 'Heteroreductives: Rancière's Disagreement with Ontology', *Parallax*, vol. 15, no. 3, pp. 50–62.

Kureishi, H. (2014) 'The Migrant Has No Face, Status or Story', *The Guardian*, 30 May. Available: www.theguardian.com/books/2014/may/30/hanif-kureishi-migrant-immigration-1 [6 June 2017].

Lindroos-Hovinheimo, S. (2012) *Justice and the Ethics of Legal Interpretation*, Oxon and New York: Routledge.
Lindroos-Hovinheimo, S. (October 2016) 'Legal Subjectivity and the "Right to Be Forgotten": A Rancièrean Analysis of *Google*', *Law and Critique*, vol. 27, no. 3, pp. 289–301.
May, T. (2010) 'Wrong, Disagreement, Subjectification', in Deranty, J.-P. (ed.) *Jacques Rancière: Key Concepts*, Durham: Acumen, pp. 69–79.
Méchoulan, E. (2004) 'Introduction: On the Edges of Rancière', *Substance*, vol. 33, no. 1, pp. 3–9.
Naffine, N. (2009) *Law's Meaning of Life: Philosophy, Religion, Darwin and the Legal Person*, Oxford and Portland: Hart Publishing.
Parker, A. (2003) 'Editor's Introduction: Mimesis and the Division of Labor', in Rancière, J. *The Philosopher and His Poor*, Durham and London: Duke University Press, pp. ix-xx.
Rancière, J. (1992) 'Politics, Identification, and Subjectivization', *October*, vol. 61, pp. 58–64.
Rancière, J. (1995) *On the Shores of Politics*, London and New York: Verso.
Rancière, J. (1999) *Disagreement: Politics and Philosophy*, Minneapolis and London: University of Minnesota Press.
Rancière, J.(2000) 'Jacques Rancière – Literature, Politics, Aesthetics: Approaches to Democratic Disagreement', *SubStance*, vol. 29, no. 2, pp. 3–24.
Rancière, J. (2005) 'From Politics to Aesthetics?', *Paragraph*, vol. 28, no. 1, pp. 13–25.
Rancière, J. (2006) *The Politics of Aesthetics: The Distribution of the Sensible*, London and New York: Continuum.
Rancière, J. (2009a) 'A Few Remarks on the Method of Jacques Rancière', *Parallax*, vol. 15, no. 3, pp. 114–123.
Rancière, J. (2009b) 'The Aesthetic Dimension: Aesthetics, Politics, Knowledge', *Critical Inquiry*, vol. 39, pp. 1–19.
Rancière, J. (2009c) *Hatred of Democracy*, London and New York: Verso.
Rancière, J. (2010) *Dissensus: On Politics and Aesthetics*, London and New York: Continuum.
Rancière, J. (2011) 'Democracies against Democracy: An Interview with Eric Hazan', in *Democracy in What State?*, New York: Chichester, pp. 76–81.
Rancière, J. (2012) 'Work, Identity, Subject', in Deranty, J.-P. and Ross, A. (eds.) *Jacques Rancière and the Contemporary Scene: The Philosophy of Radical Equality*, London and New York: Continuum, pp. 205–216.
Rancière, J. (2015) 'The Politics of Art: An Interview with Jacques Rancière'. Available: www.versobooks.com/blogs/2320-the-politics-of-art-an-interview-with-jacques-ranciere [3 March 2016].
Rancière, J. (2016) 'Critical Questions on the Theory of Recognition', in Deranty, J.-P. and Genel, K. (eds.) *Recognition or Disagreement: A Critical Encounter on the Politics of Freedom, Equality, and Identity*, New York and Chichester: Columbia University Press, pp. 83–95.
Rancière, J. and Panagia, D. (2000) 'Dissenting Words: A Conversation with Jacques Rancière', *Diacritics*, vol. 30, no. 2, pp. 113–126.
Ricoeur, P. (1994) 'Althusser's Theory of Ideology', in Elliott, G. (ed.) *Althusser: A Critical Reader*, Oxford and Cambridge: Blackwell, pp. 44–72.
Watkin, C. (2014) 'Rancière Now: Current Perspectives on Jacques Rancière (Review)', *French Studies: A Quarterly Review*, vol. 68, no. 3, p. 418.
Žižek, S. (2008) *The Ticklish Subject: The Absent Centre of Political Ontology*, London and New York: Verso.

Chapter 4

Rancière, human rights, and the limits of a politics of process

*Tom Frost**

1. Introduction

In thinking about *Rancière and Law*, as this collection exhorts us to do, I have turned my attention to one of the most well-known areas of Rancière's writings, the 'Rights of Man'. In 'Who Is the Subject of the Rights of Man?' (Rancière 2004b), Rancière aimed a broadside at the rights-scepticism which can be traced in much of critical theory to the writings of Hannah Arendt (on the left), and an older tradition on the right exemplified by Edmund Burke and Jeremy Bentham. Rancière's writings and thought cover a wide range of areas, but it is the famous focus on rights which interests me here, as it brings to bear the problematization of the 'subject' which Rancière develops in his writings.

Rancière does not take an ontological view of the subject. Rancière's writings on human rights attempt to get out of an ontological trap he sees being promulgated in relation to them (Rancière 2004b: 302). These writings on rights and the subject illustrate Rancière's conception of politics as a *process* that emphasizes a dynamic staging of conflicts and the impossibility of stepping outside that discussion and conflict.

My starting point is Daniel Defoe's *Robinson Crusoe*. This eighteenth-century piece of literature is key to this discussion about the subject of human rights, and the paradoxes which those rights contain. The novel was used in United Nations debates to justify drafting parts of the Universal Declaration of Human Rights (UDHR). In basing the subject of human rights in part on the eponymous hero of the same novel, the drafting committee (advertently or inadvertently) constructed a vision of the human subject which conflated the figures of man and citizen. The subject of human rights was not a natural man, but intimately connected and indivisible from the society in which he was living.

I connect Arendt's critique of the right to have rights to these debates at the United Nations, illustrating how they lend support to Arendt's criticisms of human rights. I then outline Rancière's counter-critique of Arendt, and his defence of politics and rights. I show how Rancière's distinction between politics and the police envisions a subject which is created through 'dissensual' acts. These acts of 'dissensus' are the very divisions, the strife or the conflict, which constitutes the stage on which politics occurs (Rancière 2009: 114–115, 122).

Rancière's subject does not need to act politically in an existing public sphere where individuals recognize each other as equal and distinct. Rather, the acts they commit help contest the very meaning of rights and politics; a politics which always entails the verification of equality as such.

I want to turn to the consequences of this processual politics. I use Rancière's writings on politics and his defence of rights to illustrate how, in his schema, political subjects can be formed and new subjects hitherto unrecognized can be created through dissensual acts. I argue that with Rancière, any judgment on the quality of a political act, and the subject it can create, is necessarily made *ex post facto*. Rancière's separation of politics from ethics forces us to avoid pre-judgments of the political nature of acts. This carries the risk that the reader of Rancière will interpret only the acts they are already sympathetic towards as 'political' and dissensual. The political remains in the eye of the beholder.

As a result, this processual politics must be supplemented with a later judgment to be able to differentiate *between* potential political acts. In treating Rancière as a serious thinker of modernity and of rights, we need a way to distinguish between an act which is, for example, carried out by racists or those who oppress rights, and an act carried out by a demonstrator or as an act of resistance against hegemony. I argue that it is possible, following Rancière, to conceive of both as acts of dissensual politics potentially giving rise to political subjects.

This in turn highlights the key issue for me in relation to Rancière's thought. How can we distinguish between the quality of actors who act politically, without falling back on a presumed political sphere (as in Arendt) or modern liberal political philosophy? I conclude that a stronger questioning of the types of judgment needed to differentiate between political acts is required to avoid Rancière's thought being used to justify forms of action the reader finds sympathetic.

2. Human rights, Robinson Crusoe, and today's Man Fridays

My starting point may appear to be an odd one. Yet Defoe's *Robinson Crusoe* has come to shape modern debates, and the modern law, of human rights (Defoe [1719] 2003). It was used to justify the wording of Article 29 of the UDHR. The rationale for human rights, which also serves as the basis for Arendt's critique in *The Origins of Totalitarianism*, can be seen in Jacques Maritain's refrain that human rights are inherent and inalienable 'from the very fact that man is man' (Maritain 1986: 63). Human rights are seen as necessitating the free and full development of the human personality (Slaughter 2007: 4). However, even defenders of human rights note that international human rights is a notoriously feeble legal regime, only existing through formal arrangements between sovereign states or as a consequence of state practice (Slaughter 2007: 24). Perhaps the nature of this feebleness can be illustrated by the fact that the UDHR itself is just that: a declaration, and not a treaty.

Adopted in December 1948, the UDHR itself was born out of great debates held by the Third Committee of the United Nations (United Nations 1948).

Fifty-eight nations were represented at the United Nations at the time, and the Committee discussed at length the draft declaration proposed by the Commission on Human Rights (Morsink 1984: 310). These debates shed light on the underlying philosophical basis of the 'Rights of Man'.

The UDHR has been invoked as a standard by which to judge competing philosophical theories about human rights. The Committee's debates centred on whether the rights to be promulgated were to be conceived of as 'natural rights', separate from and unconnected to the state or government, or granted because the individual had a relationship with their nation state. The UDHR itself carries a strong individualistic focus, which emanates from eighteenth-century ideals of 'natural rights' (Morsink 1984: 310–311). However, Article 29 was seen as an 'escape clause', admitting that rights are balanced by and correlative to duties (Morsink 1984: 317; Morsink 1989: 22). The text of paragraph one of Article 29 originally stated that 'everyone has duties to the community which enables him freely to develop his personality'. Alan Watt, the Australian delegate to the Third Social and Humanitarian Committee of the United Nations, proposed an amendment to Article 29: 'Everyone has duties to the community *in which alone* the free and full development of his personality is possible' (United Nations 1948: 658, emphasis mine). The key word here, as Joseph Slaughter has identified, is 'alone'. This rejects individualism and asserts a clear connection between the individual and the state or society. Watt's proposal aimed to moderate the individualistic excesses of the Declaration (Slaughter 2006: 1406). Watt's amendment was opposed by the Belgian delegate, Fernand Dehousse, who was concerned that it endorsed a kind of social determinism:

> It might . . . be asserted that the individual could only develop his personality within the framework of society; it was, however, only necessary to recall the famous book by Daniel Defoe, *Robinson Crusoe*, to find proof of the contrary.
>
> (United Nations 1948: 659)

Dehousse complained that Watt's amendment implied that it was the duty of society to develop the individual's personality. Despite Australia withdrawing the amendment at this objection, the Soviet Union subsequently reintroduced it. The Soviet delegate, Alexei Pavlov, challenged the Belgian reading of *Robinson Crusoe*, claiming that the protagonist was not a natural man as Dehousse had claimed:

> [The amendment was] important in that it stressed the harmonious relations which should exist between the individual and the society in which he lived. The word 'alone' . . . seemed to him excellent. It rightly stressed the fact that the individual could not fully develop his personality outside society. The example of *Robinson Crusoe* [had] shown that man could not live and develop his personality without the aid of society. Robinson had . . . at his disposal the products of human industry and culture, namely, the tools and books he had found on the wreck of his ship.
>
> (United Nations 1948: 659–660)

Whereas Dehousse read Defoe as defending an idea of personality which developed *separately* from society, and required protecting from that society, Pavlov's reading of Defoe saw personality developing from a dialectical interaction *between* the individual and society (Slaughter 2006: 1407).

Robinson Crusoe's influence was not just restricted to the debates surrounding human rights. Jessica Whyte has written about Marx's identifying political economists' fondness for Defoe (Whyte 2014: 307; Marx 1990: 169). For Marx, all production was socially determinate production – the producing individual is always dependent on a greater social whole (Marx 1993: 84). Rather than representing a natural man outside of society, Crusoe is emblematic of the new atomized individual whose social bond is organized through the market. The newly freed individuals emerge only after they are robbed of their own means of production and of the guarantees of existence provided by the old feudal communities (Whyte 2014: 308). However, Crusoe stood as a useful device for this shift, as through his example a historically specific set of economic and social relations were naturalised and treated as the expression of the very humanity of man (Whyte 2014: 310). In Whyte's reading of Marx, the political economists' use of Crusoe is bound up with a teleological conception of history as a progressive trajectory culminating in a world of capitalism and human rights (Whyte 2014: 304).

Yet as Whyte identifies, what is missing from this UN debate surrounding Robinson Crusoe is the role, and position, of Friday. In the novel, Friday is rescued from a rival tribe and transformed into a 'faithful, loving, sincere servant' (Defoe [1719] 2003: 165). In ignoring Friday the delegates rearticulated Defoe's colonial characterization of the social relations on the island. There was no room for Friday to become a protagonist or legal person (Whyte 2014: 302; Slaughter 2007: 53). From the very beginning, international human rights law can be read as excluding certain peoples. Slaughter illustrates how *Robinson Crusoe* served Article 29 as an 'enabling fiction', where human personality entered international law as the product of and medium of social relations, but specifically Western, and colonial, social relations (Slaughter 2006: 1406). Whilst Article 2 UDHR asserted the human rights of persons in 'nonself-governing' territories, as Whyte argues, those persons had as little ability to participate in debating and shaping the terms of human personality as Friday did on Crusoe's island (Whyte 2014: 302).

3. Rancière against the Arendtian critique of rights

It is at this point that Hannah Arendt enters my argument. Her critique of rights allows Rancière's defence of rights and his processual politics to be fully understood. The rights of man arose from the same conditions for Arendt as those which Marx attributed to the Crusoe myth, namely a 'new era in which individuals were no longer secure in the estates to which they were born or sure of their equality before God as Christians' (Arendt 1960: 291). The new rights protected atomized figures of civil society. The idea of a rights-bearing natural man relies on no prior approval:

> [T]hese rights and the human dignity they bestow should remain valid and real even if only a single human being existed on earth; they are independent of human plurality and should remain valid even if a human being is expelled from the human community.
>
> (Arendt 1960: 291)

However, Arendt makes the point, like Marx, that man cannot be understood as an atomized unit, detached from the pre-existing world. The natural man of the human rights declarations did not exist:

> [M]an had hardly appeared as a completely emancipated, completely isolated being who carried his dignity within himself without reference to some larger encompassing order, when he disappeared again into a member of a people. From the beginning the paradox involved in the declaration of inalienable human rights was that it reckoned with an 'abstract' human being who seemed to exist nowhere.
>
> (Arendt 1960: 291)

The fiction of a natural man was laid bare when the inalienability of the grand rights declarations were faced with the spectre of the abandoned, the refugee (Arendt 1960: 291–292). For Arendt, the idea of human rights came apart when the world was confronted by 'people who had lost all other qualities and specific relationships except that they were still human' (Arendt 1960: 299). If human rights cannot include the Fridays of the world, then they are not 'human' rights at all.

Contrary to the declarations of rights, Arendt takes the ethical view that 'a man who is nothing but a man has lost the very qualities which make it possible for other people to treat him as a fellow-man' (Arendt 1960: 300). In this exceptional situation in which stateless people had nothing left to appeal to but their rights as human beings, they were barely recognizable as human (Schaap 2011: 23). There is on this reading an inherent tension between the ideas of 'man' and 'citizen'. In a corollary manner to Crusoe, the reality is that it is the rights of the citizen which are based in reality, not the rights of man (Arendt 1946: 139). If human rights are reducible to the rights of citizenship, they are redundant, they are the rights of those that already have rights. If they attach to the human as such, they amount to nothing.

On the face of it, the UDHR debates, and the use of *Robinson Crusoe* to describe natural man, bolsters Arendt's position. An individual can only develop their personality from within a society, as a citizen. More than this, a foundational document of human rights bases its definition of man on a book which places animals above those humans without legal personality (Defoe 2003: 118). The push-back against the teleological conception of history is evident in Arendt's work – the very nature of rights, and the paradox contained within them, means that they will never end up satisfying their aims and goals. There will always be a problematic remainder, the Friday reminding today's Crusoes that the basis of their rights is not universal, no matter how much they may protest otherwise. The paradoxes within rights that Arendt contends shows their inefficacy, but this is not a hopeless position. For Arendt, this underscores that:

> [O]nly within the framework of a people can a man live as a man among men, without exhausting himself. And only when a people lives and functions in consort with other peoples can it contribute to the establishment upon earth of a commonly conditioned and commonly controlled humanity.
>
> (Arendt 1944: 122)

For Arendt, it is as a consequence of seeing the limitations of natural rights that we become aware of the right to politics itself. Arendt's politics is a specific way of life; politics is possible only within a public sphere in which individuals already recognize each other as equal and distinct – the very thing that stateless people are deprived of (Schaap 2011: 34). This public realm is common to all, where identities and selves are revealed (Arendt 1954: 52). Only here can plurality and freedom be experienced. Politics occurs between individuals and is established as relationships which can only occur in the public sphere, not the private realm of the household (Arendt 2005: 108).

Perhaps the UDHR debates are closer to Arendt than they at first appear. By stating that personality can only be developed from within a community, the UDHR also presupposes a form of public sphere within which these political rights can be realized. In this manner, Arendt's critique can be read as one of form rather than substance; a disagreement over the manner of the public sphere, rather than the necessity of its presupposition.

For Arendt, where conditions of inequality prevail there can only be struggle for liberation (where action is subordinated to freeing oneself from domination) rather than an authentic politics where action is an end in itself (Arendt 1990: 29). There must be an equal sphere actually in existence in order for politics to occur. This is Rancière's point of contention with Arendt.

As Schaap has contended, both Rancière and Arendt are praxis theorists who want to escape political philosophy's reduction of political issues to questions of government (Schaap 2012: 146). However, Arendt believed that traditional philosophy failed to appreciate action as the proper object of political philosophy, treating politics as a matter of ruling (Schaap 2012: 147). She followed a reading of Aristotle in understanding politics in terms of its specificity as a way of life (*bios politicos*), claiming that Aristotle saw man as a living animal with the additional capacity for politics (Arendt 1954: 27). In Schaap's words, Arendt understands ordinary rights as a precondition for politics since they institutionalize an artificial equality that is constitutive of the public sphere. This is why the right to have rights amounts to the right to politics (Schaap 2011: 23).

Arendt's thesis is that the economic, biological and instinctual bases of human association are opposed to and excluded from political life. Arendt wishes to preserve the political from contamination by the private (Schaap 2012: 156). In support of this view, Arendt refers back to Aristotle's opposition of political organization with that of the home (Arendt 1954: 24, 27). Later in *The Human Condition* Arendt asserts that for the Greeks 'everything merely necessary or useful is strictly excluded' from 'the realm of human affairs', namely the political realm (Arendt 1954: 25). A hierarchy thus arises, placing the public realm of politics above the private realm of the home. The equality Arendt seeks to bring about *must* occur in the public realm.

It is this position which leads Rancière to claim that Arendt adopts an *archipolitical* position, which represses politics, rather than defending and encouraging it (Schaap 2012: 151). Rancière's complaint about Arendt is that in differentiating clearly the sphere of political life from the sphere of private life, Arendt (like the drafters of the UDHR) draws the borders around these political predicates *in advance* (Rancière 2004b: 303). This has negative consequences for how rights are conceived, and Arendt's position is explicitly rejected by Rancière as an ethical, not a political, position.

This rejection needs to be connected to Rancière's separation of politics and ethics. For Rancière, 'ethics' are not synonymous with 'morals' (Rancière 2009: 109). In *Dissensus*, he speaks about morality implying the separation of law and fact, and the division of different forms of morality and of rights (Rancière 2010: 188). In contrast, Rancière can be read as taking issue with the conceptualization of an ethical life which dissolves all distinctions necessary for judgment. The strength of Rancière's thought is his emphasis on the manner in which ethics can preclude or limit politics, by acting as a force which bounds or defines politics *in advance*. This ethical turn has two main facets.

Ethics can firstly refer to both the dwelling and way of being that corresponds to that dwelling. Ethics dissolves norm into fact and subsumes all forms of discourse and practice beneath the same point of view, or consensus (Rancière 2009: 109). This form of 'consensus' reduces the aggregate of individuals within the social body into a single people identical with the count of the population and its parts. Consensus transforms political community into an ethical community, into a community that gathers together a single people in which everyone is supposed to be counted. This comes up against a problematic remainder, the excluded, the part which has no part, the Friday to every Crusoe (Rancière 2009: 115–116). Consensus means the attempt to get rid of politics itself by ousting these surplus subjects and replacing them with 'real people' and identity groups (Rancière 2004a: 306).

The second form of ethics Rancière speaks of is the ethics of the absolute Other, and related ideas of infinite justice. This ethical life sees absolute evil as resulting from a betrayal of Otherness, the part of us we do not control (Rancière 2004b: 307–308). This form of ethics thus seeks obedience to the rights of the Other, which sweeps aside dissensus and substitutes an ontological destiny for political action (Rancière 2004b: 309). This ethical life, a constant battle between Good and Evil, erases politics.

Rancière alleges that if the gap between the abstract literalness of rights and their verification is diminished (which is what Arendt contends), then rights will appear vacuous and of no use, and the Rights of Man appear to become the rights of those who have no rights (Rancière 2004b: 307). These individuals cannot exercise the rights themselves, so others must intervene (hence the spectre of humanitarian intervention) and grant them their rights.

Rancière sharply critiques these two approaches. Neither is appropriate for understanding rights. Rights are not simply a justification for humanitarian intervention. Instead, they allow those who are excluded to litigate for their inclusion as equals. In this political community, the excluded is a conflictual actor, an actor who includes himself as a supplementary political subject, carrying a right not yet recognized or witnessing an injustice in the existing state of right. The figure of Friday, rather than Crusoe, is therefore central to Rancière's understanding of rights.

Politics is exceptional – a deviation from the normal order of things. Rights do not belong to definite subjects. Rather, politics, and democracy, is precisely about where to draw those borders, how they are constructed, and how they can be modified, helping us interrogate what we are able to think and to do (Rancière 2010: 218). Rancière does not subscribe or come back to old moral ideas, but in the current ethical turn, exemplified by Arendt's thought, he sees a movement going on which *prevents* judgments being made. I agree with Rancière that judgments need to be made. However, as I argue here, it is an ambiguity about the nature and role of judgment in Rancière's politics which needs academic focus and explication.

4. Rancière's defence of political subjectivization

Rancière's defence of rights, and construction of political subjectivization, is central to my argument that his politics is not able to distinguish between the quality of political acts. Rancière's politics focuses on the excluded, the problematic remainder which Arendt saw as undermining human rights. This focus on the excluded is why I wish to trace Rancière's defence of rights to a 1977 interview he conducted with Michel Foucault. In this interview, Foucault spoke of the 'pleb', an excluded figure to be sure. Foucault argued that the figure was irreducible to, and marked the limit of, power relations:

> The pleb does not exist in all probability, but there is something of the pleb . . . in bodies, in spirits, in individuals, in the proletariat, but, with each dimension, form, energy, and irreducibility, differs in each and every instance. This part of pleb does not represent some exteriority with regard to power relationships as much as it represents their limit, their ruin, their consequence.
>
> (Foucault 1980: 134–135)

Giorgio Agamben sees Rancière returning to this Foucauldian concept of the pleb in his work, developing it into the concept of a people, 'the part of those who have no part', the bearer of a wrong that establishes democracy as a 'community of dispute' (Agamben 2005: 57–58). Rancière has admitted his Foucauldian influence in his writings, but where Rancière differs from Foucault is that he is a defender of radical equality (Rancière 2004a: 50). There is no proper foundation for any political community, except an anarchical presupposition of equality.

Agamben is referring to *Dis-agreement*, where Rancière discusses the plebs of the Aventine Hill in Rome, who appear to be in a similar position to the natives on Crusoe's island. Like Arendt, Rancière focuses on these marginalized figures, but draws very different conclusions from considering them. The plebs are cast out from Roman society; 'there is no place for discussion with the plebs for the simple reason that plebs do not speak' (Rancière 1999: 23). The plebs were not part of a political stage because they were not recognized as equal political subjects (Rancière 1999: 26). What the plebs did, and what interests Rancière about them, was that they acted *as though they were equal political subjects*, and therefore created a conflict and a dispute over the meaning and scope of Roman citizenship and participation in civil society. This conflict over the existence of a common stage and the status of those present on it *is* 'politics' (Rancière 1999: 26–27).

Where Rancière departs from Arendt is in the consequences of following Aristotle's definition of man as a speaking animal. As Maurizio Lazzarato has explained, for Rancière Greek democracy demonstrated that the unique principle of politics is equality. In language, we find the minimum of equality necessary for a comprehension of living beings, permitting us to verify the principle of political equality (Lazzarato 2013: 155). For Rancière, what it means to be a speaking animal is a contestable issue (Schaap 2011: 29). The Aristotelian definition of man as a political animal defined politics on the essence of a mode of life (Rancière 2010: 92). This appears to create a 'test of humanity'. Political exclusion entails non-recognition of particular categories of people as subjects qualified to speak, like the pleb, or the indigenous peoples on Crusoe's island (Rancière 1999: 23).

Politics is not enacted through a presupposed stage, public sphere or society. The very existence of a stage for politics must first be established through a dispute, or *litige* – 'wrong' (Rancière 2010: 91). Subjects do not exist before any wrong, which provides that stage for political action (Rancière 1999: 26–27). In *Dis-agreement* he explains:

> Wrong is simply the mode of subjectification in which the assertion of equality takes its political shape. . . . Wrong institutes a singular universal, a polemical universal, by tying the presentation of equality, as the part of those who have no part, to the conflict between parts of society.
>
> (Rancière 1999: 39)

The wrong here involves a practice by individuals who are not recognized as speaking subjects within a social order that denies they are qualified to engage in politics (Schaap 2011: 34). This means that political subjects are in no way predetermined, but actually are 'always defined by an interval between identities, whether these identities are determined by social relations or juridical categories' (Rancière 2006: 301). Subjectivization is therefore the process of becoming a collective subject, emerging through the dissensual acting out of the presupposition of equality.

Unlike archipolitical thinkers like Arendt, Rancière reads equality as something created by people and brought into focus through disputes or actions – 'a mere assumption that needs to be discerned within the practices implementing it' (Rancière 1999: 33). These practices demand equality as individuals, like the plebs, act as though they are equal. This demonstrates the essence of equality, which has no particular character, but instead it undoes the naturalness of given orders and undercuts hierarchies, replacing them with divisions (Rancière 2007a: 32–33). Political subjects are open predicates, who emerge through disputes that end up defining the political sphere (Schaap 2011: 34; Rancière 2004b: 303).

It is here that I introduce Rancière's division between 'politics' and the 'police', two logics of human being-together (Rancière 1999: 28). The political is 'the field for the encounter between [politics] and [police] in the handling of a wrong' (Rancière 1992: 59). In order to think this encounter one has to abandon certain concepts, the first of which is the Foucauldian idea of power. Rancière writes, '[I]t is equally important to affirm that no thing is in itself political by the mere fact that power relations are exercised' (Rancière 2004a: 55–56). The police is a hierarchical form of politics, rather than an institution of power. It is a 'distribution of the sensible' within which it becomes possible to define strategies and techniques of power (Rancière 2010: 95). It is a hierarchy based on the presupposition that some are fit to govern and some are not. This distribution of the sensible is:

> [T]he system of self-evident facts of sense perception that simultaneously discloses the existence of something in common and the delimitations that define the respective parts and positions within it.
>
> (Rancière 2004a: 13)

The police disciplines conflict and disputes, subordinating agents to their place within a social order, defining the terms by which one can participate in public discourse, like the debates around *Robinson Crusoe* and the UDHR. Surplus subjects are removed by the police. The equality which exists in a police order is one granted by those who govern. In contrast, politics reconfigures the distribution of the sensible, in order:

> [T]o introduce into it new subjects and objects, to render visible what had not been, and to make heard as speakers those who had been perceived as mere noisy animals.
>
> (Rancière 2009: 25)

Those who are excluded, the Fridays, can speak. What this means is that when Rancière refers to politics, he intends that:

> 'Politics' should be used exclusively to characterise a clear-defined activity, which is also antagonistic to the former – the police. This activity, one that disrupts sensible configurations in which shares, parts or their absence are defined in regards to the presupposition that there is, by definition, no share: the share of the share-less ones.
>
> (Rancière 2009: 52–53)

Yet this does not mean that the police is always oppressive. Rancière makes the point that there is 'a better and a worse police' (Rancière 1999: 30–31). The police order can procure all sorts of good, and one kind of police may be infinitely preferable to another – but Rancière makes clear that this does not make the police any less the opposite of politics (Rancière 1999: 31). The police cannot be escaped from, or overturned in a revolutionary action; *some* police order is always inevitable (Rancière 1999: 29). Politics is a heterogeneous logic to the police, but is bound up in relation to the police order; this is because it has no objects or issues of its own. Politics runs up against the police everywhere, acting on common places and determining state institutions and their configuration (Rancière 1999: 33).

So it is clear that Rancière's politics is different from forms of politics as commonly understood (such as progressive egalitarian movements, which many readers may have sympathy for), which in his schema actually make up part of the police order. The essence of this politics is dissensus, and happens by means of the assumption of equality (Rancière 2010: 38). What determines whether an act is dissensual and political is not its outcome, but its form. A political act is one which brings the police order into conflict with the presupposition of equality (Rancière 1999: 31–32). Whilst nothing is political in itself, anything may become political if it gives rise to a meeting of these logics; the presumption of equality contradicts the police distribution of bodies in the form of a wrong (Rancière 1999: 35).

Therefore, dissensual acts are inseparably and *radically* egalitarian, engaging in a critique of the instituted divisions of the police order, and paving the way for renewing our interrogations into what we are able to think and to do (Rancière 2010: 218). Such acts reflect the capacity of the subject to work on the intervals between identities, and reconfigure the distribution of private and public, universal and particular (Rancière 2006: 302). Dissensual acts can give rise to new identities which in turn end up being recognized by the police order, changing the distribution of the sensible. Going further, democracy entails that there is never just *one* subject, since political subjects exist in the interval *between* identities, and are defined through the distribution and re-distribution of forms of subjectivization (Rancière 2010: 207). Politics brings attention to contradictory subjects which were not recognized in the police order; it is not a creation of subjects *ex nihilo*, but politics transforms identities into instances of an experienced dispute or dissensual act (Rancière 1999: 36).

Subjectivity is therefore intertwined with dissensus; acts render visible what was once not recognized, and lead to new subjects and new rights being responded to by the police order. The police order is a responsive order. Disputes create further divisions amongst received categories and distributions; the police will have to respond to these divisive acts. Politics does not focus on results. Rather, the fact that the police order would respond to political, dissensual acts immediately redistributes the sensible. Those individuals who were treated as the plebs, or Crusoe's natives, are now not so treated because of that very response. Previously, they would have simply been ignored.

5. The lack of political judgments in Rancière

Crucial to all of this is the distinct lack of pre-judgment as to the worth of the political acts that Rancière describes. Not every act is a political act. A political act is one which disrupts the police and gives voice to new subjects, to be true, but this says nothing about the nature or desirability of those new subjects, or indeed the desirability of the response of the police. We know that any presupposition of a way of life cannot be political, as politics is not a mode of being – there is no pure *bios politicos* (Rancière 2010: 42).

The lack of any presupposition, other than that of equality, must mean that it cannot be considered political to define in advance a form of life suitable for the political sphere. This is the case even with a form of life premised on principles of, say, anti-racism, non-discrimination and gender equality. By defining a political sphere in advance with such predicates, we are creating, no matter how well-intentioned, a police order and an essential way of life. This is consensus, which annuls dissensus as it nullifies surplus subjects by positing an 'end of politics' – a return to the normal state of things, through distinguishing in advance what counts as properly political action (Rancière 2010: 42–43; Schaap 2012: 158). This would include an Arendtian public sphere; Rancière views this as again distinguishing in advance what counts as political. Consensus will always exclude 'Fridays', even if those who are excluded are viewed by the vast majority of people as being correctly excluded. Consensus therefore assumes that we are not all equal, which is the only presupposition for Rancière that politics can emerge from (Mey 2013: 177). This is why Rancière argues that:

> [R]eturning the inventions of politics and art to their difference, entails rejecting the fantasy of their purity, giving back to these inventions their status as cuts that are always ambiguous, precarious, litigious.
>
> (Rancière 2009: 132)

Nor can this presupposition of equality also include the presupposition of ideas of social justice, progressive politics and egalitarianism. Rancière is clear to state that 'equality turns into the opposite the moment it aspires to a place in the social or state organisation' (Rancière 1999: 34). As soon as equality aspires to such a place, it is consensus, even if it is a progressive politics or aims for socially desirable goals such as affirmative action. Such an instrumental form of a presupposition would always presuppose a police order.

It is clear that Rancière sees politics as an active process which an individual needs to undertake, in order to act out the presumption of equality, and avoid being classified in the police order, or worse, not recognized by such an order. Passivity and spectatorship connote an individual looking at a spectacle (Rancière 2007b: 271–272), conflicting with the *practical* issues of political action and democracy (Rancière 2010: 59).

The key point for my argument is when Rancière discusses who exactly comprises the 'part of those who have no part'. For him, this is not just the 'excluded', those who are cast out by a given hegemony. Instead, it is 'anybody whoever', newcomers who are heard and allow new objects to appear as common concerns (Rancière 2010: 60). Surplus subjects here must be read as *any* subject which does not fit into the political way of life posited by consensus.

Rancière's emphasis on *common* concerns here is curious, because it appears not to fit easily with his criticism of ethics as pre-judging a way of life of the community. If acts are deemed political because they appear to fit within concerns 'common' to society, then we must ask what this common is. If it is a being-in-common, the simple dwelling together in the world that Jean-Luc Nancy speaks of (Nancy 1991: xxxvii, xl), then we again face a question of how to distinguish between political acts. If this radical equality has no world of its own, and is only traced by acts of verification (Rancière 2010: 213), then this model for revolutionary action is based on demonstration, argumentation, and interlocution (Lazzarato 2013: 164). However, following Lazzarato, if everyone is equal and can have their say, there will be as many governments as there are individuals (Lazzarato 2013: 162). Contrarily, if the 'common' Rancière refers to is a 'being-common' (Nancy 1991: xxxix), then he does nothing other than repeat the ethical pre-judgment about a way of life he so vehemently criticizes in his thought. If this is the case, then Rancière does nothing more than repeat what he criticizes in Arendt, and would lend credence to her own critique of rights Rancière opposes.

To avoid Rancière's thought being internally inconsistent, and also avoiding invoking a messianism and recasting emancipation as a multiplicity of forms of dissensus occurring in the broken time of now, we must conclude the former view (Rancière 2010: 60–61). For Rancière, the community exists through the setting up of divisions and disputes, and is constructed through the heterogeneous meeting of political acts and police hierarchies.

Because this presupposition of equality has no particular character, but undoes police orders and replaces them with divisions, it stands that Rancière cannot explain *how* we are to distinguish between these very multiplicities of political acts. No conclusion can be drawn in advance as to the worth of the dissensual activities which such subjects perform – only that the litigious actions undertaken disrupt the distribution of the given. The given could even be a 'better police order', such as a liberal democracy, or even a leftist democracy. All we know about political actions is that they institute a 'polemical universal' by tying the presentation of equality to the conflict between parts of society (Rancière 1999: 39). In short, individuals who are not recognized by police orders create a division on the basis that they presume themselves to be equal to others.

On this basis, it is possible for an individual to act out dissensual politics through activities which many would view as objectionable, distasteful, immoral, unethical, or utterly horrific. This is the case as equality is an empty predicate, and is not related to egalitarianism or forms of political belief (like socialism) that are part of the police order. The disagreement of a wrong is not connected to morality or ethics, but rather to the fact that individuals are not recognized as equals by the police order. The noises uttered by the part which has no part are recognized as sounds which could be words, but are not understood as such because of who is uttering them (Rancière 1999: xii).

This is connected to Rancière's point that some police orders may actually be preferable to others and acceptable to us – the individual espousing views and identities not accepted by the police order may act out an equality that the reader of this chapter may not want to grant them and their words. Rancière's politics is attractive as a method for opening up the social order to new forms of subjectivization, but he does not provide a schema to distinguish between the merits of those subjects. To put it crudely, how can we tell the difference between the claims of Daesh and Occupy?

6. The right to have rights

This processual, litigious account of politics provides the basis for Rancière's rethinking of human rights. Rancière reframes the subjects of the Rights of Man as supplementary subjects. The Rights of Man are 'the rights of those who have not the rights that they have and have the rights that they have not' (Rancière 2004b: 302). The subject of rights is the process of subjectivization that bridges the interval between two forms of existence of human rights. Human rights are written rights, inscriptions of equality, which are not just an abstract ideal but part of the configuration of the given. They form part of the hierarchical police order, alongside the courts and laws which sustain and uphold them. Yet the Rights of Man are also rights awarded to those who 'make something of that inscription', individuals who build a case explaining why they should be included within the inscription of the right (Rancière 2004b: 303).

In this account Rancière comes closer to liberal views of human rights than he does radical politics. In his pronouncements regarding the litigation over the meaning of political predicates Rancière brings to mind the idea of the 'living tree' approach to human rights which characterizes many progressive defences of rights.[1] However Rancière clearly does go further than the status quo, as current human rights laws appear to pre-judge a certain *ethos* with respect to rights claims.

This is the case as human rights are based around legal instruments. New rights, or extensions of existing rights, require legal recognition from the police order.

The major global human rights instruments include provisions, much like the UDHR, which limit the application of rights. In fact, many such treaties, knowingly or not, invoke the spirit of Article 29 and the assumption that personality can only be fulfilled from within an existing community (which excludes figures like Friday who do not form 'part' of that community). The International Covenant for Civil and Political Rights (ICCPR), for instance, makes the point in Article 19(2) that freedom of speech can be limited for the protection of the rights of others, or to protect 'public order'. Article 17 of the European Convention of Human Rights (ECHR) guards against the use of rights in a way which would abolish or limits other rights guaranteed in the Convention. These are part of the police hierarchy, which order claims and individuals. In addition, there is an underlying assumption that the rights protected are part of an existing order, which reflects an already existing community which has its own standards and morals. Such instruments preclude the rights claims of those persons who would destroy the rights of others through their actions. Some case examples can help illustrate my point.

In *Norwood* an individual was prosecuted for inciting racial hatred when he placed a poster on a window in his home blaming Islam for the September 11 attacks, and advocating the removal of all Muslims from the United Kingdom.[2] Norwood's claim that his conviction had breached his right to free expression was dismissed by the European Court of Human Rights on the grounds that he was setting out to destroy the rights of others through his actions. Likewise, in *Faurisson*, a scholar whose work questioned the existence of gas chambers in World War II lost his claim in challenging his conviction for such speech, on the grounds that under Article 19 ICCPR, such a restriction was permissible and necessary to serve society's struggle against racism (*Faurisson v. France* 1996).

My point is not to question these decisions. Rather, they illustrate a police order (a better one than many which exist, no doubt) which has formed a distribution of the sensible that has recognized some voices and not others. Such an order recognizes some rights claims, and some political subjects, and assumes the voicelessness of others. Could Faurisson and Norwood be dissensual political actors, and be recognized as subjects? Could they have acted from the presupposition of equality? If my argument holds, and the presupposition of equality is an empty signifier, then I think that they could. Their actions claimed that they should be included within the inscription of the abstract right of freedom of expression, as they acted *as though they were* equal to others.

Now, it may very well be objected that this was precisely what they were *not* doing, as through their actions they wanted to treat others in a discriminatory manner, and therefore they did not support equality. I think this is too easy a response. If equality is a mere assumption, and is presumed by the actor themselves in order to fracture the police order, then it cannot immediately follow that we can interpret 'equality' as a 'thick' political concept which can help us distinguish between rights claims and determine in advance which ones are political or not. By this I mean that the actor acts as though they are equal, so they must be acting from their own presupposition that they are equal to others – this says nothing about the quality or nature of their act. By a thick concept, I mean a version of equality akin to substantive forms, which already presuppose certain characteristics that equality must have.

These cases also illustrate how human rights claims are therefore inherently antagonistic. When individuals claim protection under human rights laws, they are claiming that the laws should be extended to cover their situations. In effect, they are challenging the distribution of the sensible, and asking for the given order to be redistributed in their favour. They are a part which has no part that is demanding to be counted. Such claims must be seen as political, in the Rancièrian sense.

A Rancièrian political act (such as the claims of Norwood and Faurisson) is antagonistic and involves a confrontation with a disagreement, a circumstance whereby people are treated as less than equal. Whilst it is possible to make such a judgment after the act has occurred, and it is necessary to do so, this would not detract from its political nature. The act itself would be political, as it would be interjecting itself into an order that attempted to distribute all subjects and bodies; the police order would then respond to that claim made by the new subject. This response could either reject the claim or accept it.

None of this defeats Rancière's argument and points he makes. What it does do is focus attention upon the police orders which ultimately are the responsive element to political acts. 'Better' police orders may make the judgment that the acts of Occupy need responding to, and the distribution of the sensible needs redistributing. Likewise, the acts of Daesh have been responded to differently, and are treated as though these are not, and can never be, political claims. My point is that a contrary view would be just as possible under Rancière's sketch of the police and politics. We should not read him as setting out a schematic for how broadly radical, leftist actions can help shape the world and change existing police orders. In many ways, what he does is much more important – he places the emphasis on the *response* to political acts. The police response to a dissensual act shows how an order deals with an 'outsider', a Friday. It can show us which police orders are better or worse.

7. Concluding remarks

Rancière, in his separating of ethics from politics, draws attention to the difficulty of such a separation when making judgments. Whatever our own political beliefs, deciding upon whether a political claim relates to a common concern must involve a judgment. Whilst he critiqued Arendt for an archipolitical position which does not make such a separation, I argue that it is not as easy to separate ethics and politics as Rancière suggests.

Lazzarato has critiqued Rancière on precisely this separation, arguing that if we isolate the political act, we are prone to miss the way in which the police mobilizes *both* potential political acts *and* ethics (Lazzarato 2013: 157). Lazzarato here identifies a key criticism Rancière advances against Arendt's archipolitical position. Arendt's public sphere, the *bios politicos*, delineates the borders of equality in advance. If Arendt's public sphere is a police order, then it is correct to surmise that such a police order is based on an ethical judgment. That is to say, the police order's response to antagonistic acts is precisely *not* to treat them as separate from ethics. We ultimately see as political those actions which accord with our preconceived world views and ideas of which rights claims should be recognized, and which persons should be recognized as political subjects. Arendt's writings on refugees and their status under human rights laws is a vivid example of this.

Lazzarato's point is that whereas Rancière's political subject appears to be formed in an act of instantaneous politics, the constitution of a subject is an ethical act in and of itself, and cannot be separated from a specific activity called 'politics' (Lazzarato 2013: 168–172). The cases of *Faurisson* and *Norwood* illustrate this. An underlying *ethos* influenced the legal decisions which ruled that Faurisson and Norwood were not actors whose voice should be heard. They did not fit in the police order. Just as easily, a society could form a view that actors we may see as sympathetic should not be recognized as speaking subjects, and that their political acts should give rise to new forms of subjectivity.

In my view, Rancière's critique of Arendt and her views of rights have force. Rancière illustrates the dangers in drawing the bounds of politics in advance, and how this can exclude individuals as political actors. This leads human rights to become either worthless, or to justify humanitarian intervention. Rancière shows how human rights can be reclaimed into an antagonistic political process. Surplus subjects, the Fridays abandoned by human rights declarations, stand not as examples of the failures of rights, as Arendt would have it, but as litigants who challenge the existing police order.

This brings us back to the plebs on the Aventine Hill and Crusoe's Friday. Such figures immediately appeal as those surplus subjects not recognized by existing orders. For Rancière, *contra* Arendt, the plebs and Friday seek to make something of their right to have rights, rather than always already being excluded from their inscription from the very beginning. Yet these sympathetic figures could as easily be Faurisson and Norwood, other surplus subjects not recognized as equals by the police. As Rancière states:

> By subjectification I mean the production through a series of actions of a body and a capacity for enunciation not previously identifiable within a given field of experience, whose identification is thus part of the reconfiguration of the field of experience.
>
> (Rancière 1999: 35)

Where Rancière criticizes Arendt for delineating the field of politics in advance, Rancière does not explain how the field of politics can, or will be, delineated after the act of dissensus to ensure that Friday is recognized yet Faurisson is not. How can we reconfigure the field of experience in such a way so that the actions of Occupy take precedence over Daesh? I agree with Lazzarato that the recognition of a political subject is an ethical act. It is a serious matter for scholarship to consider how Rancière's schema can be interpreted, if at all, to consider the relationship between dissensual politics and ethics. Rancière does not provide us with an easy answer. I do not think that there is an easy answer. Perhaps that is his point, and the greatest lesson we can learn from his work.

Notes

* I am extremely grateful and indebted to the incredibly detailed and thoughtful comments I received from Jo Bridgeman, Julen Etxabe, Tarik Kochi, Mónica López Lerma, Kenny Veitch, and the anonymous reviewer on earlier drafts of this paper. Any errors remain my own.
1 *Edwards v. Attorney-General for Canada* (1930) AC 124 (PC).
2 *Norwood v. UK* (2004) Application No. 23131/03 (ECtHR).

Bibliography

Agamben, G. (2005) *The Time That Remains: A Commentary on the Letter to the Romans*, translated by P. Dailey, Stanford: Stanford University Press.
Arendt, H. (1944) 'The Jew as Pariah: A Hidden Tradition', *Jewish Social Studies*, vol. 6, pp. 99–122.
Arendt, H. (1946) 'The Nation', *Review of Politics*, vol. 8, pp. 138–141.
Arendt, H. (1954) *The Human Condition*, Chicago: University of Chicago Press.
Arendt, H. (1960) *The Origins of Totalitarianism*, Orlando: Harcourt Press.
Arendt, H. (1990) *On Revolution*, London: Penguin Books.
Arendt, H. (2005) *The Promise of Politics*, New York: Schocken Books.
Defoe, D. ([1719] 2003) *Robinson Crusoe*, London: Penguin.
Edwards v. Attorney General for Canada (1930) AC 124 (PC).
Faurisson v. France (1996) Communication No 550/1993, UN Doc CCPR/C/58/D/550/1993 (ICJ).
Foucault, M. (1980) 'Powers and Strategies', in Gordon, C. (ed.) *Power/Knowledge: Selected Interviews 1972–1977*, New York: Random House, pp. 134–145.
Lazzarato, M. (2013) 'Enunciation and Politics', in Nilsson, J. and Wallenstein, S.-O. (eds.) *Foucault, Biopolitics, and Governmentality*, Stockholm: Södertörn Philosophical Studies, pp. 155–173.
Maritain, J. (1986) *The Rights of Man and Natural Law*, San Francisco: Ignatius Press.
Marx, K. ([1867] 1990) *Capital: A Critique of Political Economy*, vol. 1, translated by B. Fowkes, London: Penguin Books.
Marx, K. ([1939] 1993) *Grundrisse: Foundations of the Critique of Political Economy*, London: Penguin Books.
Mey, A. (2013) 'Rancière as Foucauldian? On the Distribution of the Sensible and New Forms of Subjectivities', in Nilssen, J. and Wallenstein, S.-O. (eds.) *Foucault, Biopolitics, and Governmentality*, Stockholm: Södertörn Philosophical Studies, pp. 175–183.
Morsink, J. (1984) 'The Philosophy of the Universal Declaration', *Human Rights Quarterly*, vol. 6, pp. 309–334.

Morsink, J. (1989) *The Universal Declaration of Human Rights: Origins, Drafting and Intent*, Philadelphia: University of Pennsylvania Press.

Nancy, J.-L. (1991) *The Inoperative Community*, Minneapolis: University of Minnesota Press.

Norwood v. UK (UK) Application No. 23131/03 (ECtHR).

Rancière, J. (1992) 'Politics, Identification and Subjectivisation', *October*, vol. 61, pp. 58–64.

Rancière, J. (1999) *Dis-Agreement: Politics and Philosophy*, translated by J. Rose, Minneapolis: University of Minnesota Press.

Rancière, J. (2004a) *The Politics of Aesthetics: Distribution of the Sensible*, translated by G. Rockhill, London and New York: Continuum.

Rancière, J. (2004b) 'Who Is the Subject of the Rights of Man?', *South Atlantic Quarterly*, vol. 103, pp. 297–310.

Rancière, J. (2006) 'Democracy, Republic, Representation', *Constellations*, vol. 13, pp. 297–307.

Rancière, J. (2007a) *On the Shores of Politics*, translated by L. Heron, London: Verso.

Rancière, J. (2007b) 'The Emancipated Spectator', *Artforum International*, vol. 1, pp. 270–281.

Rancière, J. (2009) *Aesthetics and Its Discontents*, translated by S. Corcoran, Cambridge: Polity Press.

Rancière, J. (2010) *Dissensus: On Politics and Aesthetics*, translated by S. Corcoran, London: Continuum.

Schaap, A. (2011) 'Enacting the Right to Have Rights: Jacques Rancière's Critique of Hannah Arendt', *European Journal of Political Theory*, vol. 10, pp. 22–45.

Schaap, A. (2012) 'Hannah Arendt and the Philosophical Repression of Politics', in Deranty, J.-P. and Ross, A. (eds.) *Jacques Rancière in the Contemporary Scene: The Philosophy of Radical Equality*, London: Continuum, pp. 145–166.

Slaughter, J. R. (2006) 'Enabling Fictions and Novel Subjects: The *Bildungsroman* and International Human Rights Law', *PMLA: Publications of the Modern Language Association of America*, vol. 121, pp. 1405–1423.

Slaughter, J. R. (2007) *Human Rights Inc.: The World Novel, Narrative Form, and International Law*, New York: Fordham University Press.

United Nations Third Committee (1948) *Draft International Declaration of Human Rights – Summary Transcript*. E/800. 154th Meeting, Paris, November 24.

Whyte, J. (2014) 'The Fortunes of Natural Man: Robinson Crusoe, Political Economy, and the Universal Declaration of Human Rights', *Humanity: An International Journal of Human Rights, Humanitarianism and Development*, vol. 5, pp. 301–321.

Part III

Democracy, constitution, and the state

Chapter 5

The constitution of the constitution

Democratic legitimacy and public discourse

*Eric Heinze**

The whole of politics dwells in . . . this taking-part, which must be examined as to its meaning and the conditions that make it possible.

(Rancière 1998: 224)

1. Introduction

'Such was the end of our comrade', laments Socrates' disciple Phaedo, recalling his mentor's dying breath. Phaedo dubs the philosopher 'the best, and also the wisest and most upright' among 'all those we have known' (*Phaedo* 118a, Plato 1997: 100).

No single event, for Plato, embodies corrupted politics so completely as the majority vote of a democratic assembly to sentence his mentor to death (*Apology* 39c).[1] Plato adds more systemic gripes against democracy as well. In what counts among his most durable critiques, Plato rejects market-driven individualism (*Republic* 8.561c-e, Plato 1997: 1172; cf. Heinze 2007a: 100–105) and concomitant Athenian expansionism (*Republic* 2.373d, Plato 1997: 2012). Both proceed at the expense of civic unity and shared justice.[2] Despite the *Republic*'s plan for elite rule, Plato by no means views undemocratic regimes as superior *per se*. He knows they can become far worse than democracies. Monarchy, for example, can become tyranny (τυραννὶς), 'the most severe and cruel slavery' (*Republic* 8.564a, Plato 1997: 1174).[3] Power consolidated in a few hands, making it 'capable of the greatest good', renders it equally capable of 'the greatest evils' (*Crito* 44d, Plato 1997: 1100; *Laws* 4.712a, Plato 1997: 1398).

Only by marrying power to wisdom will justice be achieved. Or rather, only by marrying the greatest possible power to the greatest possible wisdom will the greatest possible justice be achieved (see *Republic* 5.473c-d, Plato 1997: 1100; and *Laws* 4.712a, Plato 1997: 1398). That classical ideal of justice, power in pursuit of wisdom, remains vibrant today. Within pre-industrial as well as contemporary societies, we witness a clash between two principles. Political legitimacy demands, on the one hand, that government actions reflect the people's voices (Heinze 2016a: 46–47), even though that principle already faces the internal contradictions of clashing individual and group interests (Rancière 1995: 135–136; Rancière 2012: 8, 52, 131, 135, 138, 151, 172, 303; Rancière 1998: 16, 106, 244). On the other hand, political legitimacy demands that government pursue the greatest possible substantive justice, even though that result often becomes possible only by overriding some voices (e.g., *Republic* 4.420b, Plato 1997: 1053; Rancière 1995: 71).

Ideally, it is often thought, that overriding of voices is no bad thing – where, for example, those voices are unduly wealthy or powerful, whilst the voices heeded belong to the excluded. Leaving aside for a moment that familiar impulse towards redistribution of influence or of resources, such an ideal is rarely if ever realized in practice: political history discloses voices unjustly overridden even in the sincerest pursuits of justice.[4] Still, a perfect overlap of two core principles – (i) power wedded to wisdom in a way that (ii) wholly reflects the people's will (Rancière 1987: 150)[5] – continues to stand as a desired, if always unreachable endpoint. It turns out to be the very recipe for the West's most 'purist' model of political legitimacy and of democracy, namely, Rousseau's *Contrat Social* (1964: 361).

In contrast to that ideal, Jacques Rancière observes deep tension between two social spheres. On the one hand, law and government maintain processes of elite managerialism, which he calls *la police*, broadly denoting the state's overall police powers. On the other hand, we find the citizenry living subject to such power in a sphere Rancière calls *la politique* (1995: 43–67; 1998: 13, 16, 112–119). In this chapter I shall probe the encounter between those two spheres. That encounter, I shall argue, manifests only as *public discourse*, with consequences for law largely compatible with, yet unacknowledged in Rancière's theory. It is through a sphere of public discourse necessarily preserved *by* government that the disjunction between citizens and government can never be total. Public discourse ensures the irreducibly political character of a citizenry distinct from its government, yet remains always constitutive of that government.

In Section 2, I begin with Rancière's admonition against our age-old habits of equating politics with government – government which, in turn, reduces to elite managerialism. For Rancière, politics is that which occurs outside the technocratic sphere. In Section 3, I identify that more genuinely political sphere as, above all, a sphere of public discourse. Public discourse crucially thrives beyond the purview of the managerial state, and yet – either developing or departing from Rancière on this decisive point – it is also the ultimate foundation of any constitutional, hence governmental order that could ever lay any claim to political legitimacy.

2. Politics beyond the state

For Rancière, the managerial sphere of law and government is dominated by the state's police power (*la police*). Rancière envisages that police power beyond the literally coercive 'cops on the beat', who enter only in a small minority of cases (1995: 51; cf. Chambers 2011). The police power functions beyond the conventional sense of persons holding and exercising formally constituted offices (Rancière 1995: 51–53; cf. Rancière 1998: 16, 112–113, 115; Rancière 2012: 65, 104, 175, 177, 202, 218, 259–263, 265–268, 274–275, 279–280). Rancière echoes Michel Foucault's understanding of power as diffuse and disseminated:

> I do not, however, equate the police power with what we commonly designate under the name of 'State apparatus'. The notion of State apparatus ends up trapped within the presupposition of an opposition between State and society, in which the former is imagined as the machine, the 'cold monster', imposing the rigidity of its ordering upon the life of the latter. [. . .] The police power . . . is [instead] an ordering of the visible and of the speakable, operating such that one activity is visible and some other is not, one statement heard as discourse and some other as noise.
>
> (Rancière 1995: 51 [citing Foucault]. Cf. Rancière 2012: 71–76)

Rancière's concept of police power surpasses, then, the formal or official organs of state, such as legislatures, administrative agencies, courtrooms, constabularies, prisons, and the like. The state's overall legal apparatus certainly maintains those conventional nodes of authority, but also more broadly empowers an array of informal actors. These include, for example, multi-national corporations and associated institutions of credit and finance, which can provoke a critical or hostile citizenry just as forcefully as can any organ of state. Even when I am discussing government in the more traditionally institutional sense, then, I shall assume it to include a power over the legal regime in its entirety, extending power over the citizenry far beyond the scope of formally governmental norms and processes.

Our age-old usages of the terms 'politics' and 'political' have, for Rancière, never referred to that which is distinctly political, but to its opposite, namely, to the pervasively de-politicized, managerial, and technocratic sphere. It is nothing more than the state's police power which we have all along been calling 'politics', by sheer custom, through a long history in which societies constantly divide between rulers and ruled, managers and managed. Anarchic and libertarian schools have certainly long insisted that we can overcome that history (Préposiet 2002), yet with sparse success. Only in diametric opposition to, and in ongoing tension with, the managerial sphere does Rancière identify the authentically[6] political sphere, which he calls *la politique*. Politics emerges outside established norms and institutions in order to challenge them. That is all politics can be, and all democracy can be. A non-democratic politics would be a contradiction in terms. A society, or some sphere of it, de-politicizes and therefore de-democratizes insofar as it submits to statist or elitist managerialism.

Rancière raises problems, then, for Rousseau's ideal. Any concept of a unified or a collective popular will, or of its manifestation in a popular, discursive consensus, far from promoting *la politique*, works to undermine it. How so? Because 'consensus', that latter-day 'general will' (or, more commonly, 'will of the majority'), along with its implication of collective unity, are *post hoc* myths to justify elite managerialism in the face of a demos whose ongoing character is fragmentation and 'dissensus'. It is 'dissensus', the cacophony of voices and views, which creates the demos, which creates *la politique* as the ongoing challenge to *la police*, that is, as the ongoing challenge to managerial technocracy.

It would be mistaken, however, to conclude that those two classical principles of political utopia – (i) power wedded to wisdom in a way that (ii) wholly reflects the people's will – must wholly diverge. Any serious criteria of substantive justice must inevitably assume certain managerial responses to citizens' articulated needs and desires; and yet any such managerial responses must, in turn, refer back to criteria of substantive justice. Absent considerable social breakdown, those two assumptions create not a vicious circle but an irrevocable dialectic.

From Aristotle through to Hegel, Marx, and Rawls, much of what counts as justice theory, indeed as political theory, amounts to so many attempts to reconcile those two principles. They must necessarily overlap to some extent, however slight; but beyond that overlap, their respective spheres of *non*-overlap betoken conflict between, on the one hand, the demos, and, on the other hand, formal and informal structures of managerial power. It is at those points of mutual *divergence*, where some citizens' voices inevitably go unheeded, that the distinctness of democracy appears (see Rancière 1998: 41, 72–73; 2005: 54; cf. Woodford 2015). The citizenry remains distinct from those structures of government and law which 'are always practiced by the minority' within government 'upon the majority', that is, upon the citizenry (Rancière 2005: 59; cf. Rancière 1998: 65–67, 74), even while government justifies that authority with reference to free speech and to formal, electoral processes as mechanisms of 'consensus'. That gap between the government and the citizenry does not, however, entail a sheer absence of any encounter between those two spheres. To the contrary, politics *is* that encounter.

For Plato in the *Laws*, societies 'must contain some people who govern and others who are governed' (*Laws* 3.689e, Plato 1997: 1378).[7] That principle of authority equally extends beyond the formal structures of established government. It reaches into any prevailing social arrangements. 'One claim', for example, can be made 'by parents to exercise control over their children' (*Laws* 3.690a, Plato 1997: 1378). That 'title' (ἀξίωμα) (Ibid) to 'govern' issues from a more general 'decree of nature'. Be it in the family, the community, or the state, 'the ignorant (ἀνεπιστήμονα) . . . should follow the leadership of the wise (φρονοῦντα)' (*Laws* 3.690b-c, Plato 1997: 1379).

Today we would add a dozen qualifications. No, not all parents are 'wise'. No, children cannot be altogether dismissed as 'ignorant'. No, we cannot attribute to 'nature' hierarchies that are socially constructed. Yes, we admit such parental authority today only within paradigms of state oversight and human rights, notably through social services. Yes, the very meanings of 'parent' and 'child' have differed across history and across cultures, particularly in view of divergent kinship and social structures.

We could pile on further reservations. (Plato is not altogether ignorant of them. He constantly doubts, for example, Athenians' competence to raise their own children as fully capable citizens [see *Alcibiades* 110e-12d, *Meno* 92e-94e, *Protogoras* 319b-320b in Plato 1997].) Still, our default assumption of some sort of parental authority over children remains widely intact and yes – to be frank – popularly viewed as natural. Post-industrial democracies have certainly, at least formally, discarded other erstwhile 'natural entitlements' to govern, such as 'the title of those of high birth to govern those of low birth', or powers over 'slaves . . . subject to the control of their masters' (*Laws* 3.690a-b, Plato 1997: 1379). Through our electoral frameworks and our secular, post-industrial contexts, we scarcely view public officials as exercising any natural entitlement beyond an electoral mandate or a professional qualification.

But let's not overstate Plato's obsolescence. He is not committing the naturalist fallacy of uncritically ontologizing social practices. Athenians know all about societies and practices vastly different from their own. Plato grasps those practices' culturally specific – dare we say 'constructed' – character. Plato's and Aristotle's political models, often drawn from comparisons between and among Greek and non-Greek societies, confirm an openness to considering social arrangements structured in ways fundamentally different to any Athenian status quo. Indeed the assumption that renders a title to govern 'natural' in the *Laws* scarcely draws on anything like the *Republic*'s ontological commitments to Being per se as cognizable only in fundamental opposition to perception. Rather, what Plato above all maintains in the *Laws* – and this element certainly does carry over from the *Republic* – is quite simply that power ought to flow from knowledge. And we are still very far from having surpassed that view today, if indeed we would even wish to surpass it. Such knowledge, moreover, continues to manifest in our time as the expertise of the specialist (Rancière 1987: 144–152; van Reybrouck 2013: 26–29).

Even under its most capable deployments, however, the marriage of power to knowledge hardly suffices to reflect the multiple, often divergent, needs and aspirations of the various Greek *demoi*, let alone those of today's societies. In a crucial departure from the *Republic*, the *Laws* therefore demarcate boundaries on wisdom qua technical expertise. The *Laws* set limits to supposedly natural divisions between the ruler who would dispose of expertise and the ruled who would speak at best with conflicting voices, at worst in sheer ignorance. In some cases, after all, it remains unclear who or what counts as wisest: 'you [legislators] see how many titles to authority (ἄρχοντας ἀξιώματα) there are, and how they naturally (πεφυκότα) conflict with each other' (*Laws* 3.690d, Plato 1997: 1379).

Some avowedly random decision-making procedure, the arch-opposite of government through specialised knowledge, now becomes legitimate. The demos, however wise or ignorant it may be, must intervene: 'we must persuade a man to cast lots' (Ibid), a process that, by tacitly acknowledging the shortfalls even of natural, expert rule, provides by default the only legitimate arbiter. The *Republic* had subsumed politics within the total purview of government, and popular preferences within an elite administration. Through a deliberately random re-incorporation of the demos, by contrast, the *Laws* marginally re-democratize. They acknowledge the necessary disjunction, the indispensable tension, between technocratic expertise and popular sentiments. It may well be through expertise, and in that sense 'by nature', that the 'wise' claim their titles to govern; ironically, however, those titles – also 'by nature' – end up in conflict. 'Now here's a source of civil strife we've discovered for you [legislators], which you must put to rights' (Ibid) by admitting such conspicuously, such deliberately random procedures as the casting of lots. In order for there to *be* politics as such, beyond technocratic managerialism (*la police*), the various titles to govern must include some 'exceptional' title (*titre d'exception*), 'a title in addition to those by which societies great and small are "normally" governed' (Rancière 2005: 56).

A 'Nocturnal Council', to be sure, lurks always as guardian against any excesses of the masses (e.g., *Laws* 12.962c, Plato 1997: 1610). The *Laws* do not stray so far from the *Republic* as to re-kindle Athenian democracy. For as long as the tension between people and power becomes resolved in favour of a government of expertise and technocratic administration – a government of caretakers (*pasteurs*) – that resolution takes place only 'at the price of suppressing politics'. The 'exceptional' title to govern is that power which resides in the people. It is not the power 'of a population or of its majority'. Rather, it is, deliberately, the random power of 'just anyone' (*n'importe qui*) through the irrelevance (*indifférence*) of designated 'capacities to occupy positions of government and to govern' (Rancière 2005: 56; cf. van Reybrouck 2013).

Modern democracies' technocratic governments claim legitimacy through electoral mandates rendering them 'democratic' in a conventional sense. That notion of democracy assumes a citizenry whose interests end up, through the fiction of consensus, subsumed within prevailing law and policy. 'Democratic society', insists Rancière, 'is never anything more than an imaginary tableau (*peinture de fantaisie*) aimed at justifying one or another principle of good government' (Rancière 2005: 58).[8] Rancière brands all governments, including those democracies commonly viewed as successful and prosperous, as 'oligarchies' – not necessarily in the historical sense of rule by small numbers of powerful or dynastic families (although we still see a fair few of those too), but more in the literal sense of 'rule by the few'. Rancière identifies democracy, by contrast, not as the foundation of those governments we habitually call 'democracies', but as the force outside such governments. Challenging a 2,500-year heritage of constitutional topologies (e.g., *Republic* 8.544a-569c, Plato 1997: 1156–1179; *Politics* 3.7, Aristotle 1984: 2030), Rancière maintains that democracy is not 'a type of constitution' at all. It is not even properly grasped as 'a form of society'. Democracy is instead the always-residual 'power of those who claim no more title to govern than to be governed'. That 'exceptional title' to govern, exemplified in the *Laws* through the casting of lots, generates the always-inevitable 'scandal' (Rancière 2005: 54; cf. Constant 1997: 213) of democracy as that which opposes technocracy qua the marriage of power to wisdom. 'That title can be nothing but the absence of any title', yet must itself 'become a political power' (Rancière 2005: 54).

Politics emerges as 'the foundation of the power to govern in its absence of foundation' (Rancière 2005: 56). A 'democracy is neither a society to be governed nor a government of society; it is rather the ungovernable upon which all government must definitively discover itself to be founded' (Ibid: 57). Much of Rancière's writing certainly places the anarchic demos, 'the ungovernable', outside, or alongside, or parallel to government. Only this rarer declaration posits that demos, whose defining manifestation is public discourse, as *foundational* – rightly so, as I shall now be arguing. On its face, Rancière's claim here is far from obvious. Since the advent of deconstructionism and critical legal studies, and yet arguably since Plato, doubts about some identifiable foundation for legal or political systems have raged. That notion commonly suggests something pre-political, something politically neutral, or, in Kant's sense, ethically transcendental, as a necessary pre-condition for political institutions and processes *subsequently* to begin. It is no accident that the *Republic's* great lie or 'noble falsehood' (γενναῖον ψεῦδος) (*Republic* 3.414b-c, Plato 1997: 1050; cf. Rancière 1987: 160), is a conspicuously contrived – to the point of an almost deliberately comical – myth. That myth, serving the public justification of a regime supposedly harnessed to truth, furnishes a foundation for the entire regime.

Before exploring public discourse as the legitimate foundation for democracy, let's take a brief detour to revisit the very possibility of political foundations. Few problems in law are older than the question of why it ought to be obeyed (e.g., *Crito* 50a-b, Plato 1997: 44). Our reasons of immediate expedience are obvious enough: we obey to avoid such detriments as fines, prison cells, job loss, and the like. But those motives of sheer self-interest explain very little. They imply no duty or virtue of obedience wherever such repercussions could be avoided (*Republic* 2.359c-60d, Plato 1997: 1000–1001, Glaucon relating the fable of the ring of Gyges), or where any risks they pose are outweighed by the benefits of disobedience (*Gorgias* 470d-71d, Plato 1997: 814–815, Polus relating the history of Arcilaeus of Macedonia). The harder question has therefore always been whether law stakes any claim to our obedience beyond immediate individual gain; whether we ought to obey because that is the ethical thing to do, the right thing to do. We can always, of course, find sociological and psychological explanations of duty and obedience arising through social habituation, through peer pressure, through the power of authority, and so forth. However, as virtually all of Plato's writings constantly remind us, legitimacy, as opposed to a purely blind or mechanical routine, arises only insofar as we can choose, explain, and justify those behavioural patterns. After all, as the Greeks notice and as modern history confirms, purely inculcated habits of sheer conformity arise even towards the most ghastly regimes.

Again, for Rancière, public discourse remains democratic through its disjunction from governmental power. It nevertheless supplies that power with a legitimating foundation only insofar as all citizens retain – indeed only insofar as citizenship is itself defined by – some absolute and irrevocable share in public discourse. Elsewhere, with a debt to Rancière, I define democratic citizenship precisely in contrast to our mundane notions of purely administrative citizenship, consisting of mere 'pieces of paper' – birth certificates, passports, and the like (Heinze 2016a: 46, 47, 50, 57, 92, 153). I define democratic citizenship with reference to the citizens' prerogative of expression within public discourse.[9] I shall not examine that notion further here, except insofar as we are more generally enquiring about public discourse as the legitimating element of democracy and indeed of politics. We must, then, revisit the old problem of legal and political foundations. We must once again ask about the possibility of principled (as opposed to purely sociological or psychological) legal or political foundations *at all* before we can choose this or that particular foundation as that which distinctly furnishes legitimacy.

If fundamental legal and political aims or principles appear ethical, even when some or indeed many of its particular outcomes do not, then the case for obedience becomes plausible. There are certainly differences between classical approaches and more recent, post-structuralist approaches to the question about legitimate foundations. They are not differences between, on the one hand, what is often erroneously assumed to be the classics' uncritical faith in such foundations, and, on the other hand, our own more critically minded scepticism. What distinguishes Plato's approach is indeed his insistence on the necessity of a rather overtly fabricated foundationalist mythology. Nothing drives the *Republic* more powerfully than the impossibility of self-evident political or legal foundations, hence the necessity of a mythology which he conspicuously presents as such, often in a deliberately humorous and deflationist vein.

It is no accident that the *Republic*'s famous model society begins with Socrates tearing through the Greek pantheon (2.377c-3.392c, Plato 1997: 1016–1030) like Christ a few centuries later amongst the moneylenders or iconoclasts two millennia later in the cathedrals. Unlike Christ or the iconoclasts, however, Plato's campaign is executed with such parody as to render glaringly obvious that legal foundationalism does not at all supplant myth with truth. Rather, it supplants myth with myth, haphazardly traditionalist myth with scrupulously rationalised myth, solely in the hope that the latter will offer more persuasive, and therefore more socially stabilising accounts than the former had done. Hence Socrates' expressly bathetic winks of the type, 'We'll have to say this to the people even if it isn't true' (paraphrased from *Republic* 2.378a, Plato 1997: 1016) – far from the tone of, at one extreme, any blind-faith dogmatist or, at the other extreme, the unrelenting dialectician.

If the *Republic* supplies a solution, it is to the problem posed in *Gorgias*, and then later ironized in Machiavelli's *The Prince*: any ethically minded legal foundationalism can always be turned into its opposite; the pursuit of self-interest can always be paraded as promoting the common good. When the Nietzschean Callicles advocates that strategy in *Gorgias* (491e-92c, Plato 1997: 835), Socrates' reply – that the one who does injustice incontrovertibly suffers more than the one to whom it is done (492e-508c, Plato 1997: 836–852; *Republic* 1.352e, 1.254-a, Plato

1997: 996, 998) – scarcely claims any self-evidence (Heinze 2013: 3–4). Socrates instead bolsters his view with what is all too conspicuously a myth (*Gorgias* 523a-27e, Plato 1997: 865–869) to ground the supremacy of justice, hence of ethical legal foundations, over injustice, through a tale of divine justice in the afterlife. The fact that *Gorgias's* concluding myth differs from that of the *Republic* (10.614a-21d, Plato 1997: 1217–1223) and from accounts elsewhere in the corpus[10] only further confirms it *as* sheer myth, as expressly parabolic rather than apodictic.

Yet one hardly walks away from Aristotle, Hobbes, Locke, Rousseau, Kant, Hegel, or Marx with the impression that *they* need to make any such assumptions. Their theories all remain squarely embedded within epistemologies that cast truth – if not ultimate truth then certainly truth enough for us to formulate legitimate law and politics – as largely attainable, unlike Plato's view of Being as lying largely beyond humans' grasp. The *Republic* captures us in a world of illusion that must be countered by government-engineered myth; and yet those other writers' epistemological optimism casts no more doubt on critical awareness in earlier times than it does today, where every system-building Habermas has his system-sabotaging Foucault, and every rationalist Dworkin his deconstructionist Derrida.

Post-structuralists differ from Plato not, then, in their discovery of anti-foundationalism, but in their response to it. Post-industrial mass society cannot so confidently embark upon a social re-mythologizing programme in the way the *Republic* proposes, and indeed even Plato was already casting considerable doubt on it (see *Republic* 9.592a-b, Plato 1997: 1199). For Rancière it is democracy not as a foundational norm or principle, but as the demos living in perpetual disjunction and tension with government, which supplies the political foundation that government otherwise can never convincingly find.

3. Public discourse

Western political philosophy, with its distinctively programmatic and often 'blank slate' models (cf. Heinze 2013: 5–6; Heinze 2016a: 194–205), is born largely out of those ongoing crises of disjunction between citizens and government. Plato responds in the *Republic* to the horror of Athens having put to death 'the wisest and justest man of that time' (*Letter VII* 324e, Plato 1997: 1647) for voicing his dissenting views. Ancient Athens, to be sure, is not altogether an oligarchy of the type Rancière expressly locates within political modernity. Athenian legislative and even judicial powers are exercised by large bodies of assembled citizens. And yet that exercise of citizenship remains the privilege of citizen-born, male heads of households. With the vast majority of individuals, including women, non-Athenians, and slaves, all barred from government, the law's oligarchic character, in Rancière's numerical sense, remains intact.

It is no accident that the West's first systematic treatment of the problem of legal and political legitimacy arises out of a trial about citizen participation within public discourse. Plato's *Crito* offers not a casuistry of Athenian positive law governing speech, but instead, so to speak, an 'immanent critique' of democratic legitimacy, a critique starting from democracy's own assumptions. In the *Republic*, the *Laws*, or the *Statesman*, Plato may well evaluate democracy according to expressly anti-democratic criteria. In *Crito*, by contrast, Athenian democracy is held to its *own* normative criteria. Sometimes wrongly thought to teach unqualified obedience even to unjust law (e.g., Kelly 1992: 16),[11] *Crito* is in fact subtler. Plato, I shall now claim, enquires into questions of legitimating speech conditions – and, therefore, of public discourse – as they apply specifically to a citizen-driven polity. In *Crito*, Plato cannot contemplate Socrates's trial and conviction in a text imagining philosopher rulers (*Republic* 5.473c-d, Plato 1997: 1100)[12]. He must examine Socrates' real-world society, the one that had actually reached the verdict.

The imprisoned Socrates is sentenced to die on the famously bogus charges of corrupting the youth, rejecting Athenian gods, and inventing new ones (*Apology*, Plato 1997: 23; cf. Brickhouse & Smith 2004: 79, 91–97). His disciple Crito promises a safe escape. Socrates refuses. Defending even his own trumped-up death sentence, Socrates admonishes Crito that, whether the law does right or wrong, citizens cannot legitimately pick and choose the laws they obey. If our legal system as a whole lays a legitimate claim to our obedience then we must accept its individual rules and decisions, taking the bitter with the sweet. But which criteria determine that 'if'? The question as to the extent of Socrates' freedoms of speech suddenly becomes linked to a broader, ultimate question: under what conditions does the legal system *as a whole* lay a legitimate claim to our obedience?

Again, from Polus' or Callicles' standpoints in *Gorgias*, there is no reason to adhere to law when one can draw greater advantage through breaching it. That proposition responds to the question of law's legitimacy by dismissing legitimacy entirely. What interests Socrates (in a notably Kantian sense) is whether there is a categorical duty to obey law as a distinctly moral imperative, beyond considerations of material outcome or self-interest. Within his context of Athenian democracy, and indeed *solely* within that context, Socrates will reply to the question of law's legitimacy – to the question 'Why should I obey law?' – with reference to the citizen's access to public discourse. He famously seeks a reply to that question by imagining a conversation he and Crito might conduct with the 'personified' Laws of Athens.[13] As a thought experiment, Socrates imagines a conversation that would take place if those Laws could magically assume the form of a god appearing to them in the prison cell. Can Socrates persuade the Laws of Athens that, in view of the injustice done to him, he may rightly flee his imprisonment and death penalty? Or can the Laws convince him that his duty is to face the penalty, however unjust it may be?

The personified Laws begin their response with altogether general thoughts, or rather rhetorical questions, about political legitimacy and about society's claim on the citizens' obedience to law. Socrates prompts that response by asking Crito about the escape plot:

> [What if] as we were planning to run away from here . . . the laws and the state (νόμοι καὶ τὸ κοινὸν τῆς πόλεως) came and confronted us, and asked: 'Tell, me, Socrates, what are you intending to do? Do you not by this action you are attempting intend to destroy us, the laws (νόμους), and the whole city (πόλιν), as far as you are concerned?'
>
> (*Crito* 50a-b, Plato 1997: 44)

The Laws then re-phrase the question. They invoke the age-old view that violations of law, at least grave ones, do not merely offend a particular norm, but threaten the whole system, an entire social and normative fabric. As Aristotle would later phrase it, 'transgression creeps in unperceived and at last ruins the state' (*Politics* 5.8.1307^{b}32–33, Aristotle 1984: 2076; cf. de Romilly 2002: 130). The Laws exclaim, '[D]o you think it possible for a city not to be destroyed if the verdicts of its courts have no force but are nullified and set at naught by private individuals?' (*Crito* 50b-c, Plato 1997: 44). The Laws then respond to their own rhetorical questions with further such questions, while Socrates puts up little resistance,[14]

> Then what if the Laws said: '[. . .] Did we [laws] not, first, bring you to birth, and was it not through us that your father married your mother and begat you? Tell [us], do you find anything to criticize in those of us [laws] who are concerned with marriage?' And I would say I do not criticize them. 'Or in those of us [laws] concerned with the nurture of babies and the education that you too received?'
>
> (*Crito* 50d, Plato 1997: 44)

In introducing the benefits Socrates has enjoyed under Athenian democracy, that opening gambit, like much of the argument that follows, emphasizes not law's narrowly penal, 'rules backed up by force' dimension, but a more richly facilitative dimension: 'Were [Athenians] not right to instruct your father to educate you in the arts and in physical culture?'[15] These personified Laws present law not in the naïve sense of the cop or the magistrate who enters the stage from time to time within a sphere of social life otherwise 'free' of law. Socrates' imaginary interlocutors underscore law's constitution of, and its pervasiveness throughout, social life, and throughout each citizen's individual life. Violations mar not merely this or that particular community interest. They endanger, through disrespect, an entire normative system, an entire νόμος, nomos, the whole matrix not only of formal rules, but of shared habits, customs, and attitudes, without which there can be no political community. To be sure, the Laws' further queries to Socrates might appear to render democracy per se irrelevant to the question of legal legitimacy. They even seem, at first glance, to represent the 'totalitarian' Plato, constituting the individual as a subject and not as a citizen,

> [A]fter you were born and nurtured and educated, could you, in the first place, deny that you are our offspring and servant (δοῦλος[16]), both you and your forefathers? If that is so, do you think that we [i.e., you, Socrates, and we, the Laws – EH] are on an equal footing as regards the right (δίκαιον), and that whatever we do to you it is right for you to do to us?
>
> (*Crito* 50e, Plato 1997: 45)

Those analogies to Athenian legal relationships of dominance and subordination seem scarcely to offer the models we seek today,

> You were not on an equal footing with your father as regards the right, nor with your master if you had one, so as to retaliate for anything they did to you, to revile them, if they reviled you, to beat them if they beat you, and so with many other things. Do you think you have this right to retaliation against your country and its laws?
>
> (*Crito* 51a, Plato 1997: 45)

In a society imposing the death penalty, the logical conclusion suddenly begins to seem stark. The Laws ask Socrates whether he thinks,

> That if we undertake to destroy you and think it is right to do so, you can undertake to destroy us, as far as you can, in return? And will you say that you are right (δίκαια) to do so, you who truly care for virtue (ἀρετῆς)? Is your wisdom such as you do not realize that your country is to be honored more than your mother, your father, and all your ancestors, that it is more to be revered and more sacred, and that . . . you must worship it, yield to it, and placate its anger more than your father's?
>
> (Ibid)

In the next, arguably the dialogue's most famous sentence, just as we seem to have drifted far indeed from any values we would recognize today as democratic, the Laws suddenly voice their own concise reply to this inquisition. Socrates' duty to obey law is not as absolute as that relentless barrage has been suggesting. His duty now appears to come as a choice. 'You must *either persuade* [the city] *or obey* its orders' (*Crito* 51b, Plato 1997: 45, emphasis added). Public expression is not merely one of several components of legal legitimacy. It figures not merely as one among a checklist of 'human rights', as we would have it today. Rather, free speech within public discourse peremptorily constitutes democratic legitimacy (Heinze 2016a: 5, 45, 46, 50, 55–57).

The Laws repeat their formula: 'one must obey the commands of one's city and country, or *persuade* it as to the nature of justice' (*Crito* 51b-c, Plato 1997: 45, emphasis added). Accordingly, and now for the third time, 'the one who disobeys does wrong' because 'he neither obeys us nor, if we do something wrong, does he try to *persuade* us to do better' (*Crito* 51e–52a, Plato 1997: 45, emphasis added). Athens's democratically enacted laws, for the fourth time, 'do not issue savage (ἀγρίως) commands to do whatever we order; we give two alternatives, either to *persuade* us or to do what we say.'[17] In *Crito* it is nothing but free speech within public discourse that turns that 'savage' to the civilized, that coercive to the participatory, that despotic to the demotic, that arbitrary to the legitimate.

In *Crito's* otherwise terse concatenation of the attributes of authority and citizenship, its fourfold rehearsal of the 'persuade or obey' formula arises not in the kind of discussion we find in Thucydides' rendering of Pericles' funeral oration (Thucydides 1998: 91–97), which turns out to be more of a rousing encomium than a studious delimitation of citizens' prerogatives within public discourse. Not even voting per se, but rather public discourse per se (voting being but one formalised procedure within public discourse [Heinze 2016a: 46–49]) surfaces in *Crito* as the defining feature of democracy qua democracy (cf. Foucault 2009: 34).

Public discourse becomes not merely important within the already constituted order, but itself becomes constitutive *of* that order as distinctly democratic. Public discourse becomes the constitution of the constitution, the democratic *Urverfassung*. It becomes the medium of the politicised demos, itself constituting the society, and therefore its government, as legitimate. On *Crito's* principles of political legitimacy, expression within public discourse is not a *sufficient* condition for the legitimacy with which law commands our obedience. *Crito* contextually assumes other conditions, such as the government's adherence to procedures governing elections, legislation, adjudication, policing, detention, and protection of citizens. The citizen's prerogative of expression within public discourse nevertheless does emerge as a *necessary* condition for political legitimacy.

Crito may well, by today's standards, leave too little room for justified civil disobedience. That point could provoke hot debate. But the dialogue leaves the citizen's prerogative of expression within public discourse wholly intact: one is bound to obey the laws of a society within which one had the opportunity to change that law through open persuasion, even if one has failed to achieve such change. That axiom leaves *Crito* silent about any non-democracies or sham democracies in which no seriously open and robust sphere of public discourse can safely exist. As an ultimate condition for the legitimacy of law within a conventionally democratic society, the injunction 'persuade or obey' can have no serious meaning if that society punishes a speaker for trying to persuade; or, to be more precise, punishes the speaker for *that element* of speech – its viewpoint – which aims at persuasion (unlike its excessive noise or its commission of independently unlawful conduct, such as tax evasion), irrespective of how odious that viewpoint may be.

Crito effectively attributes to public discourse a 'pre-legal', and in that sense constitutive status. That status emerges not within a mythically pre-political state of nature or foundational social contract, but within a strict conceptual logic.[18]

The legal system includes a duty to obey it. Yet that duty already assumes preliminary moral and civic questions of the legal system's legitimacy. As a normative matter, then, a legal system can never be entirely self-justifying.[19] Any incursion into democratic citizenship, the essence of which, as *Crito* teaches, lies in public discourse, never enhances democracy, but only erodes it. Rancière locates democracy not *as* government but both before and beyond government, the demos always in complex disjunction from government. Ironically, it is precisely that element before and beyond government, identified here as public discourse, which itself constitutes government as legitimate. In a word, public discourse supplies democracy's *Urverfassung*. It supplies the constitution *of* the democratic constitution.

I stake that claim largely inspired by Habermas, for whom public discourse plays that legitimating role, even if Habermas does not go so far as to ascribe constitutional status to public discourse in a strictly legal sense. Also in response to Habermas, however, Rancière questions the dynamics of public discourse. Habermas, in his view, places too much faith in an arena of discourse which – indeed along liberal lines tracing back through John Stuart Mill to the Enlightenment – proceeds dialectically towards constructive outcomes. On that model, a sentence like 'Have you understood me?' ('Vous m'avez compris?') can, in the first instance, be read straightforwardly as a sheer request for confirmation.

For Rancière, by contrast, such an utterance illustrates differentials of power separating speakers. Spoken to subordinates by those in dominant positions – irrespective of the latter's subjective intentions, which may be perfectly benign – such a question translates in the sense of 'Have I made myself understood?' Far from an invitation to engage in constructive dialectic, that meaning takes on the quality of a command, in the manner of a linguistic performative. It sets forth not a desire for collective exchange but rather an indication that all necessary thinking has been completed, such that the subordinates need not do any further thinking at all (Rancière 1995: 72–77). Similar reservations have been voiced by critics of classically liberal free speech ideals.[20] Rancière sees dissensus where Habermas envisages consensus.

Yet Rancière never goes so far as to posit the public sphere as inexorably locked into static hierarchies. Such a view would un-do most of the rest of his writing, which is precisely aimed at identifying loci of effective popular action; yet such action presupposes, in turn, the effectiveness of speakers, including those in subordinate positions. As Judith Butler (1997) and Raoul Vaneigem (2003) have noted, linguistic performatives aimed at subjugation also become moments for defiance (cf. Heinze 2016b; 2017). Rancière is nothing less than visionary in so deftly locating democracy outside rather than within mechanisms of power. Yet it is precisely there, on the outside, yet within a sphere of public discourse necessarily safeguarded by the state, that the only ultimately legitimate foundation for any democratic constitution is to be found.

Notes

* I would like to thank Julen Etxabe, Mónica López Lerma, Andreas Marcou, and an anonymous reviewer for their helpful insights. Translations from modern languages are mine.

1 Unlike contemporary courtrooms, juries under Athenian democracy commonly consisted of assemblies, typically comprising several hundred male members of the citizen class.

2 On Plato's theory of justice as a unity theory as opposed to a measurement theory, see Heinze (2013: 50–78).

3 Cf. Plato's *Republic* 8.567b-c, 8.569b; see also Aristotle's *Politics* 5.11.1313a39-13b32.

4 Such a history challenges assumptions that any pursuit of justice straightfowardly entails the negation of injustice (Heinze 2013).

5 Cf. the contrast in 20th and 21st century politics between government legitimacy and technocratic efficiency, e.g., in van Reybrouck 2013: 13, 26–29.

6 The attribute of 'authentic' is not one Rancière uses much, if at all, surely because of that term's laden, essentialist usage since Heidegger (cf. Heidegger 1979: 42–43, 193, 295; cf. critically Adorno 1964). Rancière largely embraces the post-structuralist challenge to assumptions of 'real', hence tacitly fixed identities which have long accompanied discourses of authenticity (see 2012: 58). Still, some notion of the authentically or genuinely political is unmistakably implied in Rancière's challenge to conventional concepts and understandings.

7 Cf. A. E. Taylor, translating πόλεσιν as 'in a community', *in* Plato (1961: 1284). Cf. also Rancière (2005: 46) (discussing *Laws* 3.690a–c).

8 Cf. Rancière 2005: 60–62 (challenging the familiar assumption of electorally representative institutions as democratic government) and, generally, van Reybrouck 2013.

9 That interest's status as a prerogative rather than a right arises from its more primordial and constitutive character. See, Heinze (2016a: 5, 9, 14, 22, 45–47, 48 n. 40).

10 Cf. *Phaedo* 81c–82c, 107d–14c, Plato 1997: 71–72, 92–97; *Laws* 927a, Plato 1997: 1580.

11 See critically Bostock 2005; de Romilly 2002: 127, 136; Heinze 2007b: 329; Kraut 1999.

12 Cf. Statesman 309b, Plato 1997: 355 (on master 'weavers'); *Laws* 10.909a, Plato 1997: 1565 (on the 'nocturnal council').

13 Through 'the sheer fact that the Laws speak here, like living persons', writes de Romilly, 'the civic bond remains still a direct and personal bond' (2002: 134).

14 Our generally anti-democratic Plato does not, then, lack a theory of democratic legitimacy. That observation becomes confirmed by *Crito*'s essentially doctrinal content. In most of the *Republic* (after Book II) and the *Laws*, the dialogical form reduces to an effectively monologic recitation by, respectively, Socrates and the Socratic 'Athenian', whose authority in each work reigns supreme over mostly passive interlocutors. In *Crito*'s imaginary dialogue with the Laws of Athens, it is Socrates himself who, along with his disciple, assumes deferential passivity, while the democratic Laws of Athens, albeit certainly through Socrates' mouth, dominate as monological. *Crito*, then, is neither aporetic, nor even very different from Books II-X of the *Republic* or from the Laws in its more doctrinal than dialectical character, despite, as with those books of the *Republic* or with the *Laws*, its nominally dialogical form. The young disciple's counter-thesis, an effectively act-utilitarian view that the greater act of justice overrides the smaller act of injustice, does nevertheless supply *Crito* with a more genuinely dialectical exchange.

15 Anglo-American legal scholars trace this insight not to ancient Greece but to 1961. See Hart (1994: 35–38).

16 Cf. Foucault (2009: 42) (discussing the ancient notion of democracy as opposite to slavery).

17 *Crito* 52a, Plato 1997: 45–46 (emphasis added). On ancient Greeks' understandings of the consensualist foundations of their law, see de Romilly (2002: 1, 19, 20–21 (discussing Euripides), 24, 35 (discussing Thucydides)). Platonic irony in *Crito*, then, appears twofold. Its famous irony is that, in a democracy, justice commands obedience to unjust law. If Socrates' crime had been, say, robbing the rich to feed the poor, after already having failed to persuade the Athenians of more equitable distribution of resources, then the irony would stop there. Instead, the second irony is that his crime consists of exercising that very prerogative which legitimates the rest of law. He is condemned for public expression on viewpoint-punitive grounds. Such expression *cannot* legitimately be criminalised, since it forms one-half of the duty to 'persuade or obey'. If we wish to reconcile *Crito* with Plato's expressly anti-democratic writings, we can do so not, as is commonly thought, because *Crito* shows injustice arising from democracy's application of its own principles, but from its betrayal of them. The Athenians' injustice arises not merely from the *bad* laws or procedures which their democracy brings to bear against one or more of its citizens (such as, for example, an excessive tax on the poor might be), but from Socrates' punishment for exercising a necessary prerogative of citizenship.

18 Cf. Frank Michelman's notion of the conceptually pre-legal as a 'jurisgenerative politics' (in Michelman 1988: 1527; cf. also Post 1995: 133, 186). 'Responsive democracy', observes Post, 'requires that public discourse . . . will necessarily precede and inform government decision-making' (Ibid: 194).

19 Accordingly, attributions of obsessive 'individualism' (e.g., Tillmanns 2003: 29) are fair enough as challenges to extreme libertarian positions; however, to ascribe excessive individualism to democracy-based dissent is to misconstrue what democracy is. To find 'too much' individualism within public discourse is to find 'too much' citizenship there. One may legitimately wish to rescue democracy from too much individualism in the sense of, say, consumerism or selfishness. But there is no such thing as rescuing a democracy from too much citizenship.

20 See Langton (1993). See also Delgado and Stefancic 2004); Matsuda et al.(1993); Maitra and McGowan (2012); and Waldron (2012).

Bibliography

Adorno, T. W. (1964) *Jargon der Eigentlichkeit: Zur deutschen Ideologie*, Frankfurt am Main: Suhrkamp.

Aristotle (1984) *The Complete Works of Aristotle: The Revised Oxford Translations*, vol. 1 & 2, Princeton: Princeton University Press.

Bostock, D. (2000) *Aristotle's Ethics*, Oxford: Oxford University Press.

Brickhouse, T. C., and Smith, N. D. (2014) *Plato and the Trial of Socrates*, London: Routledge.

Butler, J. (1997) *Excitable Speech: A Politics of the Performative*, New York: Routledge.

Chambers, S. A. (2011) 'Jacques Rancière and the Problem of Pure Politics', *European Journal of Political Theory*, vol. 10, no. 3, pp. 303–326.

Constant, B. ([1814] 1997) 'De l'esprit de conquête et de l'usurpation dans leur rapports avec la civilisation européenne', in Constant, B. and Gauchet, M. (eds.) *Écrits politiques*, Paris: Gallimard.
Delgado, R. and Stefancic, J. (2004) *Understanding Words That Wound*, Boulder: Westview.
de Romilly, J. (2002) *La loi dans la pensée grecque des origines à Aristote*, 2nd edition, Paris: Les Belles Lettres.
Foucault, M. ([1984] 2009) *Le gouvernement de soi et des autres, Tome 2: Le courage de la vérité – Cours au Collège de France (1983–1984)*, Paris: Seuil.
Hart, H. (1994) *The Concept of Law*, 2nd edition, Oxford: Oxford University Press.
Heidegger, M. ([1927] 1979) *Sein und Zeit*, Tübingen: Max Niemeyer.
Heinze, E. (2007a) 'Epinomia: Plato and the First Theory of Law', *Ratio Juris*, vol. 20, pp. 97–135.
Heinze, E. (2007b) 'The Status of Classical Natural Law: Plato and the Parochialism of Modern Theory', *Canadian Journal of Law and Jurisprudence*, vol. 20, pp. 323–350.
Heinze, E. (2013) *The Concept of Injustice*, London: Routledge.
Heinze, E. (2016a) *Hate Speech and Democratic Citizenship*, Oxford: Oxford University Press.
Heinze, E. (2016b) *Towards a post-liberal theory of free expression*, [Online]. Available: http://criticallegalthinking.com/2016/09/06/towards-post-liberal-theory-free-expression/
Heinze, E. (2017) *Free speech debates are more than "radicals" vs "liberals"*, [Online]. Available: https://aeon.co/ideas/free-speech-debates-are-more-than-radicals-vs-liberals
Kelly, J. M. (1992) *A Short History of Western Legal Theory*, Oxford: Oxford University Press.
Kraut, R. (1999) 'Socrates and Democracy', in Fine, G. (ed.) *Plato 2: Ethics, Politics, Religion and the Soul*, Oxford: Oxford University Press.
Langton, R. (1993) 'Speech Acts and Unspeakable Acts', *Philosophy and Public Affairs*, vol. 22, pp. 305–330.
Maitra, I. and McGowan, M. K. (2012) *Speech & Harm: Controversies over Free Speech*, Oxford: Oxford University Press.
Matsuda, M., Lawrence III, C. L., Delgado, R., and Crenshaw, K. W. (1993) *Words That Wound: Critical Race Theory, Assaultive Speech, and the First Amendment*, Boulder: Westview Press.
Michelman, F. (1988) 'Law's Republic', *Yale Law Journal*, vol. 97, pp. 1493–1537.
Plato (1961) *The Collected Dialogues*, Princeton: Princeton University Press.
Plato (1997) *Plato: Complete Works*, edited by J. Cooper, Indianapolis: Hackett.
Post, R. (1995) *Constitutional Domains: Democracy, Community, Management*, Cambridge: Harvard University Press.
Préposiet, J. (2002) *Histoire de l'Anarchisme*, rev. edition, Paris: Tallandier.
Rancière, J. (1987) *Le maître ignorant*, Paris: Fayard.
Rancière, J. (1995) *La mésentente*, Paris: Editions Galilée.
Rancière, J. (1998) *Aux bords du politique*, Paris: Gallimard.
Rancière, J. (2005) *La haine de la démocratie*, Paris: La Fabrique.
Rancière, J. (2012) *La méthode de l'égalité: Entretien avec Laurent Jeanpierre et Dork Zabunyan*, Montrouge: Bayard Culture.
Reybrouck, D. V. (2013) *Tegen Verkiezingen*, Amsterdam: De bezige bij.
Rousseau, J.-J. (1964) 'Du Contrat social', in *Oeuvres Complètes*, vol. 3, Paris: Gallimard [Pléiade], pp. 340–470.
Thucydides (1998) *The Peloponnesian War*, translated by S. Lattimore, Indianapolis: Hackett Publishing.

Tillmanns, R. (2003) 'Wehrhaftigkeit durch Werthaftigkeit – der ethische Grundkonsens als Existenzvoraussetzung des freiheitlichen Staates', in Thiel, M. (ed.) *Wehrhafte Demokratie: Beiträge über die Regelungen zum Schutze der freiheitlichen demokratischen Grundordnung*, Tübingen: Mohr Siebeck, pp. 25–55.

Vaneigem, R. (2003) *Rien n'est sacré, tout peut se dire: Réflexions sur la liberté d'expression*, Paris: La Découverte.

Waldron, J. (2012) *The Harm in Hate Speech*, Boston: Harvard University Press.

Woodford, C. (2015) 'Reinventing Modes of Dreaming and Doing', *Philosophy and Social Criticism*, vol. 41, pp. 811–836.

Chapter 6

Rancière and Schmitt

Sons of Ares?

Panu Minkkinen

1. Introduction: Schmitt's formalism?

In his well-known 'Notes' on Carl Schmitt's essay *The Concept of the Political* (2007a), the young Leo Strauss reflects on the enthusiasm with which he received its publication. Here Schmitt had first presented his definition of politics as the conflictual tension that arises from the friend/enemy distinction. As a fellow critic of liberalism, Strauss immediately recognized a kindred spirit. But Strauss's admiration did not come without reservations. In his eyes, Schmitt's criticism did not, perhaps, go far enough. Strauss notes:

> He who affirms the political as such respects all who want to fight; he is just as *tolerant* as the liberals – but with the opposite intention: whereas the liberal respects and tolerates all '*honest*' convictions so long as they merely acknowledge the legal order, *peace*, as sacrosanct, he who affirms the political as such respects and tolerates all '*serious*' convictions, that is, all decisions oriented to the real possibility of *war*. Thus the affirmation of the political as such proves to be a liberalism with the opposite polarity.
>
> (Strauss in Meier 1995: 117)[1]

Strauss accuses Schmitt of falling prey to the same relativism that he is trying to criticize by reducing politics to conflict and struggle. It would seem, then, that it no longer matters what one is fighting for. The struggle for liberal institutions, such as human rights and the rule of law, would be just as 'political' as the struggle for non-liberal alternatives. The distinction is, then, formal irrespective of substance. This argument about Schmitt's 'formalism' and the relativism that allegedly follows has since been repeated by more contemporary critics as well. Despite seemingly close affinities (see, e.g., Arditi 2008), Jacques Rancière distances himself from Schmitt by limiting himself to a few vague dismissive remarks (as in Rancière and Nash 1996) and scant indirect references (e.g., Rancière 2010: 65–66 commenting on Agamben). In the only direct confrontation with Schmitt that I'm aware of, Rancière claims that:

> I do not reduce politics to a mere agonistic schema where the 'content' is irrelevant. I am far away from the Schmittian formalization of antagonism. Politics, I argue, has its own universal, its own measure that is equality.
>
> (Rancière 2011: 4)

Rancière's criticism, at least as it is presented here, touches upon the same formalism that seemed to also bother Strauss. Schmitt's concept of the political is, this argument would imply, a formal distinction that qualifies all action as political so long as it includes an antagonistic element that, in Schmitt's case, is introduced by the friend/enemy distinction. Here Rancière suggests that for him, unlike for Schmitt, that antagonistic element *as such* is never enough. In order to qualify as politics in Rancière's meaning of the term, the 'struggle' must concern a particular content, namely *equality* (on Rancière's understanding of 'active' equality, see May 2008: 38–77). Without it we would not be talking about politics in Rancière's meaning of the term.

Yet in broader terms, both Rancière and Schmitt belong to the same 'agonistic' tradition; both are 'sons of Ares'.[2] While Chantal Mouffe, to take another prominent representative in this tradition, manages to work her Schmittian premises into a theory of radical democracy (see Mouffe 2005), Rancière is clearly more reluctant to discuss his possible affiliations with the German conservative revolutionary (on the German conservative revolutionary movement in general, see e.g., Woods 1996). But why? Are the grounds for Rancière's reluctance sound? Is there something in Schmitt's *intellectual* scheme that would make it incompatible with Rancière's attempts to discern politics? Or is this just an echo of the more general disinclination of leftist French academia to engage with Schmitt, the 'convinced Nazi' (Arendt 1994: 339)?

In his native France, Rancière will, no doubt, wish to distance himself from the radical conservative *Nouvelle Droite* movement that draws heavily on Schmitt (e.g., Benoist 2003). But Schmitt appears in other lineages in France, as well. At least three can be identified. One has its origins in Raymond Aron and the liberal movement (e.g., Aron 2003; Raynaud 2014), while another is curiously situated between the liberals and the right (e.g., Freund 2003; Freund 1995; Steinmetz-Jenkins 2016). Finally, a third lineage can even trace its intellectual ancestry to the Hegelian phase of Alexandre Kojève and Georges Bataille (e.g., Geroulanos 2011).[3] So taking into account this rather complicated relationship between the 'Crown Jurist of the Third Reich' and the French, what is, if any, Rancière's affinity with Schmitt?

My argument in this chapter is that Schmitt's 'concept', as he chooses to call his delineation of the political, is not quite as 'conceptually' formal as it first seems and as Rancière in his brief remark would have us believe. Schmitt's political substance is, for sure, veiled notwithstanding facile conclusions drawn from his personal political escapades (e.g., Gross 2007). But a substance is introduced by way of what I would call the 'metapolitical necessity' of his theory. The necessity applies to both the political as a concept as Schmitt sees it and to Schmitt's notion of the constitution that I will examine more closely to illustrate my point. And it is at this metapolitical level where, I would suggest, Rancière aligns himself with Schmitt. This despite Rancière's explicit criticism of the term. In the final part of the chapter, I will attempt to show how Rancière himself may end up presenting his notion of politics in 'metapolitical' terms, as well, but understood more in the way as it is presented by Alain Badiou (Badiou 2011).

In order to develop my argument, I will read a detail extracted from Schmitt's *The Concept of the Political* against his 1928 monograph *Constitutional Theory* (2008a) in order to demonstrate how his metapolitical position arises. The historical proximity of these two texts is worth noting. *Constitutional Theory*, Schmitt's first – and some might claim only – major monograph, was published only a year after the first edition of the essay, the same year that Schmitt himself moved from Bonn to the *Handelshochschule* in Berlin (Bendersky 1983: 41–103; Kennedy 2004: 137). The Weimar Republic was just descending – again – into governmental paralysis and the economic recession that would eventually usher Hitler to power. Against this setting, my aim is to shed light on the question of the political nature of constitutional phenomena, be they Weimarian or otherwise – or, conversely, to show how focusing on constitutional phenomena may illuminate Schmitt's notion of the political. What is a political constitution? To what extent can we claim that a given constitution like the Weimar Constitution of 1919 is a 'political' charter in Schmitt's sense of the word? Is the constitution not, then, merely the *lex legum*, as the Kelsen-inspired legal tradition would imply (see also Minkkinen 2013)?

After I have developed these Schmittian themes somewhat independently, I will return to Rancière in the final parts of the chapter.

2. Schmitt: the political as enmity

The central argument that Schmitt puts forward in *The Concept of the Political* is fairly familiar territory, so it may be unnecessary to dwell on it in detail. But briefly, Schmitt criticizes previous attempts to define the political for either lack of clarity or for using the term antithetically by way of distinguishing it 'negatively' from what it is not, primarily from the moral, the aesthetic, and the economic (Schmitt 2007a: 20). Instead, Schmitt claims, the characteristics and categories that are specific to the political should be 'positively' defined. If the ultimate distinctions that allow us to define the moral are good and evil, the aesthetic beautiful and ugly, and the economic profitable and unprofitable, then, for Schmitt, the political can be defined by way of an antithetical friend/enemy distinction (Schmitt 2007a: 25–27).[4] Furthermore, the distinction introduces a polemical element into the political:

> [A]ll political concepts, images, and terms have a polemical meaning. They are focused on a specific conflict and are bound to a concrete situation; the result (which manifests itself in war or revolution) is a friend-enemy grouping, and they turn into empty and ghostlike abstractions when this situation

> disappears. Words such as state, republic, society, class, as well as sovereignty, constitutional state, absolutism, dictatorship, economic planning, neutral or total state, and so on, are incomprehensible if one does not know exactly who is to be affected, combated, refuted, or negated by such a term.
>
> (Schmitt 2007a: 30–31)

There are two things that I would like to emphasize in this quote and that, in my mind, alleviate – if not eradicate – any accusations about Schmitt's 'formalism'. Firstly, 'concepts, images, and terms'. What Schmitt means by 'the political' does not only concern concepts as theoretical categories (on Schmitt's conceptualism, see Pankakoski 2010). It also refers to the imagery and less-than-conceptual expressions that have been used in, for example, the act of constituting a state. Think of, for example, the performative complexity of the phrase, 'we the people' (e.g., Derrida 2002). Secondly, without the polemical friction within the friend/enemy groupings, supposedly political 'concepts, images and terms' are merely 'empty and ghostlike abstractions', perhaps 'formal' in the very meaning that Rancière's criticism suggests. Consequently, a constitution, for instance, is never merely a collection of conceptually formalized norms that would define and delimit the competences of the state's political and legal institutions. In its necessarily polemical character – for without it its 'concepts, images and terms' would be 'empty and ghostlike abstractions' – a constitution will always include within itself an 'existential' dimension (see, e.g., Marder 2010) that Schmitt, in his *Constitutional Theory*, elaborates with the help of the notion of an 'absolute concept'. The existential dimension is, in other words, Schmitt's way of addressing the pitfalls of 'formalization' or 'empty and ghostlike abstractions', and this dimension is introduced by way of a polemical confrontation with something 'to be affected, combated, refuted, or negated'.

So, what would an 'absolute concept of the constitution' imply? For Schmitt, the 'relative' concept of the constitution refers to the multitude of legal norms that have been legislated as constitutional norms. As such a multitude, these norms lack the 'unity' or the 'oneness' (*Einheit*) that defines the constitution as an absolute concept (see Schmitt 2008a: 67–74). The 'absolute concept' is, then, Schmitt's reference to the concrete way in which constitutional norms come together to form a political unity. Schmitt seems to assume that unity as 'oneness' is specifically political by nature. Or, to be more exact, it is the 'political unity of the people' (Schmitt 2008a: 59), a 'peculiar form of existence . . . determined through the act of constitution making' (Schmitt 2008a: 76). Individualized existence as a unity is, in other words, political existence that the unified absolute concept of the constitution represents. Although there are considerable differences here in relation to the way in which Rancière understands the relationship between the *demos* and the *ochlos*, it is worth noting that Schmitt's 'political unity of the people' is not a oneness that is 'constituted' by some charter but, rather, the unity that, for example, the Preamble of the 1919 Weimar Constitution ('The German people, united in its tribes') *presumes*: some form of unity, a contingent 'political maturity', however indeterminate and fragile it may be, is the factual prerequisite for the establishment of any political order. We reason backwards. If we can claim that a political order exists, then we must also presuppose that some 'unity' or other is responsible for its existence. Rancière, on the other hand, maintains that

> [d]emocracy is neither the consensual self-regulation of the plural passions of the multitude of individuals nor the reign of a collectivity unified by law under the shadow of Declarations of Rights. Democracy exists in a society to the degree that the *demos* exists as the power to divide the *ochlos*. This power of division is enacted through a contingent historical system of events, discourses and practices whereby any multitude affirms and manifests itself as such, simultaneously refusing both its incorporation in to the One of a collectivity that assigns ranks and identities and the pure abandonment of individual focuses of possession and terror.
>
> (Rancière 2007: 32)

But Schmitt's 'unified people' is not a unity that could only exist by way of, say, a constitution. It is, rather, the trace of a multitude that once came together successfully with the determination to establish the institutions required for its political existence of choice. And regardless of its subsequent institutional existence as, for instance, the democratic electorate 'under the shadow of Declarations of Rights', it can always re-emerge as that multitude to undo what it may have done, as we will later see. In this sense, even Schmitt's demos retains a certain 'power of division'.

Nevertheless, at this point Schmitt's more specific meaning of the word 'political' is still relatively formal, and the only hint seems to be the unitary character of the whole: the factual ability to act as a unity is what makes a whole political. Later, Schmitt further elaborates that this unity is closely related to what he calls the 'principle of identity', that is, the possibility of a people to recognize itself as a political unity in so far as 'by virtue of its own political consciousness and national will, it has the capacity to distinguish friend and enemy' (Schmitt 2008a: 247; see also Björk 2016), or to identify its 'constitutive outside'.[5] In other words, the identification of an enemy enhances the identity that enables a people to see itself as a political entity. Thus, the friend/enemy distinction also has concrete constitutional relevance.

Schmitt recognizes three dimensions in the absolute concept of the constitution.

First, in its absolute sense, the constitution can be regarded as the concrete and collective precondition of the political unity and the social order of a given state. It is 'some principle of unity and order, some decision-making authority that is definitive in critical cases of conflicts of interest and power' (Schmitt 2008a: 59). This first dimension is, in other words, a reference to how sovereign power is organized and exercised in the state. Although Schmitt does not specifically mention Bodin in this instance (see, however, Schmitt 2008a: 101), the idea is very close to the latter's notion of sovereignty as the absolute power that unifies the plurality of households into one (see Bodin 1992).

For Schmitt, the constitution may also refer to a particular political or social order, or, in other words, to a specific way of governing and subjection that is indistinguishable from the political existence of the state. In this second absolute meaning, the constitution will be identical with, for example, forms of government such as monarchy, oligarchy or democracy as the state's 'form of forms' (Schmitt 2008a: 60). Schmitt's reference to the form of the state as '*forma formarum*' may well be of Thomistic origin and especially an allusion to the famous claim made by the German Renaissance scholar Nicholas of Cusa (1401–1464) about God as the 'form of all forms [*forma omnium formarum/die Form aller Form*]' (Cusa 2013: 20, 21).

Finally, the third meaning of the absolute concept of the constitution emphasizes the principle of the dynamic development of all political unities and the force and energy that enables this. For Schmitt, no political unity can remain static as the etymological origin of the words 'state' and 'constitution' as *status* seems to falsely imply (from '*stare*' and '*statuere*', 'to stand', 'to set standing'). All unities must regenerate themselves continuously:

> Political unity must form itself daily out of various opposing interests, opinions, and aspirations. . . . The constitution is the active principle of a dynamic process of effective energies, an element of the becoming.
>
> (Schmitt 2008a: 61)

Even if the state is 'sheer status',[6] it is alive. With this third dimension, Schmitt betrays the vitalistic undertow of his theory (see also Braun 2012). This, in turn, suggests a kinship with Nietzschean contemporaries such as Max Scheler and Max Weber (see Schmitt 1996; Ulmen 1985),[7] and certainly with the aforementioned Leo Strauss.

Schmitt notes that the absolute concept of the constitution could, of course, also refer to 'fundamental legal regulation' or, in other words, to the closed system of the hierarchically ultimate legal norms as a whole, to the constitution as the 'norm of norms' (Schmitt 2008a: 62) or a sort of '*norma normans non normata*', 'the norm of norms that cannot be normed'.[8] But Schmitt's criticism against this kind of pure normativism is, firstly, that it produces distorted 'apocryphal' accounts of sovereignty, and, secondly and consequently, that a constitution would be regarded as valid merely because it has been correctly inferred from a formal competence. For Schmitt, a constitution can be valid only if, in addition to any formal criteria, it has been backed by a factual ability to constitute or, in other words, by a factual power or authority that makes the act of constituting possible to begin with. This is the decisionistic element in Schmitt's constitutional theory. The constitution is created by the will of a 'constitution-making power', and the word 'will' is, for its part, an indication of a factually existing power as the source of a command: 'The will is existentially present; its power or authority lies in its being' (Schmitt 2008a: 64). Understood politically, law is 'concrete *will* and *command* and an act of sovereignty' (Schmitt 2008a: 187). In a monarchy, the king's will is the law; in a democracy, the people's will. In order to remain internally coherent, the normativist concept of the law of the *Rechtsstaat* must remain silent about the political will that can actualize a legal norm into a valid command:

> The constitution in the positive sense originates from an *act of the constitution-making power*. The act of establishing a constitution as such involves not separate sets of norms. Instead, it determines the entirety of the political unity in regard to its peculiar form of existence through a single instance of decision. This act *constitutes* the form and type of the political unity, the existence of which is presupposed.
>
> (Schmitt 2008a: 75)

In terms of the separation of powers, the German expression for legislative power is *gesetzgebende Gewalt*. To remain consistent himself, Schmitt must refer to *verfassunggebende Gewalt* as constitution-making power in order to emphasize that we are dealing with a power more 'fundamental' than legislative power. More fundamental despite the fact that constitutional norms are formally 'legislated' in similar ways as conventional laws. The literal translation of Schmitt's term is rather clumsy, but it can be clarified with the help of the distinction between constituent and constituted power. For Schmitt, a 'separated' legislative power is clearly an expression of constituted power, a power that the legislator exercises within its constitutional competence. Constitution-making power, on the other hand, is a constituent power exercised in a democracy by the people, and it cannot be framed within pre-existing competences, not even logically (on the distinction, see Sieyès 2003; Loughlin and Walker 2007). In German, the expression *verfassunggebende Gewalt* is, in fact, often used as a synonym for Sieyès's *pouvoir constituant*.

Already in these conceptual preliminaries that frame the juridical analyses in *Constitutional Theory*, one can rather easily detect the polemical confrontation that Schmitt is seeking with the positivistic tradition of public law (with Hans Kelsen in particular, see, e.g., Vinx 2015). A constitution is, in other words, not simply the 'charter' of a *Rechtsstaat* that limits its own powers through constitutional competences as this tradition would have it. It is the outcome of a constitution-making power through which the constituent subject – in this case the people – both establishes the institutions and practices that are essential for its political existence as a unified 'one' and secures them against potential threats. Constitutional institutions and practices are, then, 'constituted' for the very reason that they are potentially under threat from 'enemies', and it is the threat of such 'enemies' that also makes constitutions political in Schmitt's meaning of the word.

But the subject of the constitution-making power does not exercise that power only at the initial moment when it establishes the institutions and practices of its political existence. As a constituent power, it can never exhaust itself into the institutions that it has constituted. So, for example, a people that uses its constitution-making power to establish a representative democracy does not, by so doing, reduce itself to a constituted electorate despite the fact that the established institutions may be functioning normally. Or, in Schmitt's terms, a people 'anterior to and above' the constitution, that is, the presupposed people behind every democracy, can never quite reduce itself into a people 'within' the constitution, that is, into the people that the constitution identifies and recognizes as an institution (Schmitt 2008a: 268). A constituent residue will, namely, always remain dormant in the institutions that the people may have constituted, and it will re-emerge and activate itself if its political existence becomes threatened. We can use Bruce Ackerman's well-known expression 'constitutional moments' (Ackerman 1991) or Jason Frank's 'constituent moments' (Frank 2010) to depict such points of re-emergence even if the emphasis in both is slightly different. But we could equally well call them 'constitutional crises'.[9] From Schmitt's point of view it is, however, worth noting that such 'moments' or 'crises' are not pathologies but, rather, expressions of the state's political vitality, measures in which 'the superiority of the existential element over the merely normative one reveals itself' (Schmitt 2008a: 154).[10]

3. Rancière: politics as disagreement

If Schmitt's friend/enemy distinction is well-known to the point of becoming analytically almost redundant, then the same can, perhaps, be said of Rancière's attempts to distinguish politics proper from the more conventional practices of government that he famously terms 'police' (for a good introduction, see May 2010: 1–28). There is, however, a twist here. For Rancière's police is neither an allusion to the forced compliance executed by what he calls the 'petty police' nor an amalgam for the various coercive operations of the state apparatus (cf. Foucault 1995: 213). It is, rather, a particular distribution of places and roles that may arise from the regularities of social relations just as well as within state practices. It is the 'implicit law' that defines a share or its lack in a configuration of what can be perceived. Police is, then,

> an order of bodies that defines the allocation of ways of doing, ways of being, and ways of saying, and sees that those bodies are assigned by name to a particular place and task; it is an order of the visible and the sayable that sees that a particular activity is visible and another is not, that this speech is understood as discourse and another as noise.
>
> (Rancière 1999: 29)[11]

Rancière's notion of police, with its emphasis on an order of the perceptible – what is visible, audible, or understandable, and how – is, of course, far from Schmitt's state-centric view of the world in which politics is relevant. The state may well contribute to the order of the police, and its practices may even be central to the way in which something is perceived. But no equation marks can be written between the two. There are, however, other similarities and differences that would justify a comparison. Schmitt's starting-point, his 'police', if you will, is an orderly view of the world as well, an order that cannot be reduced to any type of legal order even if legal norms play an important role in it. It is, rather, an existential order in which individuals and institutions will have relatively stable assigned roles. For Schmitt, such an existential order can become conciliated into 'party politics' if the original antagonisms essential for any political existence and made public through the friend/enemy distinction have been lost (Schmitt 2007a: 29–30). In other words, one of the motivations for Schmitt's essay is to recognize and to re-articulate the antagonisms that are necessary for the political after they have been pacified or even neutralized in 'party politics'. Schmitt's line of argumentation runs, then, from an antagonistic political ontology towards a gradual depoliticization of all social relations. And this depoliticized world is, if you will, both Schmitt's 'police' and the 'enemy' that he wishes to confront.

In a similar agonistic vein as Schmitt, Rancière reserves the word 'politics' for 'dissensual' disagreement, for rather exceptional interventions that are extremely 'antagonistic to policing' (Rancière 1999: 29), and that disrupt the everyday routines of government:

> Politics is by no means a reality that might be deduced from the necessities leading people to gather in communities. Politics is an exception in relation to the principles according to which this gathering occurs.
>
> (Rancière 2010: 35)

But Rancière's 'exceptional politics' does not operate as a 'constitutive outside'. His argument proceeds in a different way. If, for Schmitt, the antagonistic nature of politics is his starting point as a political ontology from which a depoliticized existence may potentially follow, Rancière's ontology, if he even has one, only extends to the social order of police into which politics intervenes as rare and singular intrusions. Although Rancière's politics has a logic, it is, rather, anti-ontological: politics throws the ontology of police into disarray. As Samuel Chambers notes, 'on this particular point – the refusal to ontologize, the rejection of all ontology – Rancière's approach to politics may mark him not just as distinct, but perhaps even as unique' (Chambers 2013: 20; see also Deranty 2003). Disregarding all the other more nuanced differences, the main difference between the two political thinkers is at this 'ontological' level. The arguments move in parallel but opposite directions: for Schmitt, an antagonistic political ontology has made way for the pacified social order of liberalism (and so needs to be reinvigorated), whereas for Rancière all political ontologies are police regimes into which antagonistic politics may occasionally intervene.

This applies to the state's constituted arrangements *à la* Schmitt, as well:

> [P]olitics cannot be identified with the model of communicative action. This model presupposes partners that are already pre-constituted as such and discursive forms that entail a speech community, the constraint of which is always explicable. Now, the specificity of political dissensus is that its partners are no more constituted than is the object or stage of discussion itself. Those who make visible the fact that they belong to a shared world that others do

> not see – and cannot take advantage of – is the implicit logic of any pragmatics of communication.
>
> (Rancière 2010: 38)[12]

Seen from this perspective, any constituted exchange between, for example, branches of government would, in Rancière's terms, be police as opposed to politics proper. If, for example, the judiciary exercises its constitutional competence to 'check' the powers of the elected branches, it would engage in police regardless of how 'strong' or 'weak' (Tushnet 2008) the constitutional framework for its intervention may be. In stable liberal democracies, government will by convention gravitate towards consensual outcomes even if it means accepting interpretations that one or the other branch was originally in disagreement about. And one could well argue that Rancière's police, just like Foucault's apparatuses of security and government (Foucault 2007: 1–27; see also May 2008: 41–42; Baiocchi and Connor 2013), is not unequivocally a 'negative' phenomenon.

However, occasionally a civilized disagreement may grow from simple government into a confrontation that could have the potential of qualifying as politics even in Rancière's specific meaning. An example of this might be the so-called *Belmarsh 9* case (*A v. Secretary of State for the Home Dept* [2004] UKHL 56) where the House of Lords, the UK court of last resort at the time, held under Section 4 of the Human Rights Act 1998 (HRA) that the indefinite detention of foreign prisoners in Belmarsh prison without trial (Section 23 of the Anti-terrorism, Crime and Security Act 2001) was incompatible with Article 14 of the European Convention on Human Rights. While the UK government acknowledged the court's declaration of incompatibility by amending the situation with new legislation (Prevention of Terrorism Act 2005) – and this would be an example of how disagreements tend to defuse themselves and to be reincorporated back into the consensual order of police – it also triggered a heated discussion about whether the powers of the courts had grown beyond what was conceived as constitutionally acceptable (see Malleson 2007). For one thing, the case dealt specifically with the inequality between terrorism suspects based on nationality that the 2001 legislation had introduced – though an allusion here to Rancière's notion of equality would be a bit of a stretch. But more importantly, the intervention of the judiciary advocating the Convention rights of those 'miscounted' as 'foreign terrorism suspects' – and not as equal participants in social life – disrupted the established order in which the courts were expected to simply accept their restrained role in liberal democracy. The same discussion concerning the role of the judiciary continues after the 2015 elections when the conservative government reaffirmed its intention to repeal the HRA and to distance the British constitution from European human rights mechanisms (on the plans, see Horne and Miller 2015; for analysis, see Dimelow and Young 2015). After the 2016 referendum the situation is, of course, even more volatile.

Many of Rancière's examples would seem to imply that 'dissensual' political action can only come about in rare and extraordinary circumstances, and the illustrations that he uses are often 'heroic' in nature (e.g., the case of Auguste Blanqui, Rancière 1999: 37–38). As Samuel Chambers asks: 'If all we take from Rancière are rare and beautiful political moments, which are easily boiled down to revolutionary moments, then how do we orient thinking or action within the realm of police orders that are our lives?' (Chambers 2011: 21; see also Chambers 2013: 65–87). It may well be that all politics can do is reveal, for a passing ephemeral moment, the true nature of the order under which we all live. This position is, of course, very different to Schmitt's political ontology. Even if the essentially antagonistic nature of political life has been pacified in liberalism, for Schmitt the individual events that interrupt the monotony of government as sovereign and exceptional gestures serve as abrupt reminders of that ontology. In *Constitutional Theory*, Schmitt uses the somewhat plausible example of a head-of-state who prematurely dissolves a squabbling and inefficient parliament and calls for new elections even in situations when the constitution does not recognize such powers (Schmitt 2008a: 148). Schmitt's more concrete example of Louis-Napoléon Bonaparte's 'exception' during the 1851 *coup d'état* is, perhaps, not as innocent as he would have us believe (e.g., Halsted 1972), but the political existence that these exceptional measures are meant to protect can substantively even be 'democratic' (e.g., Varol 2012). If any entrenched political existence, be it democratic or undemocratic, can be protected in this way, then Schmitt's scheme does, indeed, come across as 'formalistic' in the way in which Rancière's criticism suggests. Nietzsche, who is usually regarded as a slash and burn critic of liberalism, can also argue that even liberal institutions promote freedom. So long as they are being 'fought for', these institutions have entirely different effects than what they would normally have and, consequently, they promote freedom rather than hinder it: '[I]t is the war that produces these effects, the war *for* liberal institutions which, being a war, keeps illiberal institutions in place' (Nietzsche 2005: 213).

In Schmittian terms, this type of struggle *for* liberalism is a reference to the actualized threat of a potential enemy. For Schmitt, the polemical confrontation with the enemy need not actualize. The threat of such a confrontation is enough. In other words, government – or some version of Rancière's police – will, for Schmitt, remain antagonistically political so long as the *potential* threat exists. In Michael Marder's view,

> there is no such thing as an actual political sphere because every sphere is *potentially* political or politicizable due to a possible increase in the intensities of association and dissociation structuring it. The fact of politicization will be retrieved only retrospectively, *a posteriori*, after the interpretive decision on the sphere's transfiguration has been made. That is why no liberal de-politicization can do away entirely with the political, which is not a domain amenable to being supplanted, but the overarching principle of displacement and, hence, the dynamic governing de-politicization as well.
>
> (2010: 65)

Perhaps one would not be too far off the mark to suggest that even Rancière's way of distinguishing between the relative permanence of the police order and the occasional – indeed, rare – interventions of politics could also be seen through a similar scheme of potentiality and actuality. In such a scheme, politics is a possible way in which, for example, the democratic shortcomings of the police order are challenged and possibly even rectified, at least for that brief moment of the intervention itself.

4. Conclusion: the metapolitical necessity

To finally return to the Schmittian argument, what is a political constitution? What makes a constitution political? The reply is fairly self-evident: every constitution is political in Schmitt's meaning of the word. The political characteristics of a constitution reveal themselves in two different ways.

Firstly, in its constitution or its basic law, the subject of the constitution-making power – in our case, 'we the people' – defines its own enemies by providing heightened protection to the institutions and practices that are essential for its political existence of choice. In its simplest form, such heightened protection is provided by entrenchment clauses that either prevent amendments to these institutions and practices or otherwise protect them from change. Heightened protection from legislative amendments is deemed necessary for the very reason that the stability and continuity of these institutions and practices is always at least potentially threatened by 'enemies'. Constitutional protection is always an indication of a threat, because without a threat no entrenchment would even be necessary.[13] Rancière's counterpoint is difficult to fathom because he does not dwell on the possible desired features of one police order or another. But most likely we would be talking about some kind of 'distribution of the sensible' (e.g., Rancière 2004: 15) that has developed to protect one form of democratic existence or another from the threats that may potentially arise. For Rancière, all such arrangements protecting the institutions of political existence are police regimes, regardless of what their perceived 'democratic' advantages may be. This is the problem that Samuel Chambers refers to in the passage quoted earlier. Are all police regimes 'undemocratic'? Or are they each as undemocratic as the other regardless of, for example, how well or poorly they distribute wealth in society? Is all politics necessarily revolutionary politics, and, conversely, does all revolutionary action qualify as politics regardless of the nature of the police order from which they arise and into which they intervene?

Secondly, from time to time the threats, so far acknowledged as only potential, will materialize and become actual. In such cases the subject of constitution-making power – or even a branch of government acting at least nominally on its behalf as the preceding example of the judiciary was intended to illustrate – may reveal itself and exceptionally even violate some individual norm of the constitution in order to secure the continuity of the political existence enshrined in it. It is important to note that this is not a constituted institutional subject such as the 'people', as defined in a constitutional framework but, rather, a presupposed subject – the people 'before and above' the constitution, that can only be identified after the fact: whoever or whatever factually rises to the task. The constitution is violated against at those individual moments of danger, when the residue of constituent power that is dormant in the constituted institutions and practices it has created awakens to protect them. There are limitations to finding a parallel in Rancière's work, even if some secondary literature comes close.[14] For even the most exceptional of Schmitt's constitutional violations aim, in the end, to normalize a given situation and to return to the ordered political existence that was deemed worthy of protection to begin with. The exceptional interruptions to the police order that Rancière qualifies as politics seemingly have but one aim: to reveal and to overturn the very logic on which any police order, democratic or undemocratic, is built. Schmitt's conservatism includes no possibilities for such revolutionary ambitions.

But Schmitt's notion of a political constitution includes a third dimension, one that is seldom mentioned and one that, I would claim, aligns him closer with Rancière than the latter would want to admit. Schmitt continues the passage from *The Concept of the Political* quoted earlier:

> Above all the polemical character determines the use of the word political regardless of whether the adversary is designated as nonpolitical (in the sense of harmless), or vice versa if one wants to disqualify or denounce him as political in order to portray oneself as nonpolitical (in the sense of purely scientific, purely moral, purely juristic, purely aesthetic, purely economic, or on the basis of similar purities) and thereby superior.
>
> (Schmitt 2007a: 31–32)

If, as Schmitt here claims, the polemical character of politics (cf. Fried 2000) concerns academic debates as well – or, in other words, if the property of the 'purely scientific' is merely an attempt to find an appropriate detour around the inevitably political nature of all academic debates – then that same polemic will by necessity inform Schmitt's own academic musings as well, including the allegedly 'conceptual' distinction between friend and enemy that he here puts forward. There are, then, two levels at which Schmitt exercises his own decisionistic polemics. Firstly, this particular 'conceptual' distinction is presented in order to confront some other conceptual definitions of politics that Schmitt sees as threats. The ultimate threat is, of course, a totally depoliticized world (e.g. Schmitt 2007a: 80–96). Any definitions of the political advancing such an existence are his 'enemies'. Secondly, in order for the distinction to perform its polemical task, 'friend' must first be conceptually discerned from and set against 'enemy'. The distinction does not come about itself. It cannot be extracted from some pre-existing scheme of signifying binaries or inferred through the detached observation of social and cultural phenomena. It is, as Derrida notes, an *Entscheidung*, not merely a decision, but a 'determined opposition' or a 'discrimination' (Derrida 1997: 85). In other words, Schmitt must himself *make the distinction* by setting friend against enemy before he can present it as a criterion for the political. Making such a distinction is, in Rancière's 'methodological' terms, a 'polemical intervention' (Rancière 2009; see also Müller 1999) into the world that Schmitt wants to protect from the dangers of depoliticization. By making the distinction as a 'polemical intervention', *The Concept of the Political* also confirms the identity of its own enemies. And especially in terms of Schmitt's constitutional theory, those enemies are rather easy to identify. To paraphrase Schmitt himself, the notion of a 'political constitution' would be incomprehensible unless one knows who it is targeted at.

The Concept of the Political is, namely, a *metapolitical theory*, a *political theory of the political* in the same way as Rancière's 'political theory'. This will require some justification, as Rancière uses the term 'metapolitics' to specifically distance himself from a particular tradition in political philosophy, a tradition typically exemplified by Marxism (Rancière 1999: 61–93; see also Bosteels 2010; Bosteels 2011: 20–25). For Rancière, metapolitics is an approach to political phenomena that performs a double-sleight-of-hand, if you will. On the one hand, it takes existing political practices for illusions that merely serve to obscure a political 'truth' as, for example, the institutions of liberal democracy do to the relations of production in the Marxist account of capitalist economies. And yet, at the same time, this 'truth' will always remain *beyond* politics, an inoperable complement to the struggles that it is meant to stand for. This is what Rancière means by metapolitics. By contrast, Alain Badiou uses the term to equate politics and thinking in that 'every philosophy is conditioned by a real politics' (Badiou 2011: 16) and, conversely, that 'politics itself is, in its being, in its doing, a thought' (Badiou 2011: 24). It is in this latter sense attributed to Badiou that I use the term 'metapolitical necessity' here.

When making its central claims, Schmitt's theory must itself make a similar distinction between friend and enemy as it claims all things political to require (see also Schmitt 2008a: 112–113). Such a distinction is always entwined in the act of 'distincting', of 'discerning' in the sense of *krinein* and *krisis*, of the Heideggerian notion of 'de-ciding' or '*ent-scheiden*' (see Heidegger 2012: 69–81).[15] The same 'metapolitical necessity' informs Schmitt's constitutional theory, as well: it is a political theory about a political phenomenon. Its enemies are, in the first instance, its positivistic public law counterparts (generally, see Stolleis 2004), not because they are 'wrong' in some epistemological meaning of the word, but because their blanched or even non-existent polemical binaries are a threat to all political existence:

> Nobody can valuate without devaluating, revaluating, and serving one's interests. Whoever sets a value, takes position against a disvalue by that very action. The boundless tolerance and the neutrality of the standpoints and viewpoints turn themselves very quickly into their opposite, into enmity, as soon as the enforcement is carried out in earnest. The valuation pressure of the value is irresistible, and the conflict of the valuator, devaluator, revaluator, and implementor, inevitable.
>
> (Schmitt 1996: 23)

In a similar way, Rancière's distinction between politics and police is in itself 'always already' political because it can only come about through a 'polemical intervention' that must precede the distinction itself. The distinction or, rather, the intervention through which the distinction has been introduced into the world mimics the same intrusions that characterize the 'heroic' examples of Rancière's politics. Rancière's reluctance to define his own work as political philosophy or political theory, his own evasive 'rationality of disagreement', will also allow him to resist this 'metapolitical necessity'. But only to a certain point. It would, namely, be fairly simple to show how the interrelated logics of police and politics run the risk of falling into the same metapolitical trap that Rancière identified in Marxism, or at least into a 'quasi-metapolitical supra-politics' to use Suhail Malik's somewhat complex expression (Malik and Phillips 2011: 122). But my claim here is, rather, that Rancière's exposition, just like Schmitt's, is metapolitical in Badiou's meaning of the term. The position from which Rancière observes and analyzes the world of politics, be that position philosophical, theoretical, or any other 'named' position that he himself has either endorsed or refuted, is necessarily interwoven into the political phenomena that are being observed, analyzed, and explained. The political actor that identifies himself as 'Rancière' is politically embedded in the world in which he 'thinks'.

Rancière's criticism of Schmitt's 'formalism' is, then, not entirely genuine. Schmitt may well attempt to cloak his polemics in the seemingly formal language of German public law conceptualism, but in the end that formalism is mostly used as a means to identify and to engage with a very specific enemy, that is, a particular tradition of public law scholarship. Formalism is, in other words, the common ground that Schmitt needs in order to confront his enemy tête-à-tête. But Schmitt's metapolitics is in no way intended to stop at mere forms. He has a clear conservative agenda that he subsequently furthers by polemically identifying his enemy. Rancière's 'polemical interventions', on the other hand, identify a very different enemy, but they identify one nonetheless:

> For me, the fundamental question is to explore the possibility of maintaining spaces of play. To discover how to produce forms for the presentation of objects, forms for the organization of spaces, that thwart expectations. The main enemy of artistic creativity as well as of political creativity is consensus – that is, inscription within given roles, possibilities, and competences.
>
> (Rancière in Carnevale and Kelsey 2007: 263)

If Schmitt is seeking a 'polemical intervention' with the legal positivism of the *Rechtsstaat*, then perhaps we can shorthand the different expressions that Rancière uses for his enemy as 'political philosophy'. What is common to the two enemies, Schmitt's and Rancière's, is that they both represent an attempt to 'scandalously' expunge the political from the seemingly political phenomena that they claim to be explaining. Similarly, despite all their differences at a more nuanced level, both

Schmitt and Rancière intervene in order to restore the political, or some part of it, by presenting a distinction that will allow us to see a levelled playing field – basically, political liberalism – through an antagonistic scheme.

So Rancière's beef with Schmitt is, I would conclude, substantive or even prescriptive rather than a criticism of formalism per se. As a thinker, Rancière is normatively committed to a particular brand of revolutionary politics, a politics that is incompatible with Schmitt's radical conservatism. But both identify their commitments through an 'enemy'. Perhaps Rancière does see Schmitt merely as the intellectual herald of the *Nouvelle Droite* despite the alternative French lineages and wishes to keep his distance accordingly. This would explain why, as Samuel Chambers correctly notes, Mouffe's democratic 'mobilization' of Schmitt provides a much better comparison with Rancière than Schmitt himself ever would (Chambers 2013: 174). But as 'sons of Ares', both Schmitt and Rancière intervene into a world where the antagonistic relations that are necessary for politics are in danger of collapsing. Both do so with a 'polemical intervention' which discerns the distinction that each respectively then uses to identify an enemy.

Notes

1 The English 'enlarged edition' of Schmitt's essay also includes Strauss's 1932 'Notes' as an annex (Schmitt 2007a: 97–122; see also Keedus 2015: 79–80).

2 Ares, son of Zeus, the Greek god of war: 'You are most hated to me of the Gods who inhabit Olympos. Always dear to you are strife and war and battles' (Homer 2013: 157, book 5 lines 900–902, spoken by Zeus).

3 Of particular interest in this respect is the correspondence that preceded Kojève's 1957 seminar visit to Düsseldorf at Schmitt's invitation (Kojève and Schmitt 2001; see also Kojève 2000: 134–135).

4 Schmitt further elaborated on the distinction much later in his *Theory of the Partisan* (Schmitt 2007b), 'radicalized and properly uprooted', as Jacques Derrida would approvingly say (Derrida 1997: 146).

5 '[A]ntagonism is the "constitutive outside" that accompanies the affirmation of all identity' (Laclau 1990: 183).

6 This passage identifying the state as '*der Status schlechthin*' (Schmitt 1991: 20) that has received much attention (e.g., Derrida 1997: 109; Vries 2002: 355) has been omitted from the English edition. Schmitt later introduces a tension between *status* and *kinesis* ('movement') as the twin sides of *stasis* in the 'Postscript' of his final 1970 book *Political Theology II* (Schmitt 2008b: 123).

7 Schmitt's relationship to Nietzsche is clearly an understudied theme (see however McCormick 1997: 83–117; Aydin 2008).

8 This Latin expression is central in the ever-continuing theological disputes about the relationship between Scripture and interpretation (e.g., '*Dei Verbum*' 2014).

9 Levinson and Balkin distinguish a 'constitutional crisis' from an 'emergency' by way of the former's relevance to conflicts about the legitimate use of power. A 'crisis' is not so much about the possible emergency at hand, but rather comes about 'because there is

a dispute between constitutional actors about the nature of the emergency and the legitimate way to respond to it' (Levinson and Balkin 2009: 717).

10 A fitting example of such 'moments' is the election scene in the opening chapters of José Saramago's satirical novel *Seeing* (2006: 1–16; see also Minkkinen 2016).

11 The etymological origins of Rancière's 'police' would merit further investigation as it is not entirely self-evident that it should be associated with law enforcement in any way (on the etymological affinities of 'police' and 'civilization', see Starobinski 1993: 1–35).

12 See also Schaap (2011).

13 This initial decisionistic moment at which a people constitutes the institutions and practices of its own political existence operates in a similar founding-myth-like fashion (see also Salter 2012), as the claim made in the opening chapter of *The Nomos of the Earth* about the first appropriation of land as the 'primeval act' (*Ur-Akt*) of law (Schmitt 2003: 42–49).

14 In, e.g., Gabriel Rockhill's 'Glossary', the 'people' are 'the *political subjects* of *democracy* that supplement the *police* account of the population and displace the established categories of identification' (Rancière 2004: 88). This could well go for one definition of the 'constituent residue'.

15 One of the translators of the first English edition of the *Beiträge* provides a detailed reading of this difficult passage (Maly 2008: 58–65).

Bibliography

Ackerman, B. A. (1991) *We the People, Volume 1: Foundations*, Cambridge: Belknap Press.

Arditi, B. (2008) 'On the Political: Schmitt Contra Schmitt', *Telos*, vol. 2008 no. 142, pp. 7–28.

Arendt, H. ([1951] 1994) *The Origins of Totalitarianism*, new edition with added prefaces, San Diego, New york, London: Harcour Brace Jovanovich.

Aron, R. ([1962] 2003) *Peace and War: A Theory of International Relations*, New Brunswick: Transaction Publishers.

Aydin, C. (2008) 'The Struggle between Ideals: Nietzsche, Schmitt, and Lefort on the Politics of the Future', in Siemens, H. W. and Roodt, V. (eds.) *Nietzsche, Power and Politics: Rethinking Nietzsche's Legacy for Political Thought*, Berlin and New York: De Gruyter, pp. 801–817.

Badiou, A. (2011) *Metapolitics*, translated by J. Barker, London: Verso.

Baiocchi, G. and Connor, B. T. (2013) 'Politics as Interruption: Rancière's Community of Equals and Governmentality', *Thesis Eleven*, vol. 117, no. 1, pp. 89–100.

Bendersky, J. W. (1983) *Carl Schmitt, Theorist for the Reich*, Princeton: Princeton University Press.

Benoist, A. (2003) 'Schmitt in France', *Telos*, vol. 2003, no. 126, pp. 133–152.

Björk, M. (2016) 'Representation and the Unrepresentable: Ernst Jünger, Carl Schmitt, and the Limits of Politics', in Arvidsson, M., Brännström, L. and Minkkinen, P. (eds.) *The Contemporary Relevance of Carl Schmitt: Law, Politics, Theology*, Abingdon: Routledge, pp. 120–133.

Bodin, J. ([1576] 1992) *On Sovereignty*, translated by J. H. Franklin, Cambridge: Cambridge University Press.

Bosteels, B. (2010) 'Archipolitics, Parapolitics, Metapolitics', in Deranty, J.-P. (ed.) *Jacques Rancière: Key Concepts*, Durham: Acumen, pp. 80–92.

Bosteels, B. (2011) *Badiou and Politics*, Durham: Duke University Press.
Braun, K. (2012) 'From the Body of Christ to Racial Homogeneity: Carl Schmitt's Mobilization of "Life" against "the Spirit of Technicity"', *The European Legacy*, vol. 17, no. 1, pp. 1–17.
Carnevale, F. and Kelsey, J. (2007) 'Art of the Possible: Fulvia Carnevale and John Kelsey in Conversation with Jacques Rancière', *Artforum International*, vol. 45, no. 7, pp. 256–269.
Chambers, S. A. (2011) 'The Politics of the Police: From Neoliberalism to Anarchism, and Back to Democracy', in Bowman, P. and Stamp, R. (eds.) *Reading Rancière*, London: Continuum, pp. 18–43.
Chambers, S. A. (2013) *The Lessons of Rancière*, Oxford: Oxford University Press.
Cusa, N. ([1440] 2013) *De docta ignorantia/Die belehrte Unwissenheit, Buch II. Lateinisch – Deutsch*, Dritte Aufl, translated by H. G. Senger, Hamburg: Meiner.
Deranty, J.-P. (2003) 'Rancière and Contemporary Political Ontology', *Theory and Event*, vol. 6, no. 4. Available: https://muse.jhu.edu/article/44780 [8 June 2017].
Derrida, J. (1997) *Politics of Friendship*, translated by G. Collins, London: Verso.
Derrida, J. (2002) *Negotiations, Interventions and Interviews, 1971–2001*, translated by E. Rothenberg, Stanford: Stanford University Press.
Dimelow, S. and Young, A. L. (2015) *"Common Sense" or Confusion? The Human Rights Act and the Conservative Party*, London: The Constitution Society.
Foucault, M. (1995) *Discipline and Punish: The Birth of the Prison*, 2nd edition, translated by A. Sheridan, New York: Vintage.
Foucault, M. (2007) *Security, Territory, Population: Lectures at the Collège de France, 1977–1978*, translated by G. Burchell, Basingstoke: Palgrave Macmillan.
Frank, J. (2010) *Constitutent Moments: Enacting the People in Postrevolutionary America*, Durham: Duke University Press.
Freund, J. (1995) 'Schmitt's Political Thought', *Telos*, vol. 1995, no. 102, pp. 11–42.
Freund, J. ([1965] 2003) *L'Essence du politique*, Paris: Dalloz.
Fried, G. (2000) *Heidegger's Polemos: From Being to Politics*, New Haven: Yale University Press.
Geroulanos, S. (2011) 'Heterogeneities, Slave-Princes, and Marshall Plans: Schmitt's Reception in Hegel's France', *Modern Intellectual History*, vol. 8, no. 3, pp. 531–560.
Gross, R. (2007) *Carl Schmitt and the Jews: The "Jewish Question", the Holocaust, and German Legal Theory*, translated by J. Golb, Madison: University of Wisconsin Press.
Halsted, J. B. (ed.) (1972) *December 2, 1851: Contemporary Writings on the Coup d'État of Louis Napoleon*, Garden City: Anchor Books.
Heidegger, M. ([1936–1938] 2012) *Contributions to Philosophy (Of the Event)*, translated by R. Rojcewicz and D. Vallega-Neu, Bloomington and Indianapolis: Indiana University Press.
Homer (2013) *The Iliad*, translated by B. P. Powell, Oxford: Oxford University Press.
Horne, A. and Miller, V. (2015) *A British Bill of Rights? Briefing Paper, Number 7193, 19 May 2015*, London: House of Commons Library.
Keedus, L. (2015) *The Crisis of German Historicism: The Early Political Thought of Hannah Arendt and Leo Strauss*, Cambridge: Cambridge University Press.
Kennedy, E. (2004) *Constitutional Failure: Carl Schmitt in Weimar*, Durham: Duke University Press.
Kojève, A. ([1943] 2000) *Outline of a Phenomenology of Right*, translated by B.-P. Frost and R. Howse, Lanham: Rowman & Littlefield.
Kojève, A. and Schmitt, C. (2001) 'Alexander Kojève: Carl Schmitt Correspondence and Alexandre Kojève, "Colonialism from a European Perspective"', *Interpretation*, vol. 29, no. 1, pp. 91–130.

Laclau, E. (1990) *New Reflections on the Revolution of Our Time*, London: Verso.
Levinson, S. and Balkin, J. M. (2009) 'Constitutional Crises', *University of Pennsylvania Law Review*, vol. 157, no. 3, 707–753.
Loughlin, M. and Walker, N. (eds.) (2007) *The Paradox of Constitutionalism: Constituent Power and Constitutional Form*, Oxford: Oxford University Press.
Malik, S. and Phillips, A. (2011) 'The Wrong of Contemporary Art: Aesthetics and Political Indeterminacy', in Bowman, P. and Stamp, R. (eds.) *Reading Rancière*, London: Continuum, pp. 111–128.
Malleson, K. (2007) 'Judicial Reform: The Emergence of the Third Branch of Government', in McDonald, A. (ed.) *Reinventing Britain: Constitutional Change under New Labour*, Berkeley: University of California Press, pp. 133–150.
Maly, K. (2008) *Heidegger's Possibility: Language, Emergence – Saying Be-ing*, Toronto and London: University of Toronto Press.
Marder, M. (2010) *Groundless Existence: The Political Ontology of Carl Schmitt*, London: Continuum.
May, T. (2008) *The Political Thought of Jacques Rancière: Creating Equality*, Edinburgh: Edinburgh University Press.
May, T. (2010) *Contemporary Political Movements and the Thought of Jacques Rancière: Equality in Action*, Edinburgh: Edinburgh University Press.
McCormick, J. P. (1997) *Carl Schmitt's Critique of Liberalism: Against Politics as Technology*, Cambridge: Cambridge University Press.
Meier, H. (1995) *Carl Schmitt and Leo Strauss: The Hidden Dialogue*, translated by J. H. Lomax, Chicago: University of Chicago Press.
Minkkinen, P. (2013) 'Political Constitutionalism versus Political Constitutional Theory: Law, Power and Politics', *International Journal of Constitutional Law*, vol. 11, no. 3, pp. 585–610.
Minkkinen, P. (2016) '"Electoral Shenanigans": The Constituted Electorate, the Constituent People, and the Porous State', in Griffiths, A., Mustasaari, S. and Mäki-Petäjä-Leinonen, A. (eds.) *Subjectivity, Citizenship and Belonging in Law: Identities and Intersections*, Abingdon: Routledge, pp. 72–83.
Mouffe, C. (2005) *On the Political*, Abingdon: Routledge.
Müller, J. (1999) 'Carl Schmitt's Method: Between Ideology, Demonology and Myth', *Journal of Political Ideologies*, vol. 4, no. 1, pp. 61–85.
Nietzsche, F. ([1889] 2005) *The Anti-Christ, Ecce Hommo, Twilight of the Idols, and Other Writings*, translated by J. Norman, Cambridge: Cambridge University Press.
Pankakoski, T. (2010) 'Conflict, Context, Concreteness: Koselleck and Schmitt on Concepts', *Political Theory*, vol. 38, no. 6, pp. 749–779.
Rancière, J. (1999) *Disagreement: Politics and Philosophy*, translated by J. Rose, Minneapolis: University of Minnesota Press.
Rancière, J. (2004) *The Politics of Aesthetics: The Distribution of the Sensible*, translated by G. Rockhill, London: Continuum.
Rancière, J. (2007) *On the Shores of Politics*, translated by L. Heron, London: Verso.
Rancière, J. (2010) *Dissensus: On Politics and Aesthetics*, translated by S. Corcoran, London: Continuum.
Rancière, J. (2011) 'The Thinking of Dissensus: Politics and Aesthetics', in Bowman, P. and Stamp, R. (eds.) *Reading Rancière*, London: Continuum, pp 1–17.
Rancière, J. and Nash, K. (1996) 'Post-Democracy, Politics and Philosophy: An Interview with Jacques Rancière', *Angelaki*, vol. 1, no. 3, pp. 171–178.

Raynaud, P. (2014) 'Raymond Aron lecteur de Carl Schmitt', *Commentaire*, vol. 148, no. 4, pp. 813–818.

Salter, M. (2012) *Carl Schmitt: Law as Politics, Ideology and Strategic Myth*, Abingdon: Routledge.

Saramago, J. (2006) *Seeing*, translated by M. J. Costa, London: Harvill Secker.

Schaap, A. (2011) 'Enacting the Right to Have Rights: Jacques Rancière's Critique of Hannah Arendt', *European Journal of Political Theory*, vol. 10, no. 1, pp. 22–45.

Schmitt, C. ([1927–1932] 1991) *Der Begriff des Politischen: Text von 1932 mit eimen Vorwort und drei Corollarien*, 3. Aufl. der Ausbage von 1963, Berlin: Duncker & Humblot.

Schmitt, C. ([1967] 1996) *The Tyranny of Values*, translated by S. Draghici, Washington, DC: Plutarch Press.

Schmitt, C. ([1950] 2003) *The Nomos of the Earth in the International Law of the Jus Publicum Europaeum*, translated by G. L. Ulmen, New York: Telos Press.

Schmitt, C. ([1927–1932] 2007a) *The Concept of the Political*, exp. edition, translated by G. Schwab, Chicago: Unviersity of Chicago Press.

Schmitt, C. ([1963] 2007b) *Theory of the Partisan: Intermediate Commentary on the Concept of the Political*, translated by G. L. Ulmen, New York: Telos Press.

Schmitt, C. ([1928] 2008a) *Constitutional Theory*, translated by J. Seitzer, Durham: Duke University Press.

Schmitt, C. ([1970] 2008b) *Political Theology II: The Myth of the Closure of Any Political Theology*, translated by M. Hoelzl and G. Ward, Cambridge: Polity.

Second Vatican Council (2014) *Dei Verbum: Dogmatic Constitution on Divine Revelation. Promulgated by His Holiness Pope Paul VI on November 18, 1965*, Vatican City: The Vatican Publishing House.

Sieyès, E.-J. ([1789] 2003) *Political Writings: Including the Debate between Sieyès and Tom Paine in 1791*, translated by M. Sonenscher, Indianapolis: Hackett Publishing.

Starobinski, J. (1993) *Blessings in Disguise, or: The Mortality of Evil*, translated by A. Goldhammer, Cambridge: Harvard University Press.

Steinmetz-Jenkins, D. (2016) 'Plettenberg Not Paris: Julien Freund, the New Right and France's Liberal Moment', in Stewart, I. and Sawyer, S. W. (eds.) *In Search of the Liberal Moment: Democracy, Anti-Totalitarianism and Intellectual Politics in France Since 1950*, Basingstoke: Palgrave Macmillan, pp. 39–59.

Stolleis, M. (2004) *A History of Public Law in Germany, 1914–1945*, translated by T. Dunlap, Oxford: Oxford University Press.

Tushnet, M. (2008) *Weak Courts, Strong Rights: Judicial Review and Social Welfare Rights in Comparative Constitutional Law*, Princeton: Princeton University Press.

Ulmen, G. L. (1985) 'The Sociology of the State: Carl Schmitt and Max Weber', *State, Culture and Society*, vol. 1, no. 2, pp. 3–57.

Varol, O. O. (2012) 'The Democratic Coup d'État', *Harvard International Law Journal*, vol. 53, no. 2, pp. 292–356.

Vinx, L. (ed.) (2015) *The Guardian of the Constitution: Hans Kelsen and Carl Schmitt on the Limits of Constitutional Law*, translated by L. Vinx, Cambridge: Cambridge University Press.

Vries, H. (2002) *Religion and Violence: Philosophical Perspectives from Kant to Derrida*, Baltimore: Johns Hopkins University Press.

Woods, R. (1996) *The Conservative Revolution in the Weimar Republic*, Basingstoke: Palgrave Macmillan.

Part IV

Law and aesthetics

Chapter 7

Undoing law

Public art as contest over meanings

Petr Agha

This chapter explores the relationship of symbolic, performative, and discursive exchange in the public sphere and the effect it has on the practices and processes of cultural and legal signification. We shall consider the mutually interdependent relationality between law and (public) art, understood as a contest over meanings, modes of interpretation, and knowledge-production, with an eye to examining how artistic activities contribute to ongoing legal, political, and cultural discussions in society. This chapter will in particular consider whether and how street art, graffiti art, and performance art can produce new concepts and ideas, and whether they are able to re-shape existing symbolic, legal, and political boundaries by first producing new (symbolic) spaces and secondly reinterpreting existing ones. While 'monumental art', the kind we encounter in public streets and plazas of cities, is a key pillar of maintaining the existing order, 'street art' may provide unusually powerful challenges to these dominant ideological forms. Art in public space therefore plays a double role – in terms of both domination and emancipation. These networks of cultural patterns, spatial arrangements, and aesthetic and democratic imagination consequently provide the coding for legal and political reality. Artistic activities become co-creators of legal and political reality and by extension the expressive material of art becomes a creative part of the law. Street artists have the capacity to re-imagine public space by populating it with images and instances of rupture. If we link aesthetics with debates in law, a much richer and more substantial base for thinking about the law emerges. What I aim to do here is to chart some of the parameters within which this kind of work might be undertaken. The question we will ask in different forms is this: How do a couple of lines sprayed in the shape of, for example, a heart across a wall have the power to change our perception of the world we live in?

This chapter will look at the role that artworks placed within a certain context in public space can contribute to ongoing legal, political, and cultural discussions in society. Firstly, it will juxtapose the character and role of official art, namely so-called monuments, with artworks which populate public space spontaneously, un-commissioned and sometimes even un-wanted, that we generally call street art and use the example of the so-called Lennon Wall to illustrate the different effects these artworks may have. We will than examine Rancière's distinction between the order of the police and politics in order to further see if and how the presence of street art can influence public debate. This distinction, together with the story of the Lennon Wall, will navigate our thoughts on the role of art in ongoing legal, political, and cultural discussions in society as well as providing reflections on the existing distribution of places, meanings, and identities. Rancière's analysis of the role of spectators in receiving and decoding the message of the artist will serve as the crux of our analysis of the possible effect of art on the legal world.

1. The paradox of monuments and the ephemeral nature of street art

In his famous essay, 'Monuments', Robert Musil describes monuments as often 'invisible' and 'impregnated with something that repels attention'. Something paradoxical resides in his aphorism 'there is nothing in the world as invisible as monuments' (Musil 1987: 61). The job of monuments, according to Musil, has always been to 'grab our attention and give our feelings a pious direction; and at this their main business monuments fail always' (Ibid.: 62). Indeed, not only do monuments fail to achieve this, but they also eventually become unnoticeable or even 'gaze-repellent'. The invisibility of large artworks in public space is, according to Musil, caused by their failure to gain attention from their prospective audience, despite their size and prominent positioning in public space. In other words, all material artwork or any sort of presence in public space requires a spectator, someone who engages with its presence; otherwise it becomes invisible (Rancière 2009a: 8). The most important quality of monuments, according to Musil, and for the purposes of this chapter, is that monuments are primarily an assigned place of memory or dominant narrative, made and installed to occupy the public space of a city and to direct our imagination. They are imposed in an attempt to restore traditional hierarchies and return things to their officially authorized place (Rancière 2002: 140).

Street art consists, very much like monuments, of artwork placed within a certain context in public space. However it differs from official art, as represented, for example, by monuments, in many important respects. The first of these is that, unlike official art, which tends to co-opt, impose, or even take over the surrounding space and its symbolic economy, street art is much less ambitious in its projected impact and scope. Secondly, street art is art which is produced without the consent of either the property owner or even the audience which will be confronted with its presence. This is an important quality, given the fact that art sponsored by public money often depends on the consent of those who commission it – the message, form, and location are all largely pre-determined and reflect dominant narratives. Street art, on the other hand, typically ignores, disregards, or defies such sentiments and regulations. Thirdly, street art does not come as a permanent installation. This adds to its temporal, immediate, and ephemeral nature – a direct result of its un-commissioned and often provocative nature. Related to this is yet another key feature which effectively sets street art apart from other forms of art present in public space, namely that it may be changed and altered beyond the control of the artist , not merely removed by authorities but painted over by other artworks or altered or even co-opted and included with other artworks which appear later.

In order to illustrate how street art differs from monuments and monumental art in its effect on public space and, by extension, public discourse and imagination, we will follow the story of the so-called Lennon Wall in downtown Prague, located on the opposite side of the River Vltava, on the cobbled Wallenstein Square, one of the loveliest plazas in downtown Prague. This story will help illustrate how spontaneous artistic activities contribute to ongoing political, cultural, and legal discussions in society and how, unlike monumental art, which tends to impose and solidify particular narratives and modes of legitimation, street art can lend a forum through which different sections of the population can, in many different forms and contexts, spontaneously experience new temporal avenues of imagination and different ways of thinking about the order in place and its legitimacy. In the 1980s, following John Lennon's assassination, this secluded square, home to the now famous wall, across from the French Embassy, became the famous 'Lennon Wall' overnight when it received its first decoration by an unnamed artist who painted an image of John Lennon with Beatles lyrics across the rear flank of the Grand Priory of the Knights of Malta. To the pacifist youth of Central and Eastern Europe during communist rule, Lennon was a symbol of peace and a hero. And since Western images, culture, and symbols were largely banned, the image on the wall was quickly covered over by the police. Suddenly, what was once an ordinary white wall, which stretches approximately 20 metres, standing quietly as a part of the cityscape of downtown Prague, a space along which people moved from one place to another, devoid of meaning or personal connection, quickly became a space for protest against the communist regime, thanks to the painted-over image of John Lennon. The Lennon Wall represented not only a memorial to John Lennon and his ideas for peace, but also a spontaneous monument to free speech and the non-violent rebellion of Czech youth against the regime. This image, despite its short-lived presence, inspired a whole generation of young people as well as a steady stream of graffiti that kept appearing on the wall despite the many efforts of the police. The communist authorities tried every way they could to keep the wall clean either by repainting it or installing surveillance cameras, even an overnight guard. The wall would be filled with graffiti the very next day and continued being covered with quotes, lyrics and graffiti until it gradually became known as a place for anti-communist political graffiti, which neither surveillance cameras nor an overnight guard stationed at the wall could prevent. Slowly, the wall was filled with the feelings and dreams of a generation. The wall became the one place where people in Prague expressed their opinions by graffiti messages and paintings of Lennon along with lyrics of his songs. From that moment onwards, the once ordinary wall became a symbol, a forum, a place of resistance and as such re-established and visibly expressed a relationship between the desires and alternative narratives of a generation within the communist regime and the dominant order, visible in other public 'monumental' spaces, much more visible and imposing.

This example is fitting to identify what happens when a wall is sprayed over with an image, in this case the image of an assassinated musician, a publicly known figure who represented ideals which certain parts of the population could relate to. One such effect is the emergence of this kind of spontaneous art, art through which parts of the population can experience and problematize the existing city, its streets and parks as well as its values. Until the wall was decorated with Lennon's image, it was a place of passage, a wall beside a thoroughfare. The sudden eruption of artworks on this particular wall suggested the existence of an alternative to the straightforward day-to-day role that the wall, as well as the streets connected to it, would normally play (Young 2014). The image of Lennon was surely not an artwork which was well received by all sections of society. Indeed, the same could be said of the many messages related to the symbolic space the painting had created and that their authors tried to communicate. However, by inserting these works directly into the ordinary world of daily lives, the presence of this particular artwork constructed a forum, where, depending on the audience, passers-by might start imagining the world differently, possibly even re-inventing the very place, the wall and the little plaza in the heart of Prague, they would normally just pass through (Rancière 2003: 22; Rancière 1999: 29–30). It generated a certain dissensual discourse, a sense of revolt, the presence of alternative ideas and concepts; it also made visible the rigour with which the police and other state organs tried, unsuccessfully, to subdue the spontaneous emergence of all those many paintings and messages which would keep appearing again and again in the very same place where the original Lennon image was painted.

2. Public space as a place of law

Law is a potent and powerful force active in public space, but still it is only one amongst many others. Law represents the more formal way of managing the boundaries in society: other ways are less formal and less visible but may be even more powerful. The contest over meanings and modes of interpretation between official and un-official narratives in public space is often and on many different levels demarcated and defined by law (different regulations concerning property, freedom of assembly and expression, as well as other norms). Law not only represents but also promotes dominant social norms, other conventions and standards in social behaviour. These shared but informal sets of understandings that underpin legal rules and regulations are embedded in social structures which help in policing these symbolic boundaries of the community. Those same boundaries are held in place by shared expectations, habits, and customs as well as the 'practice' itself and as such help regulate the visibility and speak-ability of certain modes of living and thinking as well as with the consequent distribution and redistribution of spaces, places, and identities. However, the power and immanence of these boundaries, be it official (visible) or unofficial (invisible), lies mostly in how these boundaries are recognized and how they emerge from sustained interaction among individuals. Therefore legal rules and regulations connect to narratives and metaphors we find in public space and that we use to communicate about and describe the world with. Alison Young calls this the 'commons of the image' which provides us with particular visual codes which are linked to particular contexts (Young 2014).

The ongoing interplay between different modes of interpretation, official and un-official narratives in public space, is perhaps best captured by Rancière's influential distinction between *politics* and the *police*, which are two distinct but mutually intertwined categories. The police, for Rancière, signifies what is commonly understood by the term 'politics'.

> Politics is generally seen as the set of procedures whereby the aggregation and consent of collectivities is achieved, the organization of powers, the distribution of places and roles, and the systems of legitimizing this distribution. I propose to give this system of distribution and legitimization another name. I propose to call it the police.
>
> (Rancière 1999: 28)

The logic of the police is therefore to distribute, legitimate, and assign each its proper place. In order to determine where each belongs and to define their share in the common, the police decides how and what part of the common is visible and identifiable as a part, whether or not its speech will be heard as intelligible, meaning that a particular activity is visible and another is not, that this particular speech is understood as discourse and another as noise. The police order is based on stability, which captivates the imagination of people and restricts perception to legitimated ways of thinking, speaking, seeing, and being. It is a 'system of self-evident facts of perception based on the set horizons and modalities of what is visible and audible as well as what can be said, thought, made or done' (Rancière 2004: 85). It appears as a full, complete, and objective account. The police is perhaps best understood as delimitation of the field of possible sensory experience, the distribution of the sensible (*le partage du sensible*) as Rancière calls it. It is important to highlight that the police is here not understood as some form of repressive force, but rather as 'a form of intervention that prescribes the visible and the invisible, the sayable and the unsayable' (Rancière 1999: 28). Therefore, it first of all organizes and only secondly reproduces a particular distribution of the sensible.

Effectively, the police order creates a configuration where each and everyone have their place; it provides all of us with language, meanings, and symbolic efficiency. This connects with the second prong of Rancière's distinction – politics. Politics is that which disrupts this distribution of the sensible, and thus reconfigures that which is visible and sayable. Politics, in Rancière's understanding 'revolves around what is seen and what can be said about it, around who has the ability to see and the talent to speak, around the properties of spaces and the possibilities of time' (Rancière 2004: 12–13). The small-scale (visual) dialogue we have witnessed on one of the many walls of Prague in 1980s communist Czechoslovakia shows how street art can become a form of dynamic communication, turning once passive recipients into members of the political community, and, in the same vein, providing space for exchange between the order of the police and politics.

The matter of visibility and speak-ability, in other words, that which is able to appear within the configuration of the visible, brings our attention back to the role of street art in the public sphere. Although the police establishes a particular space and forms of visibility (for example in what we have defined as 'monumental art'), street art may actually disrupt these 'ways of doing, ways of seeing and ways of speaking' (Rancière 1999: 29). Street art speaks of alternatives, promises, and expectations but it also speaks of impossibilities, fragmentation, and division. Given its nonlinear and fragmentary form as well as its ephemeral nature, street art is not necessarily representative of any dominant or long-standing narrative that pervades public space, which is why street art may have the ability to bring to the fore a multiplicity of 'other' forms and contents. However, is the ability to represent and make visible the multitude of manifestations of alternatives in public space enough to bring about significant change in the state of affairs? Indeed, in his book *The Right to the City*, Henri Lefebvre remains cautious about the possibilities for transformation that might arise out of different appropriations of space in the city, as he does not believe that such appropriations would coalesce into substantial transformation: 'there are holes and chasms. These voids are not there due to chance. They are the places of the possible. They contain the floating and dispersed elements of the possible, but not the power which could assemble them' (Lefebvre 1996: 156). Rancière, aware of the inherent limitations of street art in achieving long-lasting and profound changes in the deep seated orders that govern public space, is nonetheless convinced of its impact and highlights two moments which show how the presence of street art may have implications on how we perceive the world, despite the limited, multiple and impossible effects of street art. Granted, street art is random, fragmented in both form and in substance, but what it can do is to involve spectators, attract attention, and inspire interaction. As a result, those who happen to interact with such artworks become active translators not just of an isolated artwork (as is often the case in galleries) but of the context in which the artwork is positioned and thus cease to be mere passive recipients and passers-by. Rancière addresses the intuition of Henri Lefebvre by putting forward the ability of random artworks to assemble the many dispersed users of public space into temporary social agents constructing their own realities and meanings and most importantly to involve different segments of the population in re-imagining the space we all share. Public space is therefore no longer just a network of the streets we walk, the walls we pass by, buildings we enter. Public space is transformed and shaped through people's social exchanges, memories, images, and daily use of the material space, scenes and actions that produce, convey, and consume meaning(s).[1] Public space engages its audience by telling different stories. These stories are not one-directional, like 'invisible' monuments, but require the participation of those who happen to pass by. This sphere consists of, and is created out of, myriads of interactions, events, images, rules, norms, procedures, and appearances. Therefore, the multiple manifestations of alternative narratives which we encounter through spontaneous artistic projects not only enable us to observe the different narratives in place and the impact they have. Beside its ability to shed light on the contours of the dominant order, the greatest value of street art perhaps lies in its flexibility, in its immanence and in the way it brings forth, through the cracks, what the official narrative lacks. In other words, it presents passers-by, random spectators, with alternative visions of the common world. However, practices, narratives, and norms are never fixed – they are complex in character, as they are both conditions for installing and maintaining forms of hegemony and for articulations of alternatives and dissenting narratives.

Monuments attempt to dominate the field of discursivity, to arrest the flow of images, ideas and spontaneous open-ended interactions, and to construct a point from which they seek to stabilize the flow that drifts through public space. Graffiti on the wall, on the other hand, has neither permanent visibility nor a known place; instead, it takes many forms and sends different, sometimes contradictory, messages, while together pointing, from its various positions, to the cracks in the official narrative(s), populated by floating elements and the possibility of their articulation by many different and even opposite camps. Street art, by its very presence, therefore, destabilizes hegemonic articulations in place by illustrating and commenting on the nature of public space as well as its dominant frameworks. Varying degrees and intensities of the familiar converge and blur the distribution of the sensible to create a novel experience by highlighting a so far un-seen aspect of the common world. Street art brings to the mix something which Derrida described as the 'aesthetic of the outside' or 'an aesthetic of touching'. This 'affective nature of the spectator's encounter' (Young 2014: 161) invites viewers to engage directly, not just to look or touch but to leave one's own trace, thus breaking the 'law of untouchability' (Derrida 1993). This quality then stands in sharp contrast to the regulated interactions of monuments, which are highly circumscribed and monitored.

Rancière shows how aesthetic protest can create dissensus, or ruptures in common sense, and a gap in the sensible, which works ultimately to show that what we see, according to our usual division of the sensible, could be otherwise – thus demonstrating the contingency of the entire perceptual and conceptual order. In this context, the ambivalence of street art is not to be thrown away, because it seems to escape and open up regulated interactions, represented by monuments, since it is precisely this 'affective nature' of the viewer's encounter with street art which has the capacity to generate (new) meaning(s). In the words of Rancière '[art] reframe[s] the way in which practices, manners of being and modes of feeling and saying are interwoven in a commonsense' (Rancière 2006: np). In the same vein, Rancière opposes the very idea, and sometimes the professed desire, of art to contribute directly to the production of specific effects: 'There is always this idea, this temptation, that art speaks and becomes an action precisely because it is programmed to produce a specific kind of efficiency, but, in my view, what emancipates is precisely the possibility of the reader or the viewer constructing or reconstructing that efficiency himself or herself' (Rancière 2008: 11). Rancière asserts that viewers are not passive and thus do not need to be encouraged to actively engage with a work, as they are already involved in an active process of interpretation (Rancière 2009a: 17ff). This is a material form of active interpretation, a form of engagement, akin to the creative performativity of 'making art', and which verifies: 'the capacity of anonymous people, the capacity that makes everyone equal to everyone else. [This] involves active interpretation and translation – we link what we see to what we have seen and said, done and dreamed' (Rancière 2009a: 17). The affective register which street art brings back to a largely depoliticized public space (Young 2014) presents a disruption with the 'monumental' distribution of public space and demonstrates that what we ordinarily see could be otherwise.

Rancière looks for how such interventions are capable of producing 'an alteration of resemblance' (Rancière 2007a: 6), 'a discrepancy, a dissemblance' (Rancière 2007a: 7). Rancière is not interested in big revolutionary moments involving the masses (Rancière 2009a: 79–80); indeed, his approach is based on little narratives of social history. What is therefore important is how these 'little narratives' can introduce new ideas and images into existing social orders and how these stories can rupture those spaces. The emergence of street art cannot be equated to some kind of radical emancipatory moment which would, by its very existence, change the entire order (*partage du sensible*). If the artist would try to influence the spectator into seeing their work of art in a certain way, this would utterly spoil the moment which is crucial for the spectator's understanding of the role of art: 'Emancipation begins . . . when we understand that viewing is also an action that confirms or modifies this distribution [of the sensible]' (Rancière 2007b: 277) and that 'interpreting the world' is already a means of transforming it, of reconfiguring it' (Rancière 2007b: 277).

However, for Rancière it is not the message of the artist which is the most important effect of street art; the crucial point is that the perceptive order of spectators is reconfigured in order to make sense of the artistic encounter. This relation is characterized more generally by the constant process of both constituting and being constituted by street art, where meanings are interchangeably produced, challenged, and negotiated. The meaning of street art is therefore in continual production: it is constantly generated and re-generated. The public space of plazas, streets, and other parts of the city are therefore fertile grounds for the emergence of multiple unpredictable, fleeting, and polyphonic subjects.

Artistic practices may tentatively help to reconfigure the landscape of the visible, though not in any revolutionary way; what they do instead is to corroborate other actions or contribute to the commencement of certain debates, making visible what was hidden from the public eye, and opening up novel lines of communication and connections. Rancière writes:

> Being a spectator is not some passive condition that we should transform into activity. It is our normal situation. We also learn and teach, act and know, as spectators who all the time link what we see to what we have seen and said, done and dreamed.
>
> (Rancière 2009a: 17)

The moments when ordinary walls painted in white in forgotten squares in Prague are turned into arenas for contestation have the capacity to briefly rupture everyday public space. The public is drawn out of passivity and transformed into active participation, interpreting what is made visible by the intervention of street art. But the activation of the viewer begins when we dismiss the opposition between looking and acting, that is, when we realize that '[w]e all observe, select, compare, interpret and relate what we observe with the many other things we have observed on other stages, in other kind of spaces, and make our own poem with the poem performed in front of us' (Hallward 2006: 115).

Any form of public action necessarily involves an aesthetic dimension in which participants perform and stage their claims; this process of 'staging' political action should not be reduced to occupation of the physical spaces of the city. As Rancière puts it: 'Politics is primarily conflict over the existence of a common stage and over the existence and status of those present on it' (Rancière 1999: 26). No pre-given stage is proper to politics. And yet, political action involves behaving 'as though such a stage existed, as though there were a common world of argument – which is eminently reasonable and eminently unreasonable, eminently wise and resolutely subversive, since such a world does not exist' (Rancière 1999: 52). Therefore any space has the potential to become a stage for politics, because it stages a place for polemics, but for this any (potentially) significant action needs a material 'space of appearance', a place in which acts become present, seen, and heard.

3. Street art, politics, and sense of community

It is the inconsistency of street art and its dependence on interaction with spectators that guarantees the political life of the polis by posing a challenge to common (and institutionalized) assumptions about the sources and production of meaning (and authority). The mode of thinking and imagining brought about by the presence of art in the public domain is linked to a highly specific form of political efficacy: imagination. Imagination becomes the medium that paves the way to the multiplicity and indeterminacy through which we can hold subjective positions and engage in politics. Even though we cannot equate (street) art to politics or place it right in the domain of the political, it nonetheless stimulates the world of politics to be inconsistent and developing, setting up the basic ground where diverse views can be contested – questioning the presumed results and the assumptions on which they are based. Street art is not, and cannot be, either a vehicle or substitute for politics, but it may contribute to attempts at 'switching scene, by passing from the appearances of democracy and the forms of the State to the infra-scene of underground movements and the concrete energies that comprise them' (Rancière 2009b: 33). What this alternative articulation creates is quite simply a common space (albeit only one space amongst many), a particular topography with certain relational arrangements of elements which exist through their reciprocal relational determinations. This is enabled by allowing our various partnerships with things, objects, and space to become a part of our democratic milieu. This newly established structure is only the result of contingent and temporary constructions, and thus always open to contestation and alternative visions.

What street art can do is to take objects, ideas, and images out of their usual constellations and throw them into new ones, all this by connecting the spectator with their immediate surroundings, precisely through the installation of a work of art within ordinary public space. This moment presents to some of its members an alternative account which contests the very notion of existing definitions of the polis, which suddenly, after having interacted with a work of street art, no longer appears as unified and whole. Therefore, in this way, the (artistic) imagination has always moved borders between the political, legal, and social spheres. But even though artistic interventions influence the distribution of the sensible, they do so not because they are in any way superior to any other rationale present in the public domain, but rather because they publicly demonstrate new options for participation. Their performative nature stages polemical scenes, sometimes paradoxical, sometimes contradictory (Rancière 2002). This novel assemblage has the capacity to suspend the ordinary coordinates of existing sensory experience and reframe the network in place. Street artworks allow for re-interpretation of the various elements within the existing distribution of the sensible with which they come into contact. In that way, street art is capable of producing temporary communities of intersubjective encounters from within public space, which allows for diverse subjectivities to emerge (and disappear again). This is why Rancière claims that 'an emancipated community is a community of narrators and translators' (Rancière 2009a: 22). What an encounter with artistic intervention can do is to set up a temporary and spatially defined community of emancipated and equal spectators united by the various effects of street art placed in the public domain. Public space is suddenly invigorated: think about how this once ordinary white-painted wall suddenly becomes a place of revolt and artistic creativity, and as such a forum for the articulation of diverse subjectivities and configurations. These communal spaces are highly polemical and unstable, depending on chance encounters and random interpretations between spectators and objects.

Thanks to the dynamic nature of the space opened up by street art, the community it creates is a '*community structured by disconnection*' (Rancière 2010: 59). Disidentification and the staging of a gap produces a situation which differs from that which has so far been seen, spoken, thought, or sanctioned by the authorities (Rancière 2010). The sudden emergence of street art in the public domain momentarily confronts and, albeit provisionally, replaces the police distribution of order, mostly by creating alternative spaces and inviting spectators to engage and re-configure that very order. This rupture does not break away from the world as it is, creating alternatives detached from the ordinary; rather, it presents us with a juncture, within the existing distribution of the sensible, which makes something visible, makes it heard, and makes it appear differently from the way it previously appeared precisely by having enabled these contact zones between different dynamics, normative systems, and different people (Rancière 2015). Street art does not necessarily bring people together and foster a sense of community; rather, it lays the foundation for a possible rupture, a change in perception. The many messages and paintings on the Lennon Wall did not bring about the fall of the regime or significantly change the atmosphere in society. Nonetheless, it played a vital role, in that the Wall as a form of street art disclosed that the life of the polis is not based on one single principle and therefore cannot be identified with one form of co-existence as expressed in the juridico-political form in place, although it is of course not indifferent to it. In this light, street art can perhaps best be described as some form of supplement which reveals to us the fundamental contingency and indeterminacy of each social order and its unfinished nature (Rancière 1999: 15). The emergence of street art represents one of those points in the political life of the polis where it becomes noticeable that there is no ultimate foundation or legitimacy, and that the order in place relies on nothing else but contingency.

Street art is not capable of producing direct political effects nor is it crucial because of its ability to present to us the structures and conflicts in society. Street art does not bring about solutions, normative frameworks, and new legal regulations; it is, however, capable of providing new configurations of visibility and of seeing, saying, doing, and imagining. The new meaning(s) that come into existence may be divergent not just from the *partage du sensible* but may also differ even from the very work of art that inspired the exchange between various elements and that led to such a change. Even though this process transpires within the existing contours of the distribution of the sensible, connecting its constitutive elements, only in different combination, it still involves a certain level of dis-identification from the *partage du sensible* as well as reflections on the existing distribution of places, meanings, and identities which inspired the emergence of the artwork in the first place. This is enabled by the fact that 'spectators' of artworks are in fact active 'participants', invited to join in by the particular artwork.

4. The politics of artistic practices

Art's legal and political implications, while potentially not insignificant, are ambiguous and fleeting, as it is doubtful whether art can deliver, compel, teach, or make its audiences do anything, since there is no 'straight line between perception, affection, comprehension and action' (Rancière 2009a: 103). However, the interplay between one particular white wall in downtown Prague, which, were it not for the Lennon painting, would have remained one amongst many, and the spontaneous and colourful graffiti, breaking the image of cohesion and unidirectionality of public space as represented by the white wall carrying the message of the status quo, not only inspired the expression of that which remained hidden away but also provided a context, unregulated feedback and commentary. It is along such lines that we have explored Rancière and his ideas and the history of the Lennon Wall in downtown Prague.

Later, after the 1989 Velvet Revolution, the wall became a site for calls to activism worldwide. Over the years, visitors continued to add lyrics from Beatles tracks, messages of love and peace and their own names – the wall has been allowed to thrive, becoming a bloom of colours, shapes, scrawls, and signatures. The original portrait of Lennon is long gone, lost under layer upon layer of spray-paint. In 1998, work on reconstructing the wall covered the political message of the 1980s with a larger cement 'tombstone'. The original stone was replaced by a solid white surface, which was repainted afterwards during an organized painting session by Czech and Western young people. Effectively and quite ironically it slowly morphed into something of a monument, as described by Musil. It received official recognition, the wall was transformed from a spontaneous space into a large plaque, very much akin to any official plaques we come across in cities, installed by the authorities. Gradually the Wall, once filled with anti-communist graffiti, has been not only recognized and co-opted by the authorities, but also by the travel industry, as one of the landmarks of Prague, appearing on many 'must-see' lists for visitors to Prague, not so much a framework for protest any more, but surely a place to scratch the message 'Pepé 4 Bianca, Praha 2015'.

However, on November 17th 2016, on the 25th anniversary of the Velvet Revolution, Prague residents woke up to a very different Lennon Wall than the one they had known since the 1980s – a completely white space, with years of artwork painted over save for bold black text proclaiming (in English), 'Wall Is Over!' A group of students calling themselves Prague Services painted over the famous landmark to make space for the next generation of artists. 'Twenty-five years ago, one big totalitarian wall fell', read a statement. 'Students of art are expressing their commemoration [of 1989] and opening room for new messages of the current generation'. The words 'Wall Is Over!' represented an attempt to move once again from an order bound and preoccupied with matching any given object with its appropriate form and place to a regime that embraces the endless confusion of mutually unintelligible subjects (opposites) otherwise unknown to exist, to make the Wall relevant again as a site of contestation.

Aesthetic practices are, for Rancière, one of the primary means of creating dissensus. Instances of dissensus are moments in which the supposed obviousness of the distribution of bodies, voices, and capacities breaks down. They trouble traditional patterns of assigning meaning to that which appears to our senses. Street art is a rejection of the idea that things have a single and definitive meaning. Art's sensible heterogeneity is what holds out the promise that the sensible more generally can be reconfigured. It is therefore one of the means by which the meanings of an object, a body, a policy or a group of people can be contested. Aesthetic practices are political because they contest, impact, and alter what can be seen and said. In their resistance to simple interpretation, they function as a reproach to the idea that what appears to our senses could ever be supplied with a uniform meaning or constellation in public space.

The once-again white surface of the Lennon Wall suddenly no longer hid, confirmed, and conformed but became a scene against which different ideas could (perhaps) once again find an audience and, more importantly, interact. The emergence of a white wall painted over years of graffiti, which gradually lost its original meaning and became a tourist site, thus once again disconnected the Wall and its legacy from 'the logic of the proper'. Besides, this unexpected occurrence yet again presented a certain challenge in relation to the world of carefully distributed roles and tasks within the order of the community. Because the order of the police denies the existence of alternatives it is important again and again to stage, to construct a scene on which the metaphors of alternative can be played out.

Street art is immensely potent since it breaks with the order (of communication and expression) in place and because it has not been sanctioned by the authorities despite the fact that its message always appears against the background of the order of the police. Nevertheless, dissenting alternatives somehow do not exist outside the order of the police: they always occur within the existing order, represented by streets, plazas, parks, and legal regulations, through a kind of anarchic, free gesture that authorizes itself through its own possibility. Street art creates multiple common stages where dissensus may be played out and temporarily disrupt the established order. These common stages, born out of dissensus, are based not on normative frameworks but is founded upon (visual) uncertainty. Rancière claims that the uncertain reality of art, the shift or transport of meaning that defines metaphor, is an inherent part of every political dispute, where the argument itself bears first of all on the legitimacy or even the reality of one of the fundamental elements that configure the disagreement (its place, its object, its subjects). Art contributes to this by means of metaphors which bring a sense of rupture to the communal world. What are disrupted are not only the power arrangements of the social order, but, even more deeply, the perceptual and epistemic underpinnings of that order, the obviousness and naturalness that attaches to the order. It is also the revelation of the contingency of the entire perceptual and conceptual order in which such arrangements are embedded, the contingency of *le partage du sensible*. Art therefore

> re-frames the world of common experience as the world of a shared impersonal experience. In this way, it aids to help create the fabric of a common experience in which new modes of constructing common objects and new possibilities of subjective enunciation may be developed.
>
> (Rancière 2010: 142)

The condition of heterogeneity or, more precisely, street art's indefiniteness and identifiability, brings a blur of in-distinction to the many seemingly obvious and natural arrangements of the social order. This extends not only to what is counted as visible and say-able, but also to what counts as a proper place for debate. Street art can, by inserting an artwork which interacts with its random audience, create an-other stage for politics, a place which under existing circumstances is seen as unfit or improper. This fluidity of different orders in the public domain is important, as it gives the polis the chance to adapt to, address, and represent the constantly changing nature of such different orders present in society which later find expression in legal norms and regulations. The ability of art to impact the distribution of the sensible stems from the ambiguous and complicated relationship between different orders present in public space. Of course, encounters vary in association, but through the eye of the artist and the spectator, certain relationships within the existing world are revealed. The spectator and the artist are interchangeably the instigator and the receiver of that revelation.

Our daily lives are woven out of these entanglements, through the social interstices they create, and reveal new understandings, raising the awareness of our surroundings. While street artists have varied motivations behind what drives their work, street art tends to invite people to suspend, or at least modulate, their perception of the world by way of creating a dialogue and transactions between people, ideas, and their environments. Through street art, connections among city inhabitants are established, so that no longer is the passer-by detached without a sense of belonging, navigating through their city without meaningful interaction.

Note

1 Lefebvre (1991: 286) writes: 'space is permeated with social relations; it is not only supported by social relations but it is also producing and produced by social relations'.

Bibliography

Derrida, J. (1993) 'Le Toucher: Touch/To Touch Him', *Paragraph: A Journal of Modern Critical Theory*, vol. 16, no. 2, pp. 122–157.

Hallward, P. (2006) 'Staging Equality: On Rancière's Theatrocracy', *New Left Review*, vol. 37, pp. 109–129.

Lefebvre, H. (1991) *The Production of Space*, translated by D. Nicholson-Smith, Oxford: Basil Blackwell.

Lefebvre, H. (1996) 'The Right to the City', in Kofman, E. and Lebas, E. (eds.) *Writings on Cities*, Cambridge, MA: Blackwell Publishers, pp. 147–159.

Musil, R. (1987) *Posthumous Papers of a Living Author*, translated by P. Wortsman, Hygiene, CO: Eridanos Press.

Rancière, J. (1999) *Disagreement: Politics and Philosophy*, Minneapolis: University of Minnesota Press.

Rancière, J. (2002) 'The Aesthetic Revolution and Its Outcomes: Emplotments of Autonomy and Heteronomy', *New Left Review*, vol. 14, March–April, pp. 133–151.

Rancière, J. (2003) 'Ten Theses on Politics', *Theory & Event*, vol. 5, no. 3, pp. 1–16.

Rancière, J. (2004) *The Politics of Aesthetics: The Distribution of the Sensible*, translated by G. Rockhill, London: Continuum.

Rancière, J. (2006) 'The Politics of Aesthetics', *Mute*, [Online]. Available: www.metamute.org/editorial/articles/politics-aesthetics

Rancière, J. (2007a) *The Future of the Image*, translated by G. Elliot, London and New York: Verso.

Rancière, J. (2007b) 'The Emancipated Spectator', *Artforum*, vol. 45, no. 7, pp. 271–281.

Rancière, J. (2008) 'Aesthetics against Incarnation: An Interview by Anne Marie Oliver', *Critical Inquiry*, vol. 35, no. 1, pp. 172–190.

Rancière, J. (2009a) *The Emancipated Spectator*, translated by G. Elliot, London and New York: Verso.
Rancière, J. (2009b) *Aesthetics and Its Discontents*, translated by S. Corcoran, Cambridge and Malden, MA: Polity Press.
Rancière, J. (2010) *Dissensus: On Politics and Aesthetics*, edited and translated by S. Corcoran, London and New York: Continuum.
Rancière, J. (2015) 'The Politics of Art: An Interview with Jacques Rancière', [Online]. Available: www.versobooks.com/blogs/2320-the-politics-of-art-an-interview-with-jacques-ranciere
Young, A. (2014) *Street Art, Public City: Law, Crime and the Urban Imagination*, London: Routledge.

Chapter 8

Representing law 'in' the Holocaust or seeking the unrepresented

Undoing the legacy of Nuremberg

Wayne Morrison[1]

> Early in the Nazi regime, people of *[the civilised world]* came to look upon the Nazi Government as not constituting a legitimate state pursuing the legitimate objectives of a member of the international community. They came to view the Nazis as a band of brigands, set on subverting within Germany every vestige of a rule of law which would entitle an aggregation of people to be looked upon collectively as a member of the family of nations. . . . Once these international brigands, the top leaders of the Nazi party, the S.S., and the Gestapo, had firmly established themselves within Germany by terrorism and crime, they immediately set out on a course of international pillage.
>
> (Report to the President by Mr. Justice Jackson, June 6, 1945)

> Representation is not the act of producing a visible form, but the act of offering an equivalent – something that speech does just as much as photography. The image is not the duplicate of a thing. It is a complex set of relations between the visible and the invisible, the visible and speech, the said and the unsaid. It is not a mere reproduction of what is out there in front of the photographer or the filmmaker. It is always an alteration that occurs in a chain of images which alter it in turn.
>
> (Rancière 2009: 93–94)

1. Introduction: Jackson versus Rancière, locating the politics of representation

When contributors were invited to contribute chapters to this book it was to be entitled 'Rancière and the Possibility of Law'; however the publisher required it to be called 'Rancière and Law', ostensibly to keep it consistent with the other titles in the critical legal thinkers series. In the spirit of Rancière we might all offer ironic smiles at this little skirmish in the politics of representational regimes, perhaps seeing in it an example of how capital provides the public stage for the production and presentation of writing and fashions its price. But to most this will be seen as a minor imposition, a matter of no real concern and common sense would surely dictate that this would pass without any reaction. But, for this chapter in particular it lays out a template for answering the question 'Why Rancière and what does his presence mean for the argument of this chapter?' For, concomitantly as it being a calling in of power, it is an imposition of grammar: the possibility of law becomes law.

A grammar that represents nature itself. For if we have 'law' and not 'the possibility of law' then we reinforce the sense that when there is not law there is not law. This Rancière calls the 'concordance between sense and sense'. At this stage many readers may think we are in the realm of the total banal, of the repetition of the sensible, approaching the nonsensical. Thus this chapter.

My scholarly background is in criminology and jurisprudence. Latterly, I teach a course on Law, Modernity and the Holocaust; in doing this I confuse many for I am not Jewish nor were any of my immediate family displaced persons in World War II. Failing that rationale it is assumed that I am then one of the new disciples of the religion of modern International Criminal Law and see in its spread and growing strength a way of solving many of the ills of the world. When I disavow that role, favouring more that of spectator wishing to arouse a greater critical awareness, questions of where I stand and whom I travel with arise. In this chapter, Rancière does not provide a paradigm, or a methodology, but a presence to accompany engagement, an existential mode of being helping me call into question a major meta narrative of late modernity. Specifically that modern international criminal law – and human rights – is founded on the putting on trial a bunch of criminals, the leading Nazis, that operated in a place where law had ceased to exist, a place which had abandoned modernity andreverted to barbarism and lawlessness, namely Nazi Germany. Moreover, that place and space of lawlessness allowed the holocaust. That representation of a place outside and without law was essential to what, following Rancière, I term a policing action, namely the International Military Tribunal at Nuremberg in 1945–46 and the subsequent trials based on the London/Nuremberg Charter. The concept 'policing action' does not designate simply the process of capturing a set of people, interrogating them, constructing a 'case' for them to answer, and punishing them if found 'guilty', nor their 'disciplining'. It is more than that. It denotes a way of grasping a social totality, a mobilization of words, images, and locations by which and in which they appear as the subjects of that process, in other words the realm of social perception itself – the process by which it appears normal, sensible, and coherently rational to speak in a particular way and in this field to accept their treatment of Nazi 'crimes' and the Nazi 'criminals' as a valid precedent. And on those terms Nuremberg was successful; a fundamental axiom of late modernity is its common sense assumption that progress in international criminal law is founded upon the response to the horrors of WWII and the process of putting twenty-two of the 'major Nazi war criminals' on trial in 1945 at Nuremberg where, in the name of civilization, law came back to remedy the tragedy of a place outside of its domain (e.g., Heller 2011).

This chapter occupies a space between the two quotations I preface my introduction with. The first quote is from a report by Justice Jackson on progress in preparing the trial: the last of the US Supreme Justices to come to legal practice not through university study but apprenticeship, Jackson epitomized a common sense, honourable, pragmatic approach to legal practice and its role in society. His was a stellar legal career: a key figure in Roosevelt's New Deal politics he served as Assistant Attorney General, Solicitor General, then Attorney General and from August 1941 Associate Justice of the Supreme Court. He almost certainly would have been a Democratic candidate for President of the US if Roosevelt had not succeeded in getting the unique third term (owing to the ongoing war) in 1941. His appointment, made in principle by Roosevelt and confirmed by Truman, as Chief Prosecutor of the mooted grand trial of the surviving Nazi leaders was a powerful statement indicating how strongly the US was going to take the prosecution (the outcome of often difficult discussions between the Allies as what to do and whether it was better to simply line up 50,000 Nazis and shoot them). In the event, Jackson travelled between cities, organizing and cajoling; it is no exaggeration to say that first trial at Nuremberg by the International Military Tribunal was in the end Jackson's Nuremberg and it laid out the grounds for all subsequent trials.

Jackson's report lays out the trope of focus, an individualization: we are to view the Nazis as a band of brigands, set on subverting the rule of law. The leaders of the Nazi State are not politicians spearheading a mass political movement but members of a regime that has imposed itself upon the people; the Nazi order was not a legitimate state, every vestige of the rule of law had been destroyed creating a space beyond the family of nations; and as he emphasized in his opening address to the tribunal on November 21, 1945, civilization itself now came to judge and it brought law. That those on trial were criminals and were to be held individually liable, the consequence, as defendant Albert Speer (1970: 513) related, was that the German people were freed of complicity: 'The trial began with the grand, devastating opening address by the chief American prosecutor, Justice Robert H. Jackson. But I took comfort from one sentence in it which accused the defendants of guilt for the regime's crimes, but not the German people'. Jackson's opening address is replayed constantly in law schools today as cutting rhetoric and a great example of 'power' bowing to legal reason.[2]

Described by Sir Norman Birkett, one of the British judges, as 'the greatest trial in history', this was grand theatre; although owing to Jackson's insistence a great deal of time was used up in laboriously reading into the record documentary evidence which was preferred to the unpredictability of direct witness presentations. The use of film was an innovation with the courtroom designed with a central screen where the judges would normally be seated so that films could be shown, two of which made a great impact. In *Nazi Concentration Camps*, screened on day eight, searing images were produced that cut through language and confronted the spectators – all those in the courtroom and as the proceedings themselves were filmed, the 'world' – with images 'entirely new in human experience'. Men and women reduced 'to the condition of hollow-eyed husks or lifeless bodies no more significant than sacks of cordwood' proved 'a revelation of evil and suffering so profound as to force viewers to reconsider their understanding of human nature' (Landsman 2005: 27). Whatever qualms could be held about the technical charges the accused faced, or on the notion that the agreement setting up the Tribunal had made new – international – law that was being applied post facto, this was proof of great crimes, an obvious truth that could not be denied (for discussions on the evidential role of this film see Douglas 2001; Delage 2006; Twist 2005). Similarly *The Nazi Plan*, screened on day seventeen (12 December, 1945), a four-hour film compiled from footage of captured Nazi propaganda and newsreel image and sound recordings, was produced and presented as evidence for the main charge of the trial, namely a common conspiracy to wage aggressive war. Two contrasting but gripping sets of images: 'presented as a self-evident and overwhelming totality' both were not the subject of any form of 'cross-examination' (Landsman 2005: 28).

Instead of cross examination of their human producers in person, the films' status as evidence was achieved through sworn statements as to their manufacture and authorization appearing on screen at the beginning and in the case of the Nazi Plan through the reassurance that the film was edited from the Nazi's own 'propaganda' films and newsreels. *Nazi Concentration Camps* shocks, but it has another function in that we are told it cuts through the slippage of language; it reveals in unquestionable reality what the words 'concentration camp' mean. In *The Nazi Plan* we (are told that we) view the progress of the Nazis from simple rabble-rousers in 1925, through Party gatherings in Nuremberg onto taking power, the use of state power to destroy dissent and finally wage aggressive war. We – the civilized others – are not on screen; we are not present as actors, but are uninvolved spectators agreeing that in our name Jackson and others struggle to bring law to bear and declare that justice will be (and was) done. True, some questioned the trials at the time but while accepting that they were 'victor's justice' it was broadly accepted that this was a great advance in legality. And if during the decades of the cold war it could be thought Nuremberg was 'but a beacon behind us, growing ever fainter' (Best 1984: 26); today a consensus reigns that even allowing for its imperfections it is a shining light. Given that status it seems a betrayal of one's role as a legal professional to question this today, yet Rancière reminds us that such representation as underpinning the 'justice' and law of Nuremberg is not a simple duplicate (civilization–barbarism, law–not law, criminals–passive citizens, and so on), but a set of relations between the visible and the invisible, a construction, involving choices that are always an alteration in the chain of images. In my reading of the tactics of representation at Nuremberg the subsequent politics of legal engagement has been stripped of its core, for we are presented with a subjectification of our task as being servants of (the only) law, law whose identity was reinforced therein. By denying the Nazis 'law' we are offered a politics of uncontested identity, by contrast, for Rancière, 'the channels for political subjectivization are not those of imaginary identification but those of "literary disincorporation"' (Rancière 2006: 39–40). Perhaps nothing so much captures what Rancière has called the distribution of the sensible, in this instance the systems of divisions and boundaries define what is visible and audible about law and the Nazi State, about the unlawfulness of the Holocaust at the Nuremberg trials (for an argument on the trials' relative avoidance of the Holocaust generally see Bloxham 2001). We are presented with a philosophy of order in which the current state of affairs, the regime of Western civilization and imperialism, was to be taken for granted and reinforced; instead of Hitler and the Nazis as political subjects whom themselves challenged the distribution of the sensible, who tore 'law' from our (Western liberal) placement in grammar, they are merely criminals.

My claim herein is simple. Nuremberg was partly a trial of accused, partly a pedagogical lesson, and partly a building of foundations for the future (International Criminal Law); we were to be shocked, treated to 'incredible events' and told they were the result of 'pathological pride, cruelty and lust for power', and that through establishing and punishing as the now recognized 'crime of crimes' – that of waging aggressive war – the trial would make a lasting peace possible. But its real function was to render the modern state system immune from disaster and to reinforce our belief in the civilizing function of law; we were to learn nothing that disrupted our acceptance of the regime of the sensible, of the international elite that governed what Schmitt (2006) was later to call the nomos of the earth. Horror was to be present in courtroom via film, but it was framed in such a form, a process of individuation, that its cause lay somewhere other than where 'we' the civilized could possible inhabit and occasioned by people whose criminality made them devoid of any need to engage with them other than as objects to be corrected.

2. Living in the realm of the sensible: a personal encounter at Nuremberg

'Politics', Rancière defines, 'is an intervention in the visible and the sayable' (2010: 37); it disrupts. Policing, by contrast, is in part where the distribution of the sensible precludes any dissensus; its grip on the personal and the grammar of the 'real' is coextensive.

2015 was the seventieth anniversary of the Nuremberg Trials; as part of its 'celebrations' in November 2015, I participated in the first Conference of the newly established International Nuremberg Academy, an organization dedicated to the recognition of the role of the Nuremberg Trials and advocating their principles as the basis for developing International Criminal Law. The morning session took place in the actual courtroom from 1946, Courtroom 600 of the Palace of Justice; it was a crush, so much so that several people had to be turned away. The introduction was made by Thomas Buergenthal – President of the Academy's Advisory Board, Auschwitz survivor, and former judge of the International Court of Justice; we were thus in the presence of a human figure of victimhood, perseverance, and educated commitment. Professor Leila Sadat immediately followed evoking a martyr-like image of Justice Jackson as unshakable in his passion, commitment and desire to bring the Rule of law.[3] Assembled at this two day conference were a mixture of current judges from the ICC, politicians and individuals who had served as prosecutors or defence (sometimes interchangeably) in various ad hoc tribunals, and young students aspiring to join this new 'vocational field' as Mark Osiel puts it (Osiel 2009: preface). This was a space enthused with idealism and some hope; it was also in Rancière's terms, a heavily policed space: 'an order of bodies that defines the allocation of ways of doing, ways of being, and ways of saying, and sees that those bodies are assigned by name to a particular place and task; it is an order of the visible and the sayable that sees that a particular activity is visible and another is not, that this speech is understood as discourse and another as noise' (Rancière 2006: 40). This was an exercise 'to promote the legitimacy, legality and acceptance of International Criminal law' by judging it in terms of its accordance to the Nuremberg principles; thus I could listen to a former Chief Prosecutor for International Criminal Tribunal for Rwanda (ICTR) describe their attention to equality of arms such that when a lead defence lawyer resigned, the trial was halted for six months to allow a new chief of defence 'to come up to speed'. But that was a time when there were over 100,000 suspected perpetrators in prisons, often in appalling conditions with ten to fifteen dying per day; in the face of which the ICTR selected out a tiny number (charging 93) and for the cost of $2 billion US held trials ultimately sentencing sixty-one, acquitting fourteen, until closing on December 15, 2015.

Both the International Criminal Tribunal for the former Yugoslavia (ICTY) and the ICTR were not located in places where atrocities had taken place; housed in The Hague or in Ashura (Tanzania), they were not accountable to local political and social pressures but were places where representatives of the global elite drew upon Nuremberg to determine principles and standards of judgment. Absent, invisible, are the situated victims, voices, and demands of the locality in which terror had existed. Instead we have a 'consensus' that a tribunal with decorum would best function at a sensible distance from such ghosts, messiness, and confusion; it would be free to allow law to work itself pure. The words of the victims must be placed as evidence in appropriate appearances, witnesses chosen by the prosecution to partake in processes governed by appropriate standards; narratives in which an entitlement to be accepted as a form of international criminal law required conformity to particular principles and modes of appearance.

Now here in November 2015 we celebrated that the foundation for this was the first Nuremberg (absent of course was 'the other Nuremberg', in Tokyo, trials never accepted as fully legitimate by the Japanese where the 'souls' of those executed were in 1978 enshrined in the Yasukuni Shrine along with the two and a half million who had served in the military from 1867 to 1951).

We were participating in a ritual; Courtroom 600 was semi-consecrated on November 21, 2010, as a memorial museum to the trials and the foundation of International Criminal Law. A few of my fellow participants, such as Ambassador Stephen Rapp, had then spoken representing one or other of the Four Main Powers.[4] This was a place of linage with a sense of decorum. There was only a certain time allowed for questions in each session and my own was self-policed, not a confrontation but simply a reminder, by way of empirical contrast to the particular circumstances of the speaker, of the War Crimes Trials in Bangladesh, in which the Nuremberg trials are called forth as reference points of legitimacy but in which the defendants are rendered powerless to speak (Morrison 2017).

Why this ritual of respect, why could I not speak impolitely? We are of course in a certain distribution:

> the distribution of the sensible, the system of self-evident facts of sense perception that simultaneously discloses the existence of something in common and the delimitations that define the respective parts and positions within it. A distribution of the sensible therefore establishes at one and the same time something common that is shared and exclusive parts. This apportionment of parts and positions is based on a distribution of spaces, times, and forms of activity that determines the manner in which something in common lends itself to participation and in what way various individuals have a part in this distribution.
>
> (Rancière 2004: 12)

I should be careful not to confuse as to my thesis; it is not that the ethical burden of response to atrocities should be treated lightly. I have elsewhere been at lengths to agree that in light of the blood soaked in the twentieth century the role of the State requires reflexion and a global criminological ethos that frees criminology from the epistemology of the nation state as its core (Morrison 2006); the comforting meta-narrative is right in part to side with Jackson when in his concluding speech at Nuremberg he put forward a hope for redemption and reinforcement of narratives of rational enlightenment, industrial progress, the growth of humanism and individual freedom, was that at its mid-point – the end of World War II – the victorious allies chose to embrace the rule of law and not arbitrary revenge by subjecting the leading Nazi war criminals to a trial. Subsequently, according to the narrative, although mass killings and genocide have continued, an array of mechanisms (ad hoc tribunals, International Criminal Court, Truth Commissions) and jurisprudence (some from the ICTY, and ICTR) have increased the confidence of an international professional legal elite that impunity is over and that truth will be exposed, while human rights lawyers speak as the conscience of humankind (Osiel 2009). Thus my fellow participants and many others share the hope, even if reality still lags, for global justice and accountability, founded on the 'fact' that Nuremberg chose to combat extreme criminality and lawlessness with a civilized adoption of the rule of law and tempered violence (the sentences ranged from acquittal, through terms of imprisonment to the death penalty). I do not dispute that the trials at Nuremberg laid out important foundational principles (the principle of individual responsibility, the removal of the defence of superior orders, and so forth) but the meta-narrative needs disruption for the juxtaposition of civilization, rule of law on the one side and criminality and lawlessness on the other, is to use a term of in Rancière, a fictionalization of the real that becomes a founding myth of the late modern. The problem is that Nazi exterminatory violence in the case of the Holocaust was not caused by lawlessness but only made possible by law itself. The response to say that the problem was a lack of law is misplaced. The creation of the crime of genocide, for example, restricts response for it, requires that specific 'criminal' conditions are met, when many of the actions that we would like to confront are actually political confrontations – often civil wars – in which the state security forces engage in atrocity. Similarly, the Holocaust: the SD, the SS, the Einsatzgruppe, the Order Police, were security and intelligence forces. To render them criminal organizations makes them acceptable to our response, it detracts from an otherwise complex and multifaceted confrontation in which notions of the sensible and policing would be at stake (and Rancière an invaluable guide). The route to the exterminatory 'final solution' was twisted and contingent but, and in all its manifestations, was constituted by legitimate decrees that became progressively horrifically unjust and barbarous, but even then they were commands from the legitimate ruler installed according to the constitution and whose party (NSDAP) had been open about what it termed the racial and modernist challenges it would combat when in power. How was this effaced?

3. Judicial theatre and the art of representation

Nuremberg, 1945, the Palace of Justice. Ninety per cent of the city may lie in ruins but remarkably the Place of Justice with its attendant prison and the Grand Hotel are almost untouched. Intense, indeed frenzied preparations have been made for trial, involving the condensing of 'German guilt . . . into a set of indictments reserved exclusively for German Nazis, and then only a select few' (Judt 2000: 296). Nuremberg was chosen as the site of the proceedings because it was the city that the Nazi party had deemed as the most Germanic and Imperial of cities, where from the mid 1920s they gathered as a party for rallies and in 1935 announced the most (in)famous of the Nazi anti-Jewish statutes, the Law for the Protection of German Blood and Honor and the Reich Citizenship Law. To try Nazis at Nuremberg was to counter the power of those spectacles with one honouring the rule of law.

November 20, 1945, the defendants file in and take their place, some have never met before, they sit cautiously looking around and then relax as they understand that day one will consist solely in the reading of the indictment, day two is when all the newsreel coverage begins to cover; Universal newsreel of 1945/11/29 labels this 'the prosecution of the terrorists of the Nazi War Machine', begins a scanning of the defendants faces to reveal 'the arrogance with which the German war lords meet the charges of criminal injustice to civilised people'.

As Lead Prosecutor Jackson speaks for most of the day referring to the defendants as 'the Nazi conspirators'; Jackson is conscious that the appearance of the men in the dock cannot equal the gravity of the crimes outlined in the indictment. Thus he points to 'the prisoners' dock' where sit 'twenty-odd broken men . . . their personal capacity for evil is forever past. It is hard now to perceive in these men as captives the power by which as Nazi leaders they once dominated much of the world and terrified most of it'. He strives to reconcile his claim that it is not 'as individuals' the court is concerned with them for they 'represent sinister influences that will lurk in the world long after their bodies have returned to dust' with his stress on individual responsibility. 'Tenderness' towards them would be wrong, as 'civilization can afford no compromise with the social forces which would gain renewed strength if we deal ambiguously or indecisively with the men in whom those forces now precariously survive'. There is, of course, a key figure missing – Hitler – but he is evoked through the acknowledgment of the Fuhrerprinzip (leadership principle or rule by commands of the Fuher as representative of the people), which Jackson denies any jurisprudential ontology, instead calling it 'a National Socialist despotism equalled only by the dynasties of the ancient East' (Trials 2: 99–100ff.).

But for all this evocation spectators quickly disassociate the presentation of the accused and the enormity of the crimes: the haggard old men do not match the magnificence of the rhetorical portrayal as the crimes. Additionally, Jackson's strategy for proof, namely to rely upon German records and documentation and not to call many human witnesses, soon becomes boring. Rebecca West, reporting on proceedings for the New Yorker, labels it 'a citadel of boredom', boredom on huge historical scale . . . however much a man loved the law he could not love so much of it as wound its sluggish way through the Palace of Justice at Nuremberg' (West 1955: 11, 17).

As a spectacle and as a presentation of 'Justice' the trial was already in trouble – the defendants looked increasingly at ease; Goering in particular, now seen as the 'leading Nazi', with his dependency on painkillers lessened and losing weight, seemed to be almost enjoying the situation. On day eight the prosecution abruptly changed tactics and screened the film *Nazi Concentration Camps*; while admitting that this was logically out of place the film was introduced as representing 'in a brief and unforgettable form an explanation of what the words "concentration camp" imply' (Trials 2: 431–2.)

This is a dramatic confrontation: the effect was extreme. Partly in order to break down the layers of meaning in the Nazi documents ('language close woven with lies' as Steiner put it in 1971) much of the iconic imagery we today associate with the result of the Nazi reign is presented. These scenes shock, and a lens was created for viewing the Nazi regime (Hartouni 2012). But already it misleads: we see Buchenwald in particular and Belsen but not Auschwitz, as it was discovered by Soviet troops, and Treblinka had been largely covered over. As a result, the camp system is not differentiated and the particular focus of extermination camps – the industrial killing of the Jews – is missed. In part this is unavoidable: the prosecution is searching for ways in which to package what has happened, but it also reflects Jackson's focus on a claim that the crime of crimes was waging aggressive war and this was a consequence. We have a historically unguided trip into the unspeakable; the visceral horror of such imagery structured much of the early discussion on the Nazi order, working backwards it would seem that no civilized discourse, no element of modernity was present in the Nazi programme, it could only be a reversion to barbarity, of psychotic impulses, or of some radical evil.

This moment of confrontation shocked the defendants, as did in another way the testimony of Otto Ohlendorf in early January. Ohlendorf seemed a man of honour and of impeccable duty but who openly admitted his role as commander of SS-Einsatzguppen D, a mobile killing squad, that he stated had killed over 90,000 Jews. Not cruelly, he claimed, but in military style with firing squad precision so that no individual soldier knew precisely which Jew he had shot and so suffered less psychological trauma. Ohlendorf was testifying as a prosecution witness but his testimony, regarded as coming from the only person at Nuremberg who told the total truth, was so damming that in turn he was prosecuted in a later trial and executed (see Earl 2009). Ohlendorf had degrees in law and in economics, had lectured Jurisprudence and was a key economic advisor; we now suspect that he had been made commander of an SS-Einsatzguppen in part as a reaction to his complaints on corruption. For him, corruption, the pursuit of personal gain, the basking in indulgence and engagement with luxury, was totally contrary to the Nazi ideal; and whatever his personal qualms as to his Einsatzgruppen task he accepted his orders as valid and performed them impeccably.

His testimony aroused the defendants; there seemed suddenly, and almost accidentally, no escape from confronting the Holocaust. During Ohlendorf's cross examination Speer passed a slip of paper to the defence lawyers claiming to have been part of a plot to have Hitler killed and that he now wished to express again his admission of general guilt. Goering was incensed seeing Ohlendorf's testimony as an act of betrayal made the worse by Speer's reaction of admitting a general guilt (Gilbert 1995: 101–102).

Both the screening of *Nazi Concentration Camps* and Ohlendorf's testimony were, and I use the term 'conscious of its religious origins', acts of revelation, an uncovering or disclosure. In the concentration camp scenes we are in a realm that should not be, these sights should not have been, and this is a place that should not have existed. Given that, it is too easy to say therefore that 'we' could not be there. How did 'they' do this, how did 'they' come to this?

In the blacked out courtroom there is shock and silence, on screen bodies are rendered silent (and thousands of corpses are bulldozed into quickly dug mass graves to prevent disease), yet the film screams . . . this *IS* crime! This is wrong! No one can doubt the ethical appeal and the demand that retribution should be done; but the framed events cannot tell us causation . . . and yet the shock disavows, we cannot but be moved (and so many qualifiers means that qualifiers are rendered redundant); we are in the postmodern before modernity is complete. Almost as a common shared aspect of guilt both the prosecution and the defence had a stake in agreeing those sights were hidden; for the defendants' claim that they only had heard rumours and had no direct knowledge found echoes in the Allies claims elsewhere that they thought accounts were propaganda.

But what role would this play in the trial, what context would be offered? It is instructive that the screening of the *Nazi Concentration Camps* was so powerful that the Court immediately adjourned and there was no discussion of it the next day or thereafter. How it fitted into the overall charge of conspiracy was not a subject of argument. Then on December 11, *The Nazi Plan*, lasting nearly four hours, composed of Nazi newsreel and 'propaganda' film was presented as evidence in the Nazis' own words and images of a grand conspiracy.

The Nazi Plan begins with images of Weimar Germany, but what is signified? Disruption, street clashes, the threat of chaos, the threat of a breaking apart, a release of energy; what is this energy? With the benefit of history, absence is notable; the editors have chosen to narrate focusing only on one identity, the NSDAP (Nazi party) and its leaders, but without putting this into context. Weimar Germany could have been given focus with other bodies on display as in the clubs of Berlin for it was a place of the exhibition of the gay, the decadent, and the ultra-modern. Throughout the Republic, clashes, often violent, ensued. The film reflects a politics of fracture but leaves out a politics of belonging; of belonging to diverse groups and there were places – Berlin notably – where social difference was bridged in various forms of interaction. The Weimar Republic had broken with a hierarchically organized spatiality, resulting in a diversity of spaces, places, individualized, temporal yet also abstract, situating different groups, but groups that had claims of a certain modern universality. Mass culture, mass appeal, but not institutionalized, always with the hint of an opposing clash. Who could negotiate, who was trained for this political epistemology?

The success of Nazism depended on imposing a consensus, fashioning in Schmitt's terms a demos given strength by its homogeneity, a Volk, and a regime of the sensible: if we tremble at the later, almost compulsive, rendition in letters home from the East of the sight of the Jew as repulsive, as parasite, as vermin, we do so in the knowledge that such description is so common as not to need specific quotation. But this reaction – this capturing of the self as reacting to a confrontation and internalizing it as representation – is not spontaneous; it is prepared in the propaganda machines that portray a collective biological domain, with its notion of struggle and injunction to produce the healthiest people in the world.

The largest single source of *The Nazi Plan* is drawn from *Triumph of the Will*, Leni Riefenstahl's film of the 1934 Party Rally at Nuremberg, a full year after the accession to power of the NSDAP. The Nazi party had from the early 1920s conducted party rallies at Nuremberg. These were amateurish and photos from them show the diversity of the people who participated (including veterans from the genocide in German South-West Africa) but they gradually took on precise manufactured form; Leni Riefenstahl had first filmed the 1933 Rally – *Victory of Faith* – in retrospect, a learning experience for her. Before the 1934 Rally Hitler ordered all copies destroyed, for it contained images of now murdered SA leader Ernst Rohm almost as Hitler's equal[5] by 1934 a vast space, an architecture of spectacle, was created and manipulated.

Triumph of the Will is a masterpiece, a thing of terrible beauty and for Allied consumption it was first reduced from 110 minutes to 42 minutes and then intercut for placement in *The Nazi Plan*. Scenes of the preparation of the Rally, where youths are filmed in camp washing and at play, and of citizens of the old medieval town in traditional costume, for example, and generally all 'folkloric' images, were edited out. This was probably because the link between soil, folk tradition, and modern Volk was not appreciated by the external, American, editors. The prosecution team had a tricky balance to achieve: they wanted to bring the enemy face to face with their own images yet the power of *Triumph of the Will* had to be contained (in the event Roosevelt ordered public screenings banned and it has remained so in Germany). As shown at the Military International Tribunal the task was to sidestep the trope that I mostly see in the film, namely 'seduction'. If the film can seduce, show seduction, it is the result of an original seduction; in her memoirs Leni remembers first hearing Hitler speak at the Berlin Sports Palace, February 1932: 'I heard his voice . . . that very same instant I had an almost apocalyptic vision . . . I felt quite paralyzed . . . I was fascinated, and I sensed that the audience were in bondage to this man . . . I was deeply affected' (quoted and analysed in Grenier 1994, n.p). This film, which Riefenstahl claimed was true to the beauty of the occasion, shows not only the grand set piece (the regime as aesthetic) but the organization of architecture of power (or power and order[ing]). We could consider others such as the 11 July 1938 procession of 'Two Thousand Years of German Civilisation' to mark German Art Day or the 9 November 1938 Night of Broken Glass, or the 1937 Nuremberg Rally in The Cathedral of Light, the later prompting the exiled Bertolt Brecht to recognize how Hitler had turned the political into pure theatre.

> his virtuoso use of lighting
> is no different from
> his virtuoso use of the truncheon.
>
> (Spotts 2009: 56)

Triumph of the Will begins with Hitler's plane descending from the clouds over Nuremberg and the words on the screen tell of redemption: 'On September 5, 1934, 20 years after the outbreak of the World War, 16 years after the beginning of our suffering, 19 months after the beginning of Germany's rebirth, Adolf Hitler flew again to Nuremberg to must the columns of his faithful followers' (Riefenstahl 1935). Hitler is in the world, sometimes looking like he has the whole of the world's burden on him, and yet not of it. Along with the introduction to Riefenstahl's film of the 1936 Olympics in Berlin (*Olympia*, Riefenstahl 1938), where classic Greek and Roman statues fuse into images of naked Aryan men and women, we have the thesis that beauty is truth and the ideal is the nomos of an ordered and homogenous social body (individuality is lost, this is the manufacturing of the body politic) with a hierarchy of ordering (expression from the top down). The Nazi State has already declared some anti-Jewish legislation (and at the 1935 Party Rally, the centrepiece will be that the Reichstag had adopted The Law for the Protection of German Blood and Honor, an enactment that began 'Entirely convinced that the purity of German blood is essential to the future existence of the German people'). The new Reich Chancellery entrance will be flanked by Arno Breker's sculptures of 'beautiful bodies', but if Breker's work could be called inherent fantasies of flawless and idealized flesh made stone, while representing (in Alfred Rosenberg's words) the 'mighty momentum and willpower' (Wucht und Willenhaftigkeit) (see generally

Spotts 2009), here, in *Triumph of the Will*, in row after row of marching columns, we have a unifying power, and presentations of eager participation, as with 55,000 bare-topped youths with shovels declaring in unison their willingness to engage in construction projects as called by the Fuhrer (the autobahn, etc.). Susan Sontag calls this fascinating fascism, but perhaps this may also be called luxurious romanticism. The end scenes have Rudolf Hess, hardly able to give a declaration to Hitler for the continuous Sieg Heils from the ecstatic audience, finally managing to exclaim: 'The party is Hitler! Hitler however is Germany, just as Germany is Hitler!' The adoring gaze of the leaders of the Nazi party as Hitler gives his closing address demonstrates that these men felt the weight of history, they knew, they felt, they were a new political elite through whom power flowed. For Browning:

> in retrospect we can see that the inauguration of the final solution in 1941 was a monumental event in history, where old notions of human nature and progress were shattered and mankind passed forever into the post-Auschwitz era . . . we should not be surprised that such an appreciation was lost upon many of the murderers themselves. . . . For Nazi bureaucrats already deeply involved and committed to 'solving the Jewish question', the final step to mass murder was incremental. . . . They had already committed themselves to a political movement, to a career, and to a task.
>
> (Browning 1992: 142–143)

Triumph of the Will is visual jurisprudence; it ties diverse strands and provides reconciliation for many. In the 1930 novel *The Outlaws* (1931 English translation; 1930 German original) , for example, Ernst von Salomon portrayed a group of men, men who had fought and now 'recognised each other by a look, a word, a smile' that they belonged together but not loyal to the (Weimar) Government, its order no longer made sense. Not discharged from the secrets of the war, they were outcasts 'from the world of civil norms', regrouping, seeking 'their own front line'. Unable to participate in the new 'wholesome order' that had been 'praised to them in a slimy way', 'they marched through the land hither and thither', searching.

> Each of them sought something else and gave different reasons for their search; the word had not yet been given to them. They sensed the word, yes, even spoke it out loud and were ashamed of its washed out sound; they turned it over, tested it in secret fear. . . . And yet it stood over them. The word stood wrapped in deep gloom, weather-beaten, beckoning, full of secrets, beaming magical powers, felt and not yet recognised, loved and not yet bidden to them. And the word was Germany.
>
> (Von Salomon 1931: 25)

Now, as Hess pronounces at the end of *Triumph of the Will*, the word was made known, Germany was the Fuhrer and the Fuhrer was Germany. This is the reconciliation, the dreamed of magical, mystical, moment; as Hitler had said at his treason trial in 1924, only to Cleo, the Goddess of History, will he and the party give the right to stand above him and judge.

None of this of course is allowed to be gained from the reconstructed film *The Nazi Plan*.

4. The retort: visuality, the Gorgon and Nazi law

Courtroom 600, Palace of Justice, November 4, 2016: Professor William A. Schabas delivers the keynote address of the Second Conference of the Nuremberg Academy. The conference is rather subdued, several African countries are announcing they will leave the International Criminal Court, but Schabas talks of a bond that unites those who pursue the struggle for International Criminal Law and affirms Courtroom 600 as the place that symbolizes that bond. He recalls the International Military Tribunal and the later Justices trial of the Nuremberg Military Tribunals held in this room and the role of film in the courtroom and the wider role of film of the courtroom, specifically the Academy Award winning *Judgment at Nuremberg* (Stanley Kramer 1961), modelled on the Justices case. His theme is the relationship of law and politics and the fact that such trials are of course political, but a politics of choosing legality (over force and so forth). This is the story of legitimacy based, as per Jackson, on the choice of victors to establish legality, to establish procedures, to set out an operating logic and he looks to a scene from *Judgment at Nuremberg* to make his point. That scene is where the German defence lawyer contends that the defendants were not the only ones who aided, or at least turned a blind eye to, the Nazi order, specifically that the United States did not have clean hands and noted U.S. Supreme Court Justice Oliver Wendell Holmes, Jr's, support for eugenics practices (see *Buck v. Bell*); the German-Vatican Reichskonkordat of 1933 is put forward as evidence that foreign governments recognized the Nazi leadership from the beginning; Stalin's part in the Nazi-Soviet Pact of 1939 meant that Poland was actually divided between Germany and one of the victorious powers of World War II, therefore at least one of the victors was a party to the very 'aggression' that began the war; and should not the atomic bombings of Hiroshima and Nagasaki in the final stage of the war in August 1945 be called crimes? Schabas retorts that such arguments must be rejected, that the narratives that properly infuse a courtroom are those linked to an analysis of causality, responsibility, and the legitimacy of punishing the actual defendants before the court.

I hold my head and close my eyes, for this is what the International Military Tribunal at Nuremberg did; it strove to establish the legitimacy of a new project not so much through a confrontation with the Nazi state as a valid lawful state pursuing a radical (and one may easily say, 'evil') modernity, but by claiming that Nazism was totally devoid of 'civilization' for to quote Jackson again: 'the real complaining party at your bar is Civilization . . . Civilization asks whether law is so laggard as to be utterly helpless to deal with crimes of this magnitude by criminals of this order' (Trial 2:155). This founds the narrative framing of today in which mass atrocities and genocide 'happens "elsewhere" outside the frame of first world interests, activities, and direct responsibilities, in socially, culturally, politically, and fiscally distinct worlds' (Hartouni 2012: 13). These are in Rancière's terms maps of the visible and the sayable. To disrupt seems nihilist but my inner eyes turned to the contemporary British artists the Chapman Brothers and their masterpiece, 'Fucking Hell', the representation of genocide (including the Holocaust) as tens of thousands of plastic toy figures working out untold sadism and all sorts of atrocious intercoupling's and positioning's, replete with Hitler as artist and clowns. The point of that representation is to upset the hopeful narrative that if we see representations of atrocity (Goya, Picasso, etc.) our humanity will move us to prevent future atrocity, for the facts are clearly that we do not. 'Fucking Hell' is 'pure immanence': all of 'civilization' is inside, contributing. Eichmanns as clowns and clowns as *Genocidaires* (for a guide to the Chapman Brothers, see Harris 2010).

There in my mind's eye, in the invisible silence unknown to the policed space of the Courtroom, the Chapman Brothers seek to disrupt all ideas of spheres of autonomy for art, ethics, and politics in constituting (and representing) atrocity, referring constantly to Hitler as artist (one of their schemes was to purchase a set of Hitler's watercolours and add rainbows and so forth under the title 'If Hitler had been a hippy how happy we would be'). When Rancière provides in the concept of aesthetic regime for a role of experiencing art as an experience that disrupts the effects of domination in everyday life, Hitler – as Speer recounts – created a political aesthetics of domination (from the design of uniforms, to the architecture of light shows).[6] In this regime 'law' did not obey one settled regime of the identifiable, thus we can transpose Rancière:

> There are no longer rules of appropriateness between a particular subject and a particular form, but the general availability of all subjects for any artistic form whatsoever. On the other hand, there are certain characters and certain stories that cannot be altered at will, because they are not simply available 'subjects', but founding myth.
>
> (Rancière 2007: 118)

And then I raised my head and opened my eyes and saw it: I saw the Gorgon.

Behind Schabas was a door with a bronze relief sculpture. It denotes the Ten Commandments framed by the Scales of Justice. To the centre is a large Cross, which I discounted, as I knew it had been put in by the Bavarian State Government in the 1960s . . . but looking to the side is the main door, flanked by green marble and above it a large bronze sculpture relief part of the original structure of the room. At the top in the middle is a scene from the Garden of Eden with Adam and Eve where Eve is handing Adam an apple from the tree of knowledge, a young man on the left holds a sword and represents Germanic customary Law, his opposite on the right (holding an object I cannot recognize) represents Roman Law (both sources of 'modern' German law), beneath, in the centre, Medusa with hair of snakes . . . the Gorgon.

I know that Speer, who was a defendant in this room, had commissioned a magnificent desk for Hitler in the centre panel of which was Medusa's head; from 1938 the Gorgon faced anyone who formally encountered Hitler, the Fuhrer and sole source of law, he who was responsible on behalf of the Volk only to his conscience and to history. Primo Levi, another survivor of Auschwitz, knew of the power of the Gorgon (although he had no knowledge of the desk) stated that only those who had seen the Gorgon were the true witnesses. But those who had seen the Gorgon were no more, they had drowned, they were rendered speechless (Levi 1989: 83–84).

So who was left? Who and what could tell the truth of the Holocaust?

There is no set trope of representation; Auschwitz is as truthful or as untruthful as Bernhard Loesner working at his desk drafting the Nuremberg Laws, or Schmitt calmly announcing to a massive conference of lawyers that if the Nuremberg Laws did not solve the Jewish question then the matter could lawfully be transferred to the Party to solve by executive action, or the conference at the classical villa on the banks of the Wannsee, where a group of men, almost half under forty, two-thirds of them with university degrees and half with PhDs in law or economics, smoke and drink calmly agreed to the final solution. All are full of law; the law of the racial state, the police state, the state of 'social protection', the state that reinforced the Volk . . . the state and its laws, its commands that had created the corpses and the shuffling semi-corpses of the Musseleman.

But this law was not called upon: the Gorgon silenced. . . . 'The visible can be arranged in meaningful tropes; words deploy a visibility that can be blinding' (Rancière 2007: 7). To repeat: at Nuremberg the main charge was waging aggressive war (war crimes and crimes against humanity were linked to that central charge) and the main tactic of ensnaring the defendants was a common conspiracy to wage war: but not the 'war against the Jews' as Lucy Dawidowicz terms the Holocaust. The Holocaust began to emerge in film and testimony but no one was charged with it and no one officially punished for it. Conversely it may be accurate to say that the defendants were punished for the Holocaust as the central charge – that of participating in a grand conspiracy to wage aggressive war – was, in the end, outlandish. If *The Nazi Plan* revealed anything it was the reality of the Hitler myth and the Fuhrer Principle.

The Nazi Plan was produced and shown so that 'the enemy's word be heard but also *seen*' (Delage 2014: 124), but contrary to Delage's account, it was not; it was rather an American interpretation that was received. The effect on Goering of the two films is instructive: on the evening of November 29 all the defendants were depressed and shocked by the film apart from Goering who was 'apparently disturbed because it spoilt his show'. The trial had been going over his telephone conversations concerning Austria, 'and everyone was laughing with me. And then they showed that awful film, and it just spoiled everything' (Gilbert 1995: 49). Conversely, when *The Nazi Plan* was shown most of the defendants visibly perked up and Ribbentrop was overwhelmed with memories of Hitler's charisma. Goering stated simply that there was no need to show films or read documents on the rise of the NSDAP as of course he wanted to rearm, he wanted to make Germany great again and if it could be done peaceably so much the better, but if war was inevitable, so be it; the only thing he rejected was the claim that he had given orders for the execution of the atrocities on the Jews, a claim that fell apart when a signed order was produced in court. After Ohlendorf's testimony and coming down from the confrontation with Speer, Goring returned to the legality of the conspiracy charge. 'The whole conspiracy idea is cockeyed anyway. We had a Fuhrerstaat, in the last analysis. We had orders to obey from the Head of the State. We weren't a bunch of criminals meeting in the woods in the dead of night to plan mass murders like figures in a dime novel' (Gilbert 1995: 106).

Today it would be historically inept to claim there was a grand conspiracy to wage aggressive war: events simply took their dialectic course. War could have, and almost certainly would have, been prevented at various places if the French or British had intervened.

Arendt famously wrote to Karl Jaspers that the Nazi crimes, 'explode the limits of the law . . . their guilt, in contrast to all criminal guilt, oversteps and shatters any and all legal systems. That is the reason why the Nazis in Nuremberg are so smug' (cited in Lottee and Saner 1992). No, they were never smug when confronted by references to the Holocaust; they were smug as they knew they were not guilty as charged.

But modern international criminal law is founded upon avoiding the full social and legal geography of Holocaust; which would mean a confrontation between Law and Law and thus we are condemned to miss the essential lawfulness of modern atrocity.

Yes films of (some of) the camps were shown, and yes such images were needed to be shown for they form the unseen 'other' of public life in Nazi Germany . But outside of that frame no inquiry into the language of 'protective custody', work-house labour, dangerous habitual offenders, fundamental battles against criminality, tackling the 'asocials', dealing with the work shy, racial others, racial aliens, living space, Germanization; even in the language of the NMTs of legal repression and legal terror; one should not lose sight of the preface *legal*.

When one confronts the fact that in the Justices trial individuals were found guilty of 'a program of racial extermination under the guise of law', when one reads the documentation one simply finds a positivist stamp of (legal) power that some 'representations' of law are *not* law but the evidence demonstrates overlaps between older practices and new interpretations; but to come to its judgment the court must deny the technicality of the new energized legal policies, the People's community, the Volksgemeinschaft, must treat as of no effect the submersion of the individual into a communal good with individuals only having value as building blocks for the organic whole. To declare a total absence of morality when for the Aryan members of the Volk who would be called to the SS there were real injunctions, work and honour, obedience and loyalty, vigilance and action . . . the aikton, the cleansing . . . the Shoah . . .

So many contributed; those who read the memos on the gas vans, who devised the corrections to make the task more effective, the men who built the crematoriums, who repaired them, those who dealt with the receipts of the gold taken from the teeth, those who devised coats to be made from human hair, just to name a few – above all those who framed the Nuremberg laws, who solved the problem: 'who in law is the Jew?'

And what of Ohlendorf? The US psychologist, Major Leon Goldensohn, could not understand and could only conclude that he was 'a sadist, a pervert or a lunatic' to have carried out those orders without seemingly experiencing any remorse (Earl 2009: 57). But we know, he was a man of the law, a man who had found his destiny in the NSDAP, in duty, in building a place and a space fit for his children and his grandchildren; a place and a space of honour, of morality, free from the Jews. . . .

Ohlendorf was executed with his narrative self-understanding un-confronted for the court must find him a criminal and not listen with appreciation. It stripped him of his law-fullness as Jackson strove to strip the whole era of its abundance of law. And so we have a false history, the Gorgon silences, and it silences a lot. So we need mirrors, mirrors upon mirrors; the Gorgon (Law) must confront the Gorgon (Law) and then the story of the Holocaust may be told. . . .

And thus there would be the possibility of a (knowing) Law. . . .

Notes

1 This chapter reflects in part my experience of teaching an undergraduate course on Law, Modernity, and the Holocaust. In that, as in this chapter, the influence of David Fraser (Professor of Law and Social Theory, Nottingham University), ever since years ago I walked into his then office in Sydney Law School to discuss cricket and jurisprudence, criminology and its ghosts, cheese and mushrooms, should be acknowledged.

2 'The privilege of opening the first trial in history for crimes against the peace of the world imposes a grave responsibility. The wrongs which we seek to condemn and punish have been so calculated, so malignant, and so devastating, that civilization cannot tolerate their being ignored, because it cannot survive their being repeated. That four great nations, flushed with victory and stung with injury stay the hand of vengeance and voluntarily submit their captive enemies to the judgment of the law is one of the most significant tributes that Power has ever paid to Reason' (Jackson, in Trial of the Major War Criminals before the International Military Tribunal, Vol. 2, p. 98; the theme continues throughout the trial). After the International Military Tribunal finished, a number of trials also took place in the Place of Justice, Nuremberg, under devolved jurisdiction. In the trial of the Nazi Justices this tactic of denying that the Nazi era had 'law' was intensified: 'The defendants and their colleagues distorted, perverted, and finally accomplished the complete overthrow of justice and law in Germany. The "trials" they conducted became horrible farces, with vestigial remnants of legal procedure which only served to mock the hapless victims' (*United States v. Josef Altstoetter et al.*: 31). Beneath the false discourse of 'Nazi law' the Nazi court revealed the spectre of 'a judicial system deliberately fashioned into a headman's axe' (Ibid: 23, 20), where 'the dagger of the assassin was concealed beneath the robe of the jurist'. (Ibid: 985) According to

Telford Taylor (Chief Prosecutor), Nazi judges had joined in 'destroying law and justice in Germany, and . . . then utilizing the empty forms of legal process for persecution, enslavement, and extermination on a vast scale'. Law's task was clear: 'the temple must be re-consecrated. This cannot be done in the twinkling of an eye or by mere ritual. It cannot be done in any single proceeding or at any place. It certainly cannot be done at Nuremberg alone'.

3 Her address is available at www.nurembergacademy.org/events/nuremberg-forum-2015/

4 'We meet here to commemorate what began in this Palace of Justice 65 years ago today – an event of such importance that it can be said of it as Goethe said of the victory of a citizen army at Valmy, "From this place, and from this day forth, began a new era in the history of the world". . . . The trials at Nuremberg laid the foundation of a system for the enforcement of international criminal law, promising justice for victims of widespread atrocities across the globe' (Rapp 2010). Buergenthal (2004) in his well-known 2003 address at the US Holocaust Memorial Museum was clear in connecting the IMT with the Holocaust: 'Whether we realize it or not, the widely held belief in many parts of the world that strong international human rights institutions and international criminal courts are necessary to protect mankind against future genocides and crimes against humanity is a legacy of the Holocaust and of US humanitarian policies.' His speech repeatedly brackets 'Nuremberg and the Holocaust', while clearly implicitly accepting, although stopping short of explicitly say it, that Nuremberg made new international law to convict the defendants.

5 It was generally believed that all copies had been destroyed, leading Reifenstahl to even claim at one stage that it never existed, until a copy was found in Manchester University Archives.

6 See generally on aesthetics (Spotts 2009), focusing on what he terms 'High Society'.

Bibliography

Best, G. (1984) *Nuremberg and After: The Continuing History of War Crimes and Crimes Against Humanity*, Reading: University of Reading History Department.

Bloxham, D. (2001) *Genocide on Trial: War Criminals and the Formation of Holocaust, History and Memory*, Oxford: Oxford University Press.

Browning, C. (1992) *Path to Genocide*, New York: Oxford University Press.

Buergenthal, T. (2004) 'International Law and the Holocaust', *Joseph and Rebecca Meyerhoff Annual Lecture*, 28 October 2003, [Online]. Available: www.ushmm.org/m/pdfs/20050428-buergenthal.pdf

Dawidowicz, L. (1975) *The War Against the Jews, 1933–1945*, New York: Holt, Rinehart and Winston.

Delage, C. (2006) *La Vérité par l'Image*, Paris: Denoël.

Delage, D. (2014) *Caught on Camera: Film in the Courtroom from the Nuremberg Trials to the Trials of the Khmer Rouge*, Edited and translated by R. Schoolcraft and M. B. Kelly, Philadelphia: University of Pennsylvania Press.

Douglas, L. (2001) *The Memory of Judgment: Making Law and History in the Trials of the Holocaust*, New Haven: Yale University Press.

Earl, H. (2009) *The Nuremberg SS-Einsatzgruppen Trial, 1945–1958*, Cambridge: Cambridge University Press.

Gilbert, G. M. (1995) *Nuremberg Diary*, Cambridge, MA: Da Capo Press.

Grenier, R. (1994) 'The Fuehrer's Filmaker', *Commentary*, 1 August. Available: https://www.commentarymagazine.com/articles/the-fuehrers-filmmaker/
Harris, J. (ed.) (2010) *Inside the Death Drive: Excess and Apocalypse in the World of the Chapman Brothers*, Liverpool: Liverpool University Press.
Hartouni, V. (2012) *Visualizing Atrocity: Arendt, Evil, and the Optics of Thoughtlessness*, New York: New York University Press.
Heller, K. J. (2011) *The Nuremberg Military Tribunals and the Origins of International Criminal Law*, Oxford: Oxford University Press.
Jackson, R. H. (1945) 'Report of Robert H Jackson, United States Representative to the International Conference on Military Trials', [Online]. Available: http://avalon.law.yale.edu/subject_menus/jackson.asp
Judt, T. (2000) 'The Past Is Another Country: Myth and Memory in Post-War Europe', in Deák, I., Gross, J. T., and Judt, T. (eds.) *The Politics of Retribution in Europe: World War II and Its Aftermath*, Princeton: Princeton University Press, pp. 293–323.
Kramer, S. (1961) *Judgment at Nuremberg*. Film. USA: Roxlom and United Artists.
Landsman, S. (2005) *Crimes of the Holocaust: The Law Confronts Hard Cases*, Philadelphia: University of Pennsylvania Press.
Levi, P. (1989) *The Drowned and the Saved*, translated R. Rosenthal, New York: Random House.
Lottee, K. and Saner, H. (eds.) (1992) *Hannah Arendt and Karl Jaspers, Correspondence 1926–1969*, New York: Harcourt Brace Jovanovich.
Morrison, W. (2006) *Criminology, Civilisation and the New World Order*, Abingdon, Oxon: Routledge.
Morrison, W. (2017) 'Ghosts of War Crimes Past: An Account from the Front Line in Bangladesh', in Strawson, J. and Collins, B. (eds.) *Injustice, Memory and Faith in Human Rights*, Abingdon, Oxon: Routledge, pp. 11.27.
Osiel, M. (2009) *Making Sense of Mass Atrocity*, Cambridge: Cambridge University Press.
Rancière, J. (2004) *The Politics of Aesthetics: The Distribution of the Sensible*, translated with an introduction by G. Rockhill, New York: Continuum.
Rancière, J. (2006) *Hatred of Democracy*, translated by S. Corcoran, London: Verso.
Rancière, J. (2007) *The Future of the Image*, translated by G. Elliot, London: Verso.
Rancière, J. (2009) *The Emancipated Spectator*, translated by G. Elliot, London: Verso.
Rancière, J. (2010) *Dissensus: On Politics and Aesthetics*, translated by S. Corcoran, London: Bloomsbury.
Rapp, S. J. (2010) 'Remarks at Opening of the Nuremberg Trials Memoriam', [Online]. Available: https://2009-2017.state.gov/j/gcj/us_releases/remarks/2010/151884.htm
Riefenstahl, L. (1935) *Triumph of the Will*. Documentary Film. Germany: Leni Riefenstahl-Produktion.
Riefenstahl, L. (1938) *Olympia*. Documentary Film. Germany: Olympia Film GmbH.
Schmitt, C. (2006) *The Nomos of the Earth in the International Law of the Jus Europaeum*, translated by G. L. Ulman, New York: Telos Press Publishing.
Speer, A. (1970) *Inside the Third Reich*, New York: Macmillan.
Spotts, F. (2009) *Hitler and the Power of Aesthetics*, Woodstock: The Overlook Press.
Steiner, George (1971) In Bluebeard's Castle: some notes on the redefinition of culture, Yale University Press: London.
Trial of the Major War Criminals before the International Military Tribunal, Nuremberg 14 November 1945–1 October 1946, 42 Volumes, ('The Blue Series'), [Online]. Available: www.loc.gov/rr/frd/Military_Law/NT_major-war-criminals.html

Twist, S. (2005) 'Evidence of Atrocities or Atrocious Use of Evidence: The Controversial Use of Atrocity Film at Nuremberg', *Liverpool Law Review*, vol. 26, pp. 267–302.

US v. Altstoetter et al. (The 'Justice Case'), 'Trials of War Criminals Before the Nuremberg Military Tribunals under Control Council Law No. 10, vol. 3' (Washington, DC: US Government Printing Office, 1951), [Online]. Available: www.loc.gov/rr/frd/Military_Law/pdf/NT_war-criminals_Vol-III.pdf

von Salomon, E. (1931) *The Outlaws*, translated Ian F. D. Morrow, London: J. Cape.

West, R. (1955) *A Train of Powder*, Chicago: Ivan R. Dee.

Chapter 9

Justice between terror and law

Mónica López Lerma

There is no peace for the wicked, says the Lord.

(Isaiah 48:22)

This chapter explores the 'aesthetic frames' that constitute the sensory configuration of security and justice in the post-9/11 'age of terror', through Enrique Urbizu's film *No habrá paz para los malvados* (*No Peace for the Wicked*, 2011).[1] The film exposes what Michael J. Shapiro (2009) has called the 'violent cartography' of national security in the context of the Madrid terrorist attack on March 11, 2004, when a series of ten coordinated bombs exploded in three different train stations, killing 191 and injuring another 1,841 people.[2] As Shapiro explains, these violent cartographies are 'historically developed, socially embedded interpretations of identity and space' whereby 'enmities give rise to war-as-policy' and which involve 'forces, institutions, and agencies that identify the . . . spaces where bodies are judged to be dangerous' (Shapiro 2009: 18–19). The chapter places the film under the 'aesthetic frames' provided by these violent cartographies and enquires as to the extent to which it supports or challenges their underlying narratives of securitization. In doing so, the chapter seeks to assess a shift in contemporary politics and aesthetics that Jacques Rancière (2006a) has called 'the ethical turn'.

Combining thriller, film noir, and post-Western genres, *No Peace for the Wicked* tells the story of Santos Trinidad, a once respected but now drunken cowboy-like cop working in the missing persons unit. While the city of Madrid is implementing strict security measures in preparation for the G20 summit, Trinidad shoots three Colombians in a nightclub, an apparently motiveless killing. From then on, the film leads the viewer on a double hunt: Trinidad's hunt for the only witness who manages to escape him and Judge Chacón's search for the triple murderer, whose identity remains unknown to her until the end. Trinidad's quest begins as a search for the missing witness who can identify him as the killer, but he unknowingly uncovers a secret plot by a Colombian drug cartel linked to an Islamist cell planning a terrorist attack. Trinidad's actions apparently neutralize the Islamic cell – Trinidad and the terrorists kill each other in a fight to the death – yet the film ends with an image of a crowded shopping mall where a series of undetected bombs remain active, leaving the viewer with a disquieting feeling of imminent danger.

Although the events and characters in the film are fictional, they evoke the places, methods, and strategies behind the 2004 Madrid bombing attacks as they were disclosed in the 2007 court proceedings against the perpetrators.[3] Viewers can see: the Madrid neighbourhood of Lavapiés, where one of the leaders of the terrorist network owned a phone store; the countryside headquarters, where the explosive devices were actually assembled; Atocha railway station, where three of the bombs exploded; the cellphones used to detonate the bombs; and an image of the videotape that the terrorists recorded on the day of the Madrid attacks. On that tape, three hooded men read out a message in Arabic claiming responsibility for the attacks, which they justified as retaliation for Spain's participation in the US-led 'War against Islam'. They also warned that they would continue to commit more bloody attacks if Spain did not halt the 'injustices' and 'killings' of Muslims under the excuse of combating terrorism (Reinares 2010: 86, 97). By thus connecting the events of the 2004 Madrid train bombings to the scenes and narrative details of the film, *No Peace for the Wicked* invites viewers to critically examine the narratives, images, and tropes surrounding terrorism and anti-terrorism policies in the post-9/11 age of terror.

Earlier readings of the film suggest that it reinforces the violent cartography of national security and the moral landscape that Rancière has analyzed under the heading of the 'ethical turn'. By contrast, this chapter aims to demonstrate that while at the *narrative* level the film seemingly reinforces the ideological discourses of security and justice constituted by the state and the media, nevertheless at the level of *aesthetics* the film disturbs and reconfigures the frames within which the former discourses are to be understood. This approach draws on Rancière's understanding of aesthetics, by which he means not a discipline dealing with art and artworks, but a 'distribution of the sensible', a way of framing what is given to our sensorial experience or what is otherwise excluded and remains outside it (Rancière 2004). Aesthetic frames thus function as markers of what is visible or invisible, what can or cannot be heard, who is included or excluded. Additionally, aesthetic frames map a topography of appropriate or inappropriate reactions, affects, and behaviours.

The chapter begins with the religious and Wild West rhetoric that President George W. Bush used to justify an ('infinite') war against terror. Section 2 draws a contrast between, on the one hand, the construction and management of the public's perceptions of fear and terror as forms of state legitimization, and, on the other hand, the manner in which the film constructs opposing 'aesthetic frames' that allow us to challenge them. Section 3 situates the film in a post-Western aesthetics that recycles themes, tropes, and styles of classical Western cinema to actively interrupt and modify its assumptions, ideology, and values. The chapter ends with an analysis of Judge Chacón, the embodiment of law in the film, to show that even though law may be incapable of neutralizing violence, a 'different place' for justice may still exist between terror and law.

1. Infinite justice and the ethical turn

Soon after the terrorist attacks of 9/11, former United States president George W. Bush launched 'Operation Enduring Freedom' – initially named 'Operation Infinite Justice', but renamed to appease Muslim protesters who complained that only Allah could provide infinite justice (Roy 2001). Using overtly religious overtones and imagery, President Bush described his pre-emptive military strike as a 'crusade . . . against a new kind of evil' (see Lincoln 2006: 119), against a new kind of enemy who hates both freedom and the American 'way of life' (Roy 2001).[4] By constructing a Manichean worldview of good versus evil, Bush justified war as the only possible option, calling upon his allies to follow the military course without the possibility of a less belligerent approach or of staying neutral. As he put it in a well-known statement: 'You're either with us or against us in the fight against terror'.[5] Right after launching a series of airstrikes in Afghanistan, he declared: 'We're a peaceful nation. Yet . . . there can be no peace in a world of sudden terror. In the face of today's new threat, the only way to pursue peace is to pursue those who threaten it. We did not ask for this mission, but we will fulfil it'.[6] In a clear allusion to the biblical passage of the film's title, President Bush enacted the role of a holy warrior launching a mission not out of personal will, but based on (divine) mandate: a war on terror with no end in sight that is still with us more than fifteen years later.

Alongside his use of religious rhetoric, Bush's outward appearance was embedded in the mythic cowboy imagery of Wild West, so central to America's self-understanding of its history and national identity (Hoffman 2011: 325). Bush wore cowboy attire (white hat and cowboy boots) to visually associate himself with the figure of the sheriff (Hoffman 2011: 326). Like the heroic sheriff of the cinematic Old West, who would stand alone if need be in order to defeat those outside the bounds of civilization (Indians) or law (outlaws), President Bush would not hesitate to fight the new evil (terrorists) in defence of the American way of life. To demonstrate his determination, he invoked Wild West rhetoric, declaring that he wanted Osama Bin Laden 'dead or alive'; he also labelled Saddam Hussein's government as an 'outlaw regime', and gave Saddam and his sons forty-eight hours to leave Iraq (Dodwell 2004).

In *Prisoners of the Infinite* (Rancière 2010a), Rancière opposes the connection between this sheriff-like image of Bush and the representation of sheriffs in classical Western films. In his view, a difference is discernible between the morality of Westerns and Bush's call for 'infinite justice'. In contrast to classical Westerns, where sheriffs often risk their lives to save outlaws from a lynch mob and deliver them to justice, Bush's infinite justice implies a type of 'justice without limits' (Rancière 2010a: 82), a justice that erases all distinctions that can delimit its practice: 'Those which distinguish legal punishment from the vengeance of individuals, [and] which separate the law from the political, the ethical or the religious' (Rancière 2010a: 82). As examples that illustrate this erasure of distinctions, Rancière mentions the CIA's use of 'enhanced interrogation techniques' in violation of Art. 3 of the Geneva Conventions and the denial to Guantanamo Bay detainees of their status as Prisoners of War (P.O.W.), as well as their rights to legal counsel and a fair trial. In this way, traditional distinctions 'all wind up being abolished at the same time as the forms of international law are effaced' (Rancière 2010a: 83). Therefore, the term 'infinite justice' was no slip of the tongue or excess of language; quite the reverse, it meant precisely what it said: 'the assertion of a right identical with the omnipotence hitherto reserved for the avenging God' (Rancière 2010a: 83).

For Rancière, the term 'infinite justice' not only designates a retaliatory or pre-emptive strike against an enemy attack; most importantly, it entails a levelling out of the symbolic space he identifies with the 'ethical turn' he observes in contemporary politics and aesthetics (Rancière 2006a). By 'ethical turn' Rancière refers to a shift occurring in the symbolic order of society, where the specificity of political and artistic practices is dissolved, and where earlier distinctions between law and fact, between what it is and what ought to be, are erased (Rancière 2006a: 2). The 'ethical turn' alludes to a transformation of the social order of perception in so-called democratic societies after 9/11, where the space for law's abstract literariness and the polemics over its interpretations that contitute politics has shrunken (Rancière 2010b: 102). This space of dissensus so necessary for political action is being filled instead by an ethical conception of the community as a unified entity (Rancière 2010b: 104). As Rancière understands it, the term 'ethical', which is etymologically associated with the idea of an abode or way of being,[7] divides the world in two. On the side of good is a consensual practice that matches the letter of the law to a community's specific way of life, with no gaps or spaces for dissensus (Rancière 2010a: 82). On the other side lies a world of evil that is made infinite or absolute and 'can only be enacted through a war to the death' (Rancière 2010b: 104). The problem, Rancière notes, is that this evil 'cannot be righted except at the price of another evil which remains irreducible', that is, equally infinite (2010a: 115). In this new form of symbolism, war on terror and infinite justice fall within the same field of indistinction, a form of preventative justice that levels down and destroys everything that appears to threaten the ethical bond of the community (Rancière 2006a: 5).

Rancière argues that this ethical turn can be observed not only in politics and law but also in post 9/11 cinema, which borrows classical Western tropes and archetypes yet modifies them accordingly. For instance, classical Westerns used to devise scenarios that presented different forms and motivations for violence (Rancière 2010a: 115). In these films 'freelance sheriffs and righters of wrongs used to wield, without inhibition, the violence of the common law, or of morality, against the violence of those who followed the law out of mere greed' (Rancière 2010a: 114). Nowadays, however, the earlier political or aesthetic scenarios seem to have fallen into a state of indistinction, where it is no longer possible to distinguish different types of violence in their aims, character, and effects. This is precisely what the ethical turn means for Rancière: the flattening of all forms of action under the same, one-dimensional mode of perception (Rancière 2006a: 2), all of which takes place in a single, levelled down ethical scenario of (infinite) evil and justice.[8]

The biblical undertones of Urbizu's *No Peace for the Wicked* as well as its constant references to cowboy imagery seem to align the film squarely with the violent cartography identified by Shapiro and with Rancière's ethical turn of cinema in the new age of terror. According to critic Diana Norton, the film falls into a neo-imperialist trap of stereotype and institutional racism that equates terrorist potential to foreigners and immigrants (in particular, Latin American and African characters) (Norton 2015: 179). Maria Pilar Rodríguez argues further that by exposing the incapacity of the state to meet terrorist threats, the film suggests that salvation can only be achieved through the individual intervention of someone like Santos Trinidad who is willing to circumvent the rules and fight evil with the same violent means (Rodríguez 2016: 152). For Jesús Ángel González, in turn, the film's Western references establish an analogy between the traditional enemy in Westerns (Indians) and the contemporary enemy of the US-led 'war on terror' (Muslims) (González 2016: 6), with the overall purpose of warning viewers about 'the risks of applying "posthumously" the logic and moral assumptions of classical Westerns in contemporary situations' (González 2017: 70). In what follows, I confront these readings by locating the film in what Neil Campbell (2013) calls 'the politics of post-Western aesthetics', which, as I will show, challenge rather than reproduce the logic and ideology of infinite evil and justice. I do so first by analyzing how the state and media construct, manage, and legitimize feelings of insecurity, fear, and terror and then by showing how the film deconstructs these frames in the aesthetic register.

2. The media and the securitization of the state: fear and terror

The film's title sequence frames the context of the story within the post 9/11 climate of terror, drawing attention to the role that news media play in managing the public's perceptions of insecurity and danger (Cohen 2002). The sequence opens with a close-up of a slot machine: Santos Trinidad (whose name recalls Enzo Barboni's well-known 70s Trinity series) plays the machine.[9] In the background, the TV news reports that:

> The Islamic Republic now has 3000 centrifuges, 2700 more than those known of up to the present day and, say experts, enough to make an atomic bomb within a year. The president of Iran denies this and once again, insists that they are only doing uranium for peaceful purposes.

The camera then cuts to a close-up of Trinidad's cowboy boots and in a foot-level shot follows his footsteps to the counter, where another close-up shows a picture of a missing girl he is investigating. The TV news now reports that:

> There are just four days to go before Madrid is host to the forthcoming G20 summit. Madrid is taking strict security measures and it is estimated that over fifteen thousand members of the state security forces will be in place throughout the course of the summit. Violence is expected from young anti-system protesters, which have invariably accompanied the latest summits. Although border controls and access to the capital have been tightened, thousands of these violent protesters are already in the city.

The sequence closes with an image on TV of girl dancers that resemble the image of the saloon girl from the slot machine. A drunken Trinidad orders one last drink, but he is refused and is thrown out of the bar.

The media's rhetoric of the title sequence merges two disparate images to produce a single social problem. On the one hand, by portraying Iranian possession of weapons of mass destruction as an imminent threat, the media induces a diffuse sense of terror – potentially, anyone, anywhere, at any time, might become a victim. On the other hand, the media constructs the image of protesters against the neoliberal system represented by the G-20 summits as violent, calling for the need to increase security measures in anticipation of protester violence. By tying together the Iranian nuclear threat, political activists, and terrorists, the media converts disparate situations into a single object of fear (Rancière 2014: 27). In doing so, the media fosters feelings of rejection directed against this object and mobilizes a sense of the community as unified by threats to its security. The underlying message of the media is that anything that threatens the self-perceived safety of the community should equally be feared. This is what 'consensus' means for Rancière: 'not the romantic absurdity of responsible partners together discussing facts and solutions to objective problems, but the immediate identification of the subject who fears' and the object of fear (2014: 27).

Media inducement of fear and terror helps to construct a given regime of visibility and invisibility. Here, it is useful to draw a distinction between fear and terror. Fear is a concrete, tangible threat expressed by an embodied adversary (Bégin 2014: 60; Lezra 2016: 215). Fear, in other words, puts a face to the threat and 'provides it with the concrete features which will make it into an appropriate target of hatred and struggle' (Žižek 2002). Terror, on the other hand, 'is not simply a stronger type of fear, responding to a more frightening and diffuse threat. Terror is a way of feeling, naming and explaining that causes trouble both in everybody's mind and in the global world' (Rancière 2006c: 275, my translation). Put differently, terror is a 'mode of perception', a way of mapping the perceptible that imposes itself as a self-evident order and 'links a regime of thinking about causality with a moral regime of interpreting Good and Evil' (Rancière 2006c: 275, my translation).

Rancière observes that states make use of the widespread sense of powerlessness produced by terror for their own benefit: unable to protect their citizens against this invisible and elusive threat, as a result, governments take control of what is in their power, 'the production and management of [the sentiment of] insecurity' (Rancière 2010c). Rancière writes: 'To foresee dangers is one thing; to manage the sentiment of insecurity is another, one in which the state will always be more expert perhaps because it is the very principle of its power' (2010a: 113). The feeling of insecurity gives the state the justification to create a permanent state of surveillance in the name of guaranteeing security; or, more precisely, it gives the state the power to create a permanent state of insecurity in order 'to enforce its governance' (Corcoran 2010: 14) and legitimize itself (Newman 2007: 5). Terrorism and anti-terrorism run the risk of falling into a state of indistinction, in which each justifies and legitimates the other's existence and actions (Agamben 2001; Newman 2007: 5). In this way, anti-terrorism policies become floating signifiers ready to be applied indiscriminately to everything deemed to be a threat to the community's safety, and which legitimizes in advance the intervention of the state.

Unsurprisingly, the initial response from the state in the film to meet threats identified and magnified by the media is to enhance surveillance and security measures. The film presents the urban space of Madrid under a state of constant surveillance: helicopters patrolling the city; checkpoints; patrolling guards; bomb-sniffing dogs; chemical and biological weapon detectors; CCTV cameras in streets, parking lots, hotels, and nightclubs. The display of highly aesthetic images of surveillance generate what Bruce Schneier (2003) calls a 'security theatre', with a double effect: on the one hand, it creates a feeling of safety and protection promised by increased surveillance (Patel 2012: 216); on other hand, it reinforces the perception of insecurity and vulnerability portrayed by the media.

According to Diana Norton, the constant use of surveillance mechanisms within the film reconstructs the urban space of Madrid as a borderland – that is, as a contested territory characterized by racial segregation and conflict (Norton 2015: 177). In her view, the main camera of the film reproduces this segregation by recreating the static (supposedly objective) point of view of the surveillance camera. For example, in a scene that takes place in the immigrant neighbourhood of Lavapiés, the static shot participates in Trinidad's ethnic profiling of the immigrants of Lavapiés as criminals (Norton 2015: 185). However, the film does not construct a unitary viewing position, but offers contrasting perspectives that problematize rather than reinforce the omniscient gaze of the security apparatus.

One of the most notable examples is when Judge Chacón interviews members of different police departments, demonstrating not only their ineffectiveness but also their lack of coordination and cooperation. First, Judge Chacón interviews Cerdán, from the narcotics bureau, about the dismissal of an investigation into Pedro Vargas (one of Trinidad's victims) in 2004. Cerdán explains that there was a bureaucratic problem ('a civil servant forgot to lodge the prosecution appeal on time and the case was dropped'). Then, Chacón questions Inspector Mérida, from the Foreign Intelligence Unit, about why they took charge of a narcotics case: Mérida explains that one of their informants told them that Pedro Vargas was connected with El Ceutí, the leader of a group of radical jihadists, but that they have since lost track of him. Judge Chacón questions commissioner Ontiveiros, also from the Foreign Intelligence Unit, about the reasons for having lost track of El Ceutí. Ontiveiros justifies the intelligence failure by saying that 'the terrorists are unpredictable, because they move a lot, which makes it very hard to identify them, to locate them, to nail them.' In Ontiveiros' narrative, the lack of a concrete, identifiable enemy creates an 'unpredictable topography' of invisible networks, whose undetectable tactics and ability to hide in plain sight render terrorist suspects impossible to capture and guard against (Walsh 2016: 6). However, the following short dialogue brings to light a different kind of problem that belies the police narrative:

Chacón: But El Ceutí's people were still bringing cocaine to the Colombians?
Ontiveiros: That's why the case went back to narcotics.
Chacón: But in narcotics they are not aware of it. Aren't you talking to each other?

Against the state's rhetoric of undetectable terrorists working in the shadows, Chacón's interrogations suggest that the problem is not one of invisibility but of bureaucratic sloppiness, lack of coordination between different police units, and neglect to pursue known suspects. In so doing, the film invites viewers to critically examine the effectiveness and rationale of the state's management of fear and terror.

3. Trinidad and the politics of the post-Western

Some critics have argued that by showing the incompetence of the security forces the film suggests that salvation can only be achieved with the help of rogue police officers like Santos Trinidad, who navigates the same terrain as the terrorists and fights them with the same violent means. I challenge this conclusion by inscribing Trinidad in what Neill Campbell calls 'post-Western aesthetics'. Before turning to analysis of the post-Western aesthetics of the film, it is useful to briefly explain this term.

In *Post-Westerns: Cinema, Region, West*, Campbell defines post-Westerns as films that borrow from and engage with traditional Western cinema in order to comment on 'its deeply haunting assumptions and values' (2013: 31).[10] He argues that post-Westerns rescue traditions, themes, tropes, and styles established under the classical Western, 'not to emphasize their timelessness, continuity, or essential significance to identity, community, or nation' but to actively interfere, interrupt, and alter their myths, ideologies, and values (Campbell 2013: 37). For instance, if the classical Western moved towards resolution, settlement, community, and the establishment of a particular national identity, the post-Western seeks to stress 'the "provisional" and the contingent, the unfinished aspects of a people not already defined and labeled but still emerging and creating itself' (Campbell 2013: 36). For Campbell, post-Westerns are 'political' in Rancière's sense of the term because they reconfigure taken-for-granted mythic discourses and codes, even '"without being able to guarantee the absolute elimination of the social inequalities inherent in the police order" that creates and sustains them' (Campbell 2013: 352). The 'post' of the post-Western, therefore, 'does not just mean overcoming the "past"' it also means '"a process of disengagement" from the system it is in tension with' (Campbell 2013: 9).

Drawing on Campbell, I approach Urbizu's *No Peace for the Wicked* as a political post-Western. Rather than warning viewers about the inadequacy of 'applying the logic and moral assumptions of classical Westerns in contemporary situations' (González 2017: 70), the post-Western aesthetics of the film challenges the mythical, heroic cowboy narrative presumptively used to justify an infinite 'war on terror'; in doing so, the film sets up a political scenario that 'crack[s] open the unity of the given and the obviousness of the visible, in order to sketch a new topography of the possible' (Rancière 2009: 49).

***

No Peace for the Wicked declines to explain what drives Trinidad to kill three people in a nightclub, leaving the viewer wondering whether it is the news on TV that triggers Trinidad's violence, his drunkenness, his troubled past as member of a special operations unit, or the 'accidental' shooting of his partner in Cali. Trinidad is thus best understood as what Shapiro calls an 'aesthetic' rather than a 'psychological' subject (2009: 8). In contrast to psychological characters, which demand attention to the underlying causes and motivations of their personal drama, 'aesthetic subjects' are characters 'whose movements and actions (both purposive and non-purposive) map and often alter experiential, political relevant terrains' (Shapiro 2013: xiv). By focusing on the aesthetic rather than on the psychological, the film 'places an emphasis on images rather than narrative' (Shapiro 2009: 11) and encourages viewers to shift their attention away from Trinidad's personal drama towards the aesthetic realm where his movements and actions are played out.

The film associates Trinidad with Western iconography and codes from the outset. The title sequence opens with a close-up of a slot machine containing Western iconography: on the left, the image of a sheriff with a gun is set against a background of a desert where the figure of a cowboy is shown from behind; on the right, an enticing dance-hall girl appears under the doorway of a saloon. A combination of icons with dollar signs, revolvers, sheriff's stars, and cowboy hats is shown several times on the slot machine. (The name of José Coronado, the actor who plays Santos Trinidad, appears framed within these icons.) These Western references and the genre expectations that go with them, are soon subverted: the sheriff with a star-shaped badge and a gun facing saloon-hall dancers becomes the image of a drunken cop with a badge and a revolver facing dancing girls on TV; the sheriff's star becomes a police badge which is used to ask for one last drink at a nightclub; the saloon becomes a crime scene for a cold blooded triple murder; and the desert, epitome of the classical Western landscape, becomes a wasteland on the outskirts of Madrid where Trinidad burns all the evidence that links him to the murder. From there, viewers can see the four new skyscrapers that have come to symbolize the effects of the housing bubble during the 2008 Spanish financial crisis (Smith 2012: 7).

The overturning of the Western genre is indicated by the name of the main character. Trinidad evokes the name of the protagonist of Enzo Barboni's Spaghetti Western comedy series. Like Barboni's protagonist, Trinidad is also an ill-mannered, unshaven gunfighter, fearless, indifferent to the norms of law – he smashes the head of the nightclub owner against the counter just as Barboni's protagonist bangs a man's head against a cash register – and with no feeling of repentance. By associating Trinidad with the Spaghetti Western, Urbizu adds a critical layer to the character and establishes an ironic complicity with viewers (González 2017), who are encouraged to pierce the façade of the heroic, ideological cowboy narrative (see Frayling 1998).[11] Contrary to the religious connotations of his name ('Holy Trinity'), the film's Trinidad is no saint, but a crook.

The critical subversion operated by the post-Western is important in assessing the final confrontation between Trinidad and the terrorists, in which Trinidad is killed. Some critics have interpreted Trinidad's death at the end of the film as a form of redemptive sacrifice that grants him heroic status (e.g., Norton 2015).[12] Tzvetan Todorov's distinction between sacrifice and massacre can be useful here. Todorov (1985: 144) writes:

> Sacrifice . . . is a religious murder: it is performed in the name of the official ideology and will be perpetrated in public places, in sight of all and to everyone's knowledge. The victim's identity is determined by strict rules. . . . He must not be too alien, too remote. . . . [T]he sacrificial victim also counts by his personal qualities: the sacrifice of brave warriors is more highly appreciated than that of just anyone. . . . The sacrifice . . . testifies to the power of the social fabric, to its mastery over the individual.
>
> Massacre, on the other hand, reveals the weakness of this social fabric . . .; hence it should be performed in some remote place where the law is only vaguely acknowledged. [. . .] The more remote and alien the victims, the better: they are exterminated without remorse, more or less identified with animals. The individual identity of the massacre victim is by definition irrelevant (otherwise his death would be murder). [. . .] Unlike sacrifices, massacres are . . . kept secret and denied. This is because their social function is not recognized, and we have the impression that such action finds its justification in itself.

The tension between these two types of violence can be seen in the final confrontation between Trinidad and the Islamic terrorists he has unwittingly uncovered. The scene shows Trinidad killing the main leaders of the terrorist cell, one by one: he cuts the throat of one, shoots the missing witness in the head, and finally fires multiple shots into El Ceutí, who manages to fatally stab Trinidad before dying. The scene of violence can be read either as sacrifice or as massacre depending on the aesthetic frames within which the various actions are ascertained as good/heroic and evil/villainous. If framed as a religious confrontation (emphasized in the biblical title of the film), viewers are encouraged to identify Trinidad as the victim of violence rather than as its agent. Through his sacrificial death, Trinidad would become the surrogate for all potential victims of the terrorist massacre (McKenna 1991: 205). In this reading, Trinidad's violence is justified as necessary to maintain cohesion of the social fabric threatened by terrorists, who are 'the cause, the origin, of destructive violence that warrants its reciprocal and liberating response' (McKenna 1991: 205). This sacrificial scenario would bolster the ethical 'dramaturgy of infinite evil, justice, and redemption' (Rancière 2006a: 1).

This reading, however, ignores the post-Western aesthetics of the film. The final confrontation between Trinidad and the terrorists is reminiscent of the classic Western shootout-showdown, where the hero stands alone, fearless against his enemies (*Stagecoach* [1939], *High Noon* [1952], *Shane* [1953]). As John G. Cawelti explains, in the classic Western ritual of the shootout, 'the cowboy hero does not seek out combat for its own sake and he typically shows an aversion to the wanton shedding of blood. Killing is an act forced upon him' (Cawelti 1984: 87). Accordingly, one of the most important rules in Westerns is that 'the hero cannot use violence without justification' (Cawelti 1970: 268). The hero can only resort to violence in order to help others, or to protect higher values such as peace, law, and justice. In this way, the hero's 'controlled and aesthetic mode of killing' gives a sense of moral significance to violence and imposes an aesthetic order that delineates the difference between hero and savage (Cawelti 1984: 87–88). In contrast to the cowboy hero, '[t]he Indian or outlaw as savage delights in slaughter, entering into combat with a kind of manic glee to fulfill an uncontrolled lust for blood' (Cawelti 1984: 87).

No Peace for the Wicked subverts the classic Western's 'distribution of the sensible' in two ways. In contrast to the heroic figures of classical Westerns, Trinidad fights and kills the terrorists not to save society (he is unaware of the hidden bombs in the mall) but to save his own skin, and dies not as a result of selfless sacrifice in the name of a moral cause, but as a result of acting out his own self-interest. This can be more clearly discerned by comparing the scene of the moment of his death with the initial killing of the three Colombians in the nightclub, which function as mirror-like repetitions of each other. Right after the triple murder, the camera shows Trinidad sitting motionless on a chair in the darkness of his apartment with his back to the viewer. His right arm is extended and his revolver hangs with his index finger touching the trigger and pointing in his direction.[13] The same image is seen again after the final confrontation with the members of the terrorist cell: after being fatally stabbed, Trinidad is shown sitting on a chair outside the house with his back to the viewer. He holds the revolver with the finger on the trigger, but as he heaves a last sigh before dying, the revolver flips and hangs in his direction. By visually connecting these two scenes pointing the revolver ultimately towards him, the film invites viewers to identify Trinidad's death as punishment rather than redemption and his violence as a massacre rather than as a sacrifice.

Furthermore, the film denies the resolution typical of classical Western cinema in which the hero wins a clear-cut victory and a sense of order, community, and justice is restored (Campbell 2013: 27). As Rancière states, 'Victory belongs to the one who can crown the action with the words THE END' (2006b: 77). This is not the case with Trinidad. After the final shootout, two more scenes follow: first, Judge Chacón and Inspector Leiva arrive at the crime scene, where Trinidad lies dead, inviting a final scrutiny of his actions; second, the closing image shows a crowded shopping mall where a series of undetected bombs remain active, raising the question whether there might be 'no end to violence' (Young 2010).

4. Judge Chacón and the topography of the possible

In her analysis of *No Country for Old Men* (Coen Brothers 2007), Alison Young notes that the Coen brother's post-Western film shows how

> the encounter between law and violence has the character of a Sisyphean struggle, in which the agent of law toils to achieve a result, only to see it slip away, . . . or merely to reach the next stage of investigation which will never end.
>
> (2010: 169–170)

Notwithstanding this violence without end, Young also points out that viewers of *No Country for Old Men* 'should not forget the actuality of the *response* of law to violence', even though it might lead to nothing; for, in 'the actuality of law's response, there is always already the possibility of the impossible, an end to violence' (Young 2010: 171). This is why viewers can still 'see the glimmerings of . . . a "hope against the evidence" in the hopeless encounter between law and [terror]' (Young 2010: 171). Young concludes that 'the point is not that "justice" demands a particular kind of outcome but rather that there should be some kind of outcome *which can bear the name of justice*: a sense of consequence which overweighs and effaces the violence that has preceded it' (Young 2010: 153, emphasis in original). In this final section, I will try to demonstrate that Enrique Urbizu's *No Peace for the Wicked*, which some critics have explicitly compared with the Coen brothers' film, provides such a hope in the figure of Judge Chacón and her tenacious criminal investigation.

The first time Judge Chacón appears on the screen she is trapped in a traffic jam applying eye drops to her eyes, as if it were to increase her power of vision on her way to the crime scene. This visual cue is important as it ties Judge Chacón, the embodiment of law in the film, to the *sense* of sight that is to be cleared, and anticipates the external obstacles that jam her investigation. The film portrays Judge Chacón and Trinidad as opposites: although both show the same tenacity, one operates in a world of games (symbolized by the slot machine) where he plays by his own rules: he destroys evidence, searches without a warrant, and threatens people to get information; the other is a woman of integrity who strives to follow legal means towards the pursuit of justice: tracks clues; examines ballistic and forensic tests; interviews eyewitnesses; and interrogates suspects, informants, and members of different law enforcement agencies. Their antagonism also operates on an emotional register: one is 'a man who nobody loves', unable to communicate with anyone; the other combines her role as a investigating judge with motherhood – she interrupts her tasks to talk affectionately with her family on the phone.

Judge Chacón's investigation, and thus the film, places Trinidad under the scrutiny of the law. In a crucial scene in which Trinidad and Chacón encounter each other for the first time, Chacón questions Trinidad about his whereabouts at the time of the triple murder. The scene opens with the camera positioned behind Judge Chacón – shown again putting eye drops in her eyes – so that the viewer adopts her same perspective when Trinidad enters the room. The perfect square lines of the walls frame the judge, in direct contrast with the way Trinidad is seen throughout, reflected in fragmented mirrors, distorted surveillance footage, or observed through different railings. The interrogation takes place in medium close-up, where a series of shot-reverse shots emphasize the close examination. During the interrogation viewers learn that Trinidad was first of his promotion; that he received several distinctions for his work; that he killed one person (though 'he was decorated for it' Trinidad clarifies); that he later abandoned Special Operations. Viewers also learn that in recent years he has received psychiatric attention ('psychological,' he corrects); that he has had problems with alcohol, and that while working for the Spanish embassy in Colombia he 'accidentally' shot his partner in a shootout on the outskirts of Cali, after which his partner became paraplegic and later died. At this point, inspector Leiva enters the room bringing the results from ballistics, which are negative. Without any solid evidence Judge Chacón is forced to let Trinidad go free. The way Trinidad leaves the room is telling: he removes the revolver from the plastic bag in which it was returned to him and throws the plastic bag to the floor, and in typical cowboy-style puts the revolver back into its holster. From Chacón's and Leiva's point of view, Trinidad's shadowy figure is seen crossing the doorway. Chacón concludes: 'I don't get how this character can still be in the police', underscoring the outsiderness of Trinidad.

The second and final encounter between Chacón and Trinidad takes place following Trinidad's death, after the massacre has already occurred. The narrative appears to have come to an end, but the film shifts viewers' attention towards the figure of Judge Chacón, and engages in what Rancière calls 'pensiveness' (2009: 123): the image halts in a moment of suspension, where the logic of the narrative action is thwarted and every conclusion is put in suspense (2009: 123). The film engenders this suspension by showing the scene of the massacre from Judge Chacón's point of view. In sequential movement of the camera, viewers can see commissioner Ontiveiros examining the dead body of El Ceutí, who is lying on the floor. Ontiveiros looks up to Judge Chacón as she goes outside the house, where Trinidad's dead body is sitting on a chair. Following Chacón, viewers look down on Trinidad's dead body to see, for the third time, a close-up of the revolver which hangs from his bloody index finger and points towards him. Trinidad faces the camera with his dead eyes wide open. This moment of suspension encourages viewers to return to the scene of violence and to look over again and revise Trinidad's actions.

Rancière writes: 'The only good end is the one that . . . leaves open the possibility that the action may be continued, restarted' (2006b: 92). The last shots of the film show the bombs still active; instead of the proverbial words 'the end', the title of the film *No Peace for the Wicked* appears in a black background, implying that the action may be continued, restarted. But with Trinidad dead and the viewers' attention shifted towards Judge Chacón, the title acquires new meanings: On the one hand, there will be *no peace* as long as the bombs are still out there and can be detonated (Díaz 2012: 116). On the other hand, *the wicked* will continue to be persecuted. This time, however, the responsibility cannot lie in the hands of someone like Santos Trinidad, but rather of Judge Chacón. Within this new topography, the film confronts the viewer with the thought that the actuality of justice might exist elsewhere than in the outcome (Young: 20), and be practiced otherwise, between terror and law.

Notes

1 The official translation is *No Rest for the Wicked.* I have modified this translation both because it is closer to the original Spanish ('Paz') and because it is also the term used in the standard English translation of the biblical passage.
2 Judgment 65/2007, 'Audiencia Nacional', Criminal Section, Second Section.
3 See Judgment 65/2007, 'Audiencia Nacional', Criminal Section, Second Section.
4 In his speech to the Joint Session of Congress on September 20, 2001, President Bush stated: 'Americans are asking, "Why do they hate us?" They hate our freedoms – our freedom of religion, our freedom of speech, our freedom to vote and assemble and disagree with each other' (see Roy 2001).
5 Bush also said: 'Every nation has a choice to make. In this conflict, there is no neutral ground. If any government sponsors the outlaws and killers of innocents, they have become outlaws and murderers themselves. And they will take that lonely path at their own peril'. (Address to the Nation Announcing Strikes against Al Qaeda Training Camps and Taliban Military Installations in Afghanistan, October 7, 2001).
6 Ibid.
7 As Rancière notes, 'The word *ethos* signifies two things: ethos is the dwelling and the way of being, the way of life corresponding to this dwelling'. Therefore, before signifying a certain norm or rule of morality, ethics is 'the kind of thinking which establishes the identity between an environment, a way of being and a principle of action' (2006a: 2).
8 According to Rancière, *Dogville* (Lars von Trier, 2003) and *Mystic River* (Clint Eastwood, 2003) provide clear examples of the ethical turn (2010a: 115).
9 Enzo Barboni's well-known Trinity series includes *They Called me Trinity* (*Lo chiamavano Trinità*, 1970) and *Trinity Is Still My Name* (*Continuavano a chiamarlo Trinità*, 1971).

10 Campbell applies the term to films produced after World War II to demonstrate that, far from dead, as Deleuze had argued, post-Westerns continue to live on in the present by taking new forms and settings (2013: 309).

11 In *Spaghetti Westerns: Cowboys and Europeans from Karl May to Sergio Leone*, Christopher Frayling (1998) argues that the Spaghetti Western functions as 'critical cinema' in relation to classical Hollywood Western cinema and its ideology and myths. According to Frayling, Spaghetti Westerns 'employ two main strategies of critical cinema through their use of the Hollywood genre: shocking the spectator into questioning what he or she is seeing, and compelling the spectator into recognizing ideas to think about after the film is over' (1998: xxiii).

12 For Norton, Trinidad's ability to cross boundaries and his easy use of guns and fisticuffs identifies him with the cinematic American vigilante, validating his sacrifice for the Spanish nation he dies trying to protect (2015: 181).

13 Urbizu explains that this scene was inspired by John Boorman's film *Point Blank* (1967) (in Heredero 2011: 35).

Bibliography

Agamben, G. (2001) 'Security and Terror', *Theory & Event*, vol. 5, no. 4.

Bégin, R. (2014) 'The Objective: The Configuration of Trauma in the "War on Terror", or the Sublime Object of the Medium', in Flisfeder, M. and Willis, L. P. (eds.) *Žižek and Media Studies: A Reader*, New York: Palgrave Macmillan, pp. 53–63.

Cawelti, J. (1970) 'Prolegomena to the Western', *Western American Literature*, vol. 4, no. 4, pp. 259–271.

Cawelti, J. G. (1984) *The Six-Gun Mystique*, Bowling Green, OH: Bowling Green University Popular Press.

Campbell, N. (2013) *Post-Westerns: Cinema, Region, West*, Lincoln, NE: University of Nebraska Press.

Coen, J. and Coen, E. (2007) *No Country for Old Men*. Film. USA: Paramount Vantage, Miramax, and Scott Rudin Productions.

Cohen, S. (2002) *Folk Devils and Moral Panics: The Creation of the Mods and Rockers*, 3rd edition, London and New York: Routledge.

Corcoran, S. (2010) 'Editor's Introduction', edited and translated by S. Corcoran, in Rancière, J. *Dissensus: On Politics and Aesthetics*, London and New York: Continuum, pp. 1–24.

Díaz, S. (2012) 'Viaje al fondo de la noche: No habrá paz para los malvados (Enrique Urbizu, 2011)', *L'ATALANTE*, vol. Julio-Diciembre 2012, pp. 115–121.

Dodwell, K. (2004) 'From the Center: The Cowboy Myth, George W. Bush, and the War with Iraq', *The American Popular Culture Online Magazine*. Available: www.americanpopularculture.com/archive/politics/cowboy_myth.htm [22 June 2017].

Eastwood, C. (2003) *Mystic River*. Film. USA: Warner Brothers Pictures.

Frayling, C. (1998) *Spaghetti Westerns: Cowboys and Europeans from Karl May to Sergio Leone*, London: I. B. Tauris.

González, J. A. (2016) 'Transnational Post-Western in Irish Cinema', *Journal of Transnational American Studies*, vol. 7, no. 1, pp. 1–26.

González, J. A. (2017) 'A Genre Auteur? Enrique Urbizu's Post-Western Films', *Hispanic Research Journal*, vol. 18, no. 1, pp. 60–73.

Heredero, C. F. (2011) 'Entrevista Enrique Urbizu: La ética de la mirada', *Cahiers du Cinéma*, vol. 48, pp. 32–35.

Hoffman, K. S. (2011) 'Visual Persuasion in George W. Bush's Presidency: Cowboy Imagery', *Congress & the Presidency*, vol. 38, no. 3, pp. 322–343.
Lezra, J. (2016) 'Terror', in Bunz, M., Kaiser, B. M. and Thiele, K. (eds.) *Symptoms of the Planetary Condition: A Critical Vocabulary*, Lüneburg: Meson Press, pp. 211–217.
Lincoln, B. (2006) *Holy Terrors: Thinking about Religion after September 11*, Chicago: Chicago University Press.
McKenna, A. J. (1991) 'The Law's Delay: Cinema and Sacrifice', *Legal Studies*, vol. 15, no. 3, pp. 199–213.
Newman, S. (2007) 'Anarchism, Poststructuralism and the Future of Radical Politics', *SubStance*, vol. 36, no. 2, pp. 3–19.
Norton, D. (2015) 'Immigration and Spanish Subjectivity in "No habra paz para los malvados"', in Corbalán, A. and Mayock, E. (eds.) *Toward a Multicultural Configuration of Spain: Local Cities, Global Spaces*, Maryland: Fairleigh Dickinson University Press, pp. 177–188.
Patel, T. G. (2012) 'Surveillance, Suspicion and Stigma: Brown Bodies in a Terror-Panic Climate', *Surveillance & Society*, vol. 10, no. 3, pp. 215–234.
Rancière, J. (2004) *The Politics of Aesthetics: The Distribution of the Sensible*, translated with an introduction by G. Rockhill, London and New York: Continuum.
Rancière, J. (2006a) 'The Ethical Turn of Aesthetics and Politics', *Critical Horizons*, vol. 7, no. 1, pp. 1–20.
Rancière, J. (2006b) *Film Fables*, translated by E. Battista, New York: Berg.
Rancière, J. (2006c) 'De la peur à la terreur', in Novaes, A. (ed.) *Les aventures de la raison politique*, Paris: Métailié, pp. 275–291.
Rancière, J. (2009) *The Emancipated Spectator*, London: Verso.
Rancière, J. (2010a) *Chronicles of Consensual Times*, edited and translated by S. Corcoran, London: Continuum.
Rancière, J. (2010b) *Dissensus: On Politics and Aesthetics*, edited and translated by S. Corcoran, London and New York: Continuum.
Rancière, J. (2010c) 'Racism: A Passion from Above', *MR Online*, 23 September, Available: https://mronline.org/2010/09/23/racism-a-passion-from-above/
Rancière, J. (2014) *Moments Politiques: Interventions 1977–2009*, translated by M. Foster, New York and Oakland: Seven Stories Press.
Reinares, F. (2010) 'The Madrid Bombings and Global Jihadism', *Survival*, vol. 52, no. 2, pp. 83–104.
Rodríguez, M. P. (2016) 'El mal en la sociedad Española contemporánea: el cine negro de Enrique Urbizu', *Pasavento: Revista de Estudios Hispánicos*, vol. 4, no. 1, pp. 139–155.
Roy, A. (2001) 'The Algebra of Infinite Justice', *The Guardian*, 29 September, Available: https://www.theguardian.com/world/2001/sep/29/september11.afghanistan.
Schneier, B. (2003) *Beyond Fear: Thinking Sensibly about Security in an Uncertain World*, New York: Copernicus Books.
Shapiro, M. J. (2009) *Cinematic Geopolitics*, Abingdon: Routledge.
Shapiro, M. J. (2013) *Studies in Trans-Disciplinary Method: After the Aesthetic Turn*, London: Routledge.
Smith, P. J. (2012) 'Spanish Cinema Roundup', *Film Quarterly*, vol. 66, no. 1, pp. 5–8.
Todorov, T. (1985) *The Conquest of America: The Question of the Other*, translated by R. Howard, New York: Harper and Row.
Urbizu, E. (2011) *No Habrá para los malvados*. Film. Spain: Lazona Films S. L., Manto Films A. I. E., & Telecinco España S. L.
von Trier, L. (2003) *Dogville*. Film. Denmark: Zentropa Entertainments.

Walsh, J. P. (2016) 'Moral Panics by Design: The Case of Terrorism', *Current Sociology*, vol. 65, no. 5, pp. 643–662.
Young, A. (2010) *The Scene of Violence: Cinema, Crime, Affect*, Abingdon: Routledge.
Žižek, S. (2002) 'Are We in a War? Do We Have an Enemy?', *London Review of Books*, vol. 14, no. 10, 23 May, Available: https://www.lrb.co.uk/v24/n10/slavoj-zizek/are-we-in-a-war-do-we-have-an-enemy.

Index

For Product Safety Concerns and Information please contact our EU
representative GPSR@taylorandfrancis.com
Taylor & Francis Verlag GmbH, Kaufingerstraße 24, 80331 München, Germany

www.ingramcontent.com/pod-product-compliance
Ingram Content Group UK Ltd.
Pitfield, Milton Keynes, MK11 3LW, UK
UKHW011010180926
475701UK00004B/658
* 9 7 8 0 3 6 7 2 3 2 4 5 0 *